Better Homes and Gardens®

BIG BOOK OF HEALTHY FAMILY DINNERS

BETTER HOMES AND GARDENS® BOOKS
Des Moines, Iowa

If you would like to purchase any of our books, check wherever quality books are sold.

Visit our website at bhg.com or bhgbooks.com.

All of us at Better Homes and Gardens® Books are dedicated to providing you with the information and ideas you need to create delicious foods. We welcome your comments and suggestions. Write to us at: Better Homes and Gardens Books, Cookbook Editorial Department, 1716 Locust Street, Des Moines, Iowa 50309-3023.

Our seal assures you that every recipe in the *Big Book of Healthy Family Dinners* has been tested in the Better Homes and Gardens® Test Kitchen. This means that each recipe is practical and reliable, and meets our high standards of taste appeal. We guarantee your satisfaction with this book for as long as you own it.

Cover photo: Garlic Asparagus and Pasta with Lemon Cream, see recipe, page 236

Better Homes and Gardens® Books
An imprint of Meredith® Books

Big Book of Healthy Family Dinners
Project Editor: Kristi M. Fuller, R.D.
Contributing Editor: Spectrum Communication Services, Inc.
Associate Art Director: Mick Schnepf
Contributing Designer: Shelton Design Studios
Copy Chief: Catherine Hamrick
Copy and Production Editor: Terri Fredrickson
Contributing Copy Editor: Carol Boker
Contributing Proofreaders: Kathy Eastman, Beth Popplewell, Margaret Smith
Indexer: Sharon Duffy
Electronic Production Coordinator: Paula Forest
Editorial and Design Assistants: Judy Bailey, Karen Schirm
Test Kitchen Director: Lynn Blanchard
Production Director: Douglas M. Johnston
Book Production Managers: Pam Kvitne, Marjorie J. Schenkelberg

Meredith® Books
Editor in Chief: James D. Blume
Design Director: Matt Strelecki
Managing Editor: Gregory H. Kayko

Director, Sales & Marketing, Retail: Michael A. Peterson
Director, Sales & Marketing, Special Markets: Rita McMullen
Director, Sales & Marketing, Home & Garden Center Channel: Ray Wolf
Director, Operations: George A. Susral

Vice President, General Manager: Jamie L. Martin

Better Homes and Gardens® **Magazine**
Editor in Chief: Jean LemMon
Executive Food Editor: Nancy Byal

Meredith Publishing Group
President, Publishing Group: Christopher M. Little
Vice President, Consumer Marketing & Development: Hal Oringer

Meredith Corporation
Chairman and Chief Executive Officer: William T. Kerr

Chairman of the Executive Committee: E. T. Meredith III

Cooking family-pleasing meals night after night challenges the best of cooks. And, for those who aim to serve healthy and great-tasting dishes, the task becomes even more difficult. But, with the aid of the *Big Book of Healthy Family Dinners*, high-flavor, low-fat cooking is easy. In this collection, you'll find more than 250 recipes that were developed specifically for families like yours. These recipes were trimmed of fat, calories, and sodium with no sacrifice in flavor. Once your family samples the enticing appetizers, mouthwatering main dishes, colorful side dishes, and sweetly satisfying desserts, they'll be convinced that light eating is delectable eating. And you'll have the pleasure of offering delicious dishes that help the ones you love live healthier and longer.

TABLE OF CONTENTS

Lighten Up for a Lifetime

We all know that eating lighter is the best route to lifelong good health and well-being, but it's often a challenge to persuade loved ones that it can be delicious, too. So we packed this chapter with information to help get you and your family on the road to lighter eating. Discover the secrets for making recipes lighter without eliminating their taste appeal.

Techniques for Cooking Light

Adjusting to a lifestyle of light eating is really a matter of using some smart cooking techniques and substituting low-fat ingredients for the high-fat ones. Apply these techniques to your own favorite recipes so that you still can enjoy them, but in a lighter style.

Cooking Smart

- When sautéing or stir-frying, you need a lot less fat than you think. Use a nonstick skillet or wok, then a small amount of margarine or, better yet, nonstick spray coating. If you prefer to use oil, olive oil is a good choice because it appears to have a cholesterol-lowering effect.

- Opt for grilling or broiling tender cuts of meat rather than sautéing or pan-frying.

- Use cooking techniques that require no added fat, such as broiling, grilling, poaching, steaming, or baking.

- Use fats sparingly. Fat serves to prevent foods from drying out, particularly during baking or broiling/grilling. Start by brushing a small amount of oil or margarine over the food; then, during the baking or grilling process, use a fat-free salad dressing or marinade, mustard, chutney, fruit preserves, or salsa to keep the food moist.

- Often a recipe begins with sautéing or browning vegetables or meat, then adding liquid or vegetables to braise the food. Start by using just a teaspoon or two of fat or nonstick spray coating for browning in a nonstick skillet, then add a couple of teaspoons of liquid and cover, cooking the food over low heat, stirring occasionally, until softened.

- Drain off any excess fat from sautéing or browning before adding the remaining ingredients.

- Trim meat of all visible fat before cooking; remove skin and fat from poultry. Use tuna packed in water, not oil.

- Cook vegetables quickly to preserve their texture and vitamins—opt for steaming, stir-frying, or microwaving.

- Roast vegetables, when you have the time. It helps bring out their natural sweetness. Prepare more than you need as a side dish; you can toss the extras into a salad or pasta dish the next day.

- Cook fruits and vegetables in their skins whenever possible to preserve fiber and nutrients.

- Cut down on salt—never add salt during the cooking process. Wait until you serve the dish, and salt it at the table with a low-sodium product, if needed.

- Rinse and drain canned shrimp and vegetables before adding them to a recipe; you'll remove much of their salt.

- Take advantage of reduced-sodium chicken broth for stir-frying, sautéing, braising, or poaching meat or fish.

Ingredient Substitutions

- Make meat less important in your menus. Use smaller portions (2 to 4 ounces per serving) and add pasta, rice, beans, or vegetables to "flesh out" your entrées.

- Try fat-free or light mayonnaise dressing, sour cream, yogurt, milk, cottage cheese, salad dressings, pasta sauces, and fruit spreads. Nowadays, for many of your favorite condiments, there is a low-fat or fat-free product that you can substitute for the higher-fat products. Check labels however; total calories may not be reduced.

- If you are a fan of sausage, bacon, or ham, try the turkey-based version for fewer calories and less saturated fat. When a recipe calls for bacon, substitute lean smoked ham and you still will get a rich, smoky flavor.

- Select meats that look lean, without a lot of fat marbling. A good rule is to look for cuts with the word "loin" or "round" in the name. Plan for 3 to 4 ounces of cooked meat per serving (6 to 8 ounces is all we need each day).

- Substitute ground turkey breast or chicken breast for ground beef or pork in casseroles, meat loaf, and chili recipes.

- Opt for rotisserie-style chicken and extra-lean deli-sliced turkey or roast beef if you like the convenience of purchasing cooked meats from your deli.

- Use both hard and soft cheeses that are available in reduced-fat and fat-free varieties. As a rule, aim for no more than 5 fat grams per ounce. Many of these products also are low in sodium.

- Add fiber to recipes by substituting whole-wheat flour for up to half of the all-purpose flour called for in a recipe.

- Read the labels when buying breads, crackers, or grain products. The first ingredient should read whole-wheat or other whole-grain flour (wheat flour is not good enough).

- Boost your fiber. Experiment with a variety of grains, such as couscous, barley, brown rice, oatmeal, rye, wild rice, and bulgur, as well as whole-wheat pasta, corn tortillas, and rye crackers.

- Include both fresh and dried fruits in dishes other than desserts. Add them to dips, purée them for entrée sauces, or add them to salads, cold pasta dishes, side dishes, casseroles, or meat stuffings.

- Incorporate more dark green, leafy vegetables. Add greens such as spinach and kale to sandwiches, salads, and vegetable side dishes and stir-fries.

- Use shredded cabbage, especially red cabbage, as a high-fiber addition to salads, stir-fries, sandwich fillings, soups, and even meat loaf.

- Befriend those deep yellow and dark green fruits and vegetables that are rich in vitamin A, such as apricots, cantaloupe, carrots, peaches, sweet potatoes, winter squashes, spinach, broccoli, and Swiss chard.

- Replace high-fat ingredients, such as sour cream and mayonnaise, in soups, sauces, dips, and the like, with low-fat or fat-free yogurt.

- Use evaporated fat-free milk; reduced-fat, light, or fat-free milk; or buttermilk in place of whole milk in rich sauces and soups and in baked items.

- Substitute two egg whites or ¼ cup fat-free egg product for one whole egg in recipes.

- Look for fat-free refried beans and bean soups.

- Purchase canned fruits packed in their own juices or frozen, loose-pack fruits that have no added sugar or syrup.

- Read cereal labels carefully; even low-fat granola calories add up quickly, because the serving sizes listed typically are smaller than what you normally would consume. Opt for high-fiber cereals with few additions of nuts, fruit, or clusters of high-sugar or high-fat ingredients.

- Low-fat cottage cheese or part-skim or light ricotta cheese is a good substitute for whole milk ricotta cheese.

- Use just small amounts of high-fat foods to flavor dishes; be stingy with such ingredients as avocados, coconut, cheese, and nuts.

Fat-Free Flavor-Makers

One reason we enjoy high-fat foods so much is because fat adds flavor. When the fat is reduced, however, you have a wonderful opportunity to use spices, herbs, and condiments that have intriguing new tastes to offer. If you haven't tried some of these before, you'll be pleasantly surprised at the effect they can have on your taste buds. Keep a good assortment of the following on hand to flavor-up your fat-reduced recipes.

- Lemon, lime, and orange juices

- Reduced-sodium soy sauce and light teriyaki sauce

- Low-calorie fruit spreads

- Red and green onions or shallots

- Salsas—all types are low in sodium and fat

- Chutneys—mango, peach, and others

- Fresh cilantro, parsley, or watercress

- Fresh or dried herbs, from basil to thyme

- Dried herb mixtures, such as curry powder, fines herbes, Cajun seasoning, or Beau Monde seasoning

- Bottled hot pepper sauces

- Salt-free herb seasonings in a variety of flavors

- Lemon-pepper and garlic-pepper seasonings

- Reduced-calorie or fat-free salad dressings

- Mild-flavored vinegars, such as balsamic, rice, or raspberry

- Fresh garlic

- Grated fresh ginger and horseradish

- Grated fresh citrus peel (lemon, lime, orange, and grapefruit)

- Mustards in many types, from mild to hot

- Fresh or canned chili peppers, from mild to hair-raising

Reading Food Labels

As consumers, we should take advantage of the information available on food packaging. Virtually all processed food products have nutritional information on their labels. Fresh fruits and vegetables, fresh meats, fish, poultry, and items from the deli case are not required to carry nutritional labeling, although some purveyors voluntarily offer it. Many stores display nutrition information for fresh foods on posters or in brochures conveniently located in the department.

Use the Nutrition Facts label to learn about the nutrition value of foods, to make comparisons between products, and to plan your family's meals and snacks. Here are some of the features you'll find on a typical food label:

- Only foods that meet government standards can make label claims of "fat free," "light," "low fat," and "cholesterol free." For example, only those foods that are at least 97 percent free of fat can use the fat-free claim on the label. This applies to meat and poultry products as well as nonmeat products.

- Standard serving sizes are used to determine a food's calorie, fat, and nutrient count. Regulations stipulate that serving sizes must reflect amounts consumed by an average person over 4 years old.

- The FDA allows health claims to be made in only four areas: those linking fat and cancer, calcium and osteoporosis, fat and cardiovascular disease, and sodium and hypertension.

- For sugar, a product can only claim "no sugars added" if no sugar of any kind (including fructose, concentrated fruit juice, and the like) has been added during processing. Also, if the number of grams of sugar per serving appears on the nutrient breakdown.

- Products can carry the claim "cholesterol free" only if they also contain a specific low amount of saturated fat that has been shown to raise blood cholesterol levels.

The fat information you'll find on the package labels includes the amount of total fat and saturated fat contained in a serving of food. It is listed both in grams and as a "% Daily Value" on the label. The daily value percentage tells you how much fat one serving of the food contributes to a daily diet of 2,000 calories.

You can use these figures to determine how much fat and saturated fat the food will contribute to your diet. For example, if the label says a food has 6 grams of fat and the daily value is 10 percent, it means that 6 grams of fat is one-tenth (10 percent) of the total daily fat recommended for a person consuming 2,000 calories per day.

Also listed on the nutritional label is calories from fat—the number of calories supplied by the fat in one serving of the food. (This number is computed by multiplying the grams of fat by 9 calories per gram.)

Nutrition Facts

Serving Size: 1 cup (228 g)
Servings Per Container: 2

Amount Per Serving

Calories 90	Calories From Fat 30

	% Daily Value*
Total Fat 3 g	5%
Saturated Fat 0 g	0%
Cholesterol 0 mg	0%
Sodium 300 mg	13%
Total Carbohydrate 13 g	4%
Dietary Fiber 3 g	12%
Sugars 3 g	
Protein 3 g	

Vitamin A	80%	•	Vitamin C	60%
Calcium	4%	•	Iron	4%

*Percent Daily Values are based on a 2,000-calorie diet. Your daily values may be higher or lower depending on your calorie needs:

	Calories	2,000	2,500
Total Fat	Less than	65 g	80 g
Sat. Fat	Less than	20 g	25 g
Cholesterol	Less than	300 mg	300 mg
Sodium	Less than	2,400 mg	2,400 mg
Total Carbohydrate		300 g	375 g
Dietary Fiber		25 g	30 g

Calories per gram:
Fat 9 • Carbohydrate 4 • Protein 4

Here's a dictionary of the fat claims you'll find on labels and what they mean.

- Fat Free—contains less than 0.5 grams of fat per serving (it cannot have an added ingredient that is fat or oil).

- Low Fat—contains no more than 3 grams of fat per serving and per 100 grams of food.

- Fat Free and Percent Fat Free—these terms may be used only to describe the foods that meet the FDA definition of "low fat" as previously described.

- Reduced Fat—no more than half of the fat of a similar food used as a comparison; for example, "Reduced fat, 50 percent less fat than our regular oatmeal cookie. Fat content has been reduced from 10 grams to 5 grams." The FDA says the reduction must exceed 3 grams of fat per serving.

- Low in Saturated Fat—can describe a food that has no more than 1 gram of saturated fat per serving and no more than 15 percent of calories from saturated fat.

- Reduced Saturated Fat—product contains no more than 50 percent of the saturated fat than the comparison food.

- Less Saturated Fat—the food offers a reduction of 25 percent or more.

Using the Food Pyramid to Keep in Balance

When you're planning a menu, it's a good idea to become familiar with your family's actual food needs each day. Don't worry—it's not as difficult as it sounds! An easy way to do this is to refer to the Food Guide Pyramid, designed by the U.S. Department of Agriculture (opposite). It's a great tool for gaining a healthy perspective on how your food choices need to be balanced over the course of a day.

The pyramid displays each food group with the recommended daily number of servings, beginning with the breads and cereals group at its base. You need the most servings from this group. The fruit and vegetable groups are on the next tier of the pyramid, and they're second in the number of servings recommended. Meats, other proteins, and dairy products have been given less importance in terms of the amounts you need, because your body requires less of these foods. Notice you can eat fats and sugars, found at the top of the pyramid and naturally throughout the groups, in small amounts and still maintain good health.

In short, the pyramid sums up the basic principles of the U.S. Dietary Guidelines.

- Eat a variety of foods.

- Maintain a healthy weight.

- Choose a diet low in fat, saturated fat, and cholesterol.

- Choose a diet with plenty of vegetables, fruits, and grain products.

- Use sugars only in moderation.

- Use salt and sodium only in moderation.

Shopping for Healthy Foods

You will find simple tools such as the Food Guide Pyramid, the Dietary Guidelines, and food labels extremely helpful in daily menu planning. Here are some tips to use when you are shopping for food.

- When buying groceries, visualize the food pyramid, and remember to include at least a minimum number of servings from each of the five food groups daily.

- Read labels to find foods that are a good source of, or are high in, vitamins, minerals, and fiber.

- For fresh fruits and vegetables, look for voluntary nutrient listings posted in the grocer's produce section.

- Check out the serving size and calories per serving on the label to help achieve your ideal calorie intake for the day.

- Take note of the Daily Value percentages on the label for fat, saturated fat, and cholesterol; aim to keep your *total* daily intake, adding up your percentages throughout the day, below 100 percent.

- Check the label for the amount of sugars (listed in grams) in one serving of the food.

- Note the sodium values on the label, especially if you have a health problem, such as high blood pressure.

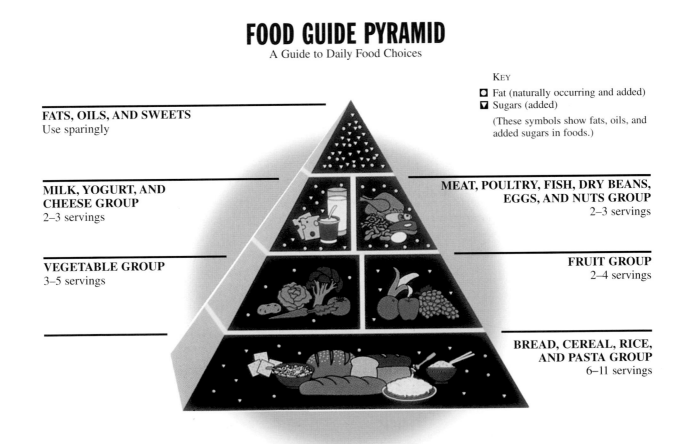

FOOD GUIDE PYRAMID
A Guide to Daily Food Choices

KEY
◻ Fat (naturally occurring and added)
▼ Sugars (added)
(These symbols show fats, oils, and added sugars in foods.)

FATS, OILS, AND SWEETS
Use sparingly

MILK, YOGURT, AND
CHEESE GROUP
2–3 servings

MEAT, POULTRY, FISH, DRY BEANS,
EGGS, AND NUTS GROUP
2–3 servings

VEGETABLE GROUP
3–5 servings

FRUIT GROUP
2–4 servings

BREAD, CEREAL, RICE,
AND PASTA GROUP
6–11 servings

Vegetable Nachos
Recipe, page 17

snacks & appetizers

herbed seafood bruschetta

This chunky seafood sensation is sure to make a splash as a snack for a casual gathering or as the prelude to a special-occasion dinner.

INGREDIENTS

- 1 tablespoon olive oil
- 1 tablespoon lemon juice
- 1 tablespoon snipped fresh chives
- 1 tablespoon snipped fresh basil
- 1 tablespoon snipped fresh mint
- 1 teaspoon bottled minced garlic
- 1 6-ounce package frozen cooked crabmeat, thawed and drained, or one 6½-ounce can crabmeat, drained, flaked, and cartilage removed
- 8 ounces peeled, deveined, and cooked shrimp, coarsely chopped
- 1 cup chopped plum tomatoes
- ½ cup finely chopped onion
- 1 8-ounce loaf baguette-style French bread
- 2 tablespoons olive oil
  Freshly ground pepper
  Fresh chives (optional)

Snipping fresh herbs, such as basil or mint, takes little time to do. Just place the herb in a glass measure or small cup and snip the herb with kitchen scissors.

Start to finish: 35 minutes

DIRECTIONS

1. In a medium bowl stir together the 1 tablespoon olive oil, the lemon juice, snipped chives, basil, mint, and garlic. Add crabmeat, shrimp, plum tomatoes, and onion; toss to coat.

2. Cut the French bread into 48 thin slices. Brush 1 side of each slice with some of the 2 tablespoons olive oil; sprinkle lightly with pepper.

3. Arrange bread, brushed side up, on a large baking sheet. Broil 3 to 4 inches from heat for 2 to 4 minutes or until toasted, turning once. Arrange, oiled side up, on a serving platter; spoon the seafood mixture on top. If desired, garnish with additional chives. Serve at once. Makes 48 servings.

NUTRITION FACTS PER SERVING:

24 calories
1 g total fat
0 g saturated fat
12 mg cholesterol
39 mg sodium
2 g carbohydrate
0 g fiber
2 g protein

INGREDIENTS

- ½ of a 10-ounce package frozen chopped spinach, thawed and well drained
- ½ of an 8-ounce package reduced-fat cream cheese (Neufchâtel), softened
- 2 tablespoons finely chopped green onion
- 1 tablespoon grated Parmesan cheese
- Dash pepper

- 1 10-ounce package refrigerated pizza dough
- Water
- 1 tablespoon milk
- Light spaghetti sauce (optional)

mini spinach calzones

Using refrigerated pizza dough takes the work out of preparing these pizza pockets. Adding spinach and reduced-fat cream cheese keeps them healthful.

Prep time: 30 minutes
Baking time: 8 minutes
Standing time: 5 minutes

DIRECTIONS

1. For filling, in a medium mixing bowl stir together the spinach, cream cheese, green onion, Parmesan cheese, and pepper. Set aside.

2. Unroll pizza dough. On a lightly floured surface, roll dough into a 15-inch square. Using a knife, cut into twenty-five 3-inch squares. Spoon 1 rounded teaspoon of filling onto each dough square. Brush edges of each square with water. Lift a corner of each square and stretch dough over the filling to the opposite corner, making a triangle. Press edges of the dough well with fingers or a fork to seal.

3. Line a baking sheet with foil; lightly grease the foil. Arrange the calzones on the baking sheet. Prick tops of calzones with a fork. Brush milk over the calzones.

4. Bake in a 425° oven for 8 to 10 minutes or until golden. Let stand for 5 minutes before serving. If desired, serve with spaghetti sauce. Makes 25 calzones.

NUTRITION FACTS PER CALZONE:

38 calories
2 g total fat
1 g saturated fat
4 mg cholesterol
63 mg sodium
5 g carbohydrate
0 g fiber
1 g protein

portobello pizzettas

Wide-brimmed portobello mushrooms—meaty and succulent—provide the perfect palette for appetizer art when stuffed with spinach, mozzarella cheese, and turkey pepperoni. Omit the pepperoni to turn this into a great vegetarian appetizer.

INGREDIENTS

- ½ of a 10-ounce package frozen chopped spinach
- 1½ cups shredded mozzarella cheese (6 ounces)
- ½ cup coarsely chopped turkey pepperoni or pepperoni
- 1 tablespoon snipped fresh basil or 1 teaspoon dried basil, crushed
- ¼ teaspoon coarsely ground pepper
- 12 portobello mushrooms (3 to 4 inches in diameter)
- 2 tablespoons margarine or butter, melted
- Fresh basil (optional)

Clean fresh mushrooms by wiping them with a clean, damp cloth or rinsing lightly, then patting dry with paper towels. Never soak fresh mushrooms. They are like sponges and it ruins their texture.

Prep time: 10 minutes
Baking time: 12 minutes

DIRECTIONS

1. Thaw spinach and press out liquid; finely chop. In a medium bowl combine the spinach, mozzarella cheese, pepperoni, basil, and pepper.

2. Clean mushrooms; remove stems. On a lightly greased baking sheet, place mushrooms open side up; brush with margarine or butter. Spoon about 2 tablespoons spinach mixture into each mushroom.

3. Bake in a 350° oven about 12 minutes or until heated through. (Or, to broil, place on the unheated rack of a broiler pan. Broil 4 inches from the heat for 3 to 4 minutes.) If desired, garnish with additional fresh basil. Makes 12 pizzettas.

NUTRITION FACTS PER PIZZETTA:

78 calories
5 g total fat
2 g saturated fat
16 mg cholesterol
201 mg sodium
2 g carbohydrate
1 g fiber
6 g protein

peasant pizza with goat cheese

Using a small amount of goat cheese on this pizza adds a tangy flavor. Look for goat cheese in the specialty cheese section of the supermarket labeled "chèvre" (pronounced SHEV), which means goat in French.

INGREDIENTS

1 16-ounce Italian bread shell (Boboli)

2 ounces fat-free cream cheese (block style)

2 ounces semisoft goat cheese or feta cheese, crumbled (about ¼ cup)

1 teaspoon dried basil, crushed, or 2 tablespoons snipped fresh basil

1 clove garlic, minced

⅛ teaspoon ground black pepper

3 plum tomatoes, thinly sliced

1 small yellow, orange, or green sweet pepper, cut into thin bite-size strips

Fresh basil (optional)

Prep time: 12 minutes
Baking time: 12 minutes

NUTRITION FACTS PER SERVING:

269 calories
8 g total fat
2 g saturated fat
14 mg cholesterol
581 mg sodium
38 g carbohydrate
2 g fiber
14 g protein

DIRECTIONS

1. Place Italian bread shell on a baking sheet.

2. In a small mixing bowl stir together the cream cheese, goat cheese or feta cheese, dried basil (if using), garlic, and black pepper. Spread over the bread shell. Place the tomato slices and sweet pepper strips on top of the cheese mixture.

3. Bake the pizza in a 400° oven about 12 minutes or until heated through. Sprinkle with the snipped fresh basil (if using). If desired, garnish with additional fresh basil. To serve, cut into wedges. Makes 6 servings.

wrap-and-roll basil pinwheels

Fresh basil and roasted sweet peppers add bursts of flavor to these tasty appetizer roll-ups. Use plain, whole wheat, spinach, or tomato tortillas to wrap up these impressive bundles.

INGREDIENTS

- 3 7- to 8-inch flour tortillas
- 1 5.2-ounce carton Boursin cheese or one 5-ounce container semisoft cheese with garlic and herb
- 12 large fresh basil leaves
- ½ of a 7-ounce jar roasted red sweet peppers, cut into ¼-inch strips
- 4 ounces thinly sliced cooked roast beef, ham, or turkey
- 1 tablespoon mayonnaise or salad dressing
   Fresh basil leaves (optional)

Prep time: 20 minutes
Chilling time: 2 hours

DIRECTIONS

1. Spread each flour tortilla with one-third of the Boursin cheese or semisoft cheese. Add a layer of the large fresh basil leaves to cover cheese.

2. Divide roasted red sweet pepper strips among tortillas, arranging pepper strips over basil leaves 1 to 2 inches apart. Top with meat slices. Spread 1 teaspoon mayonnaise or salad dressing over meat on each tortilla.

Roll up tortillas tightly into a spiral, enclosing filling. Wrap each roll in plastic wrap. Chill tortilla rolls for 2 to 4 hours to blend flavors.

3. To serve, remove plastic wrap from tortilla rolls; cut each roll into 1-inch slices on a diagonal. If desired, skewer each tortilla slice on a frilly pick or short decorative skewer. If desired, garnish with additional fresh basil. Makes about 24 pinwheels.

NUTRITION FACTS PER PINWHEEL:

52 calories
4 g total fat
2 g saturated fat
5 mg cholesterol
58 mg sodium
2 g carbohydrate
0 g fiber
2 g protein

vegetable nachos

An old Tex-Mex snack favorite takes on a bold new look and flavor when you pile tortilla chips high with fresh vegetables, pinto beans, and cilantro sour cream. (Recipe also pictured on pages 10 and 11.)

INGREDIENTS

- 1 recipe Homemade Tortilla Chips (see page 19)
- ½ cup fat-free dairy sour cream
- 1 tablespoon finely snipped fresh cilantro
- 1 small zucchini, quartered lengthwise and thinly sliced (about 1 cup)
- 1 medium red or yellow onion, chopped
- ½ cup shredded carrot
- 1½ teaspoons ground cumin
- 1 tablespoon cooking oil
- 1 15-ounce can pinto beans, rinsed and drained
- 1 4-ounce can diced green chili peppers, drained
- ½ cup seeded and chopped tomato
- ¾ cup shredded reduced-fat cheddar cheese (3 ounces)
- Fresh cilantro (optional)
- Salsa (optional)

Prep time: 25 minutes
Baking time: 10 minutes per batch; 5 minutes

DIRECTIONS

1. Prepare Homemade Tortilla Chips.

2. In a small mixing bowl stir together the sour cream and finely snipped cilantro; cover and chill.

3. In a large skillet cook zucchini, onion, carrot, and cumin in hot oil over medium heat for 3 to 4 minutes or until vegetables are crisp-tender. Stir in pinto beans.

4. Arrange tortilla chips on an 11- or 12-inch ovenproof platter or on a baking sheet. Spoon the bean mixture onto the chips. Sprinkle with chili peppers and tomato; top with cheese. Bake in a 350° oven for 5 to 7 minutes or until cheese is melted.

5. To serve, transfer nachos to a serving platter. If desired, garnish with additional cilantro. Pass the sour cream mixture and, if desired, the salsa. Makes 8 servings.

NUTRITION FACTS PER SERVING:

234 calories
7 g total fat
2 g saturated fat
7 mg cholesterol
498 mg sodium
32 g carbohydrate
4 g fiber
10 g protein

If you make the chips ahead, cool them and store in an airtight container at room temperature for up to 4 days or in the freezer for up to 3 weeks.

potted pepper dip

A rainbow of peppers lines grocery store produce bins everywhere today, unlike several years ago, when you rarely found anything but green peppers. Although they work just fine, an assortment of colors provides more eye appeal.

INGREDIENTS

2 tablespoons lemon juice

2 teaspoons olive oil or cooking oil

1 teaspoon sugar

¼ teaspoon salt

Dash black pepper

1 small onion, cut up

4 large red, green, yellow, or orange sweet peppers, seeded and cut up (see tip)

1 8-ounce package fat-free cream cheese (block style), softened

¼ cup fat-free mayonnaise dressing or salad dressing

1 teaspoon prepared horseradish

Few dashes bottled hot pepper sauce

3 medium red, yellow, and/or orange sweet peppers, tops removed and seeded

Assorted vegetable dippers and/or breadsticks

Fresh herbs (optional)

To avoid getting

tough pepper skins in the dip, blanch seeded, quartered peppers in boiling water for a few seconds. When cool enough to handle, peel off skins with a small knife and cut peppers into pieces.

Prep time: 25 minutes
Standing time: 2 hours
Chilling time: 2 hours

DIRECTIONS

1. In a blender container or food processor bowl combine the lemon juice, oil, sugar, salt, and black pepper. Add the onion and about one-third of the cut-up sweet peppers. Cover and blend or process until smooth.

2. Add remaining cut-up sweet peppers; cover and blend until smooth. Transfer to a mixing bowl. Let stand, covered, at room temperature for at least 2 hours.

3. Place pureed vegetable mixture in sieve, pressing gently to drain off excess liquid. In a medium mixing bowl combine cream cheese, mayonnaise dressing, horseradish, and hot pepper sauce. Stir in pureed vegetable mixture. Cover and chill for 2 to 3 hours.

4. Spoon into the sweet pepper shells. Place the filled peppers in the center of a serving platter; surround with vegetable dippers and/or breadsticks. If desired, garnish the dip with fresh herbs. Makes about 32 (1-tablespoon) servings.

NUTRITION FACTS PER SERVING:

16 calories
0 g total fat
0 g saturated fat
1 mg cholesterol
43 mg sodium
2 g carbohydrate
0 g fiber
1 g protein

INGREDIENTS

- **2 cups shredded lettuce**
- **1 15-ounce can reduced-sodium black beans, rinsed and drained**
- **½ cup chopped green sweet pepper**
- **2 tablespoons bottled chopped red jalapeño peppers or canned diced green chili peppers**
- **1 8-ounce carton fat-free dairy sour cream**
- **1 8-ounce jar chunky salsa**
- **½ cup shredded reduced-fat cheddar cheese (2 ounces)**
- **2 tablespoons chopped pitted ripe olives**
- **1 recipe Homemade Tortilla Chips**

layered southwestern dip

If you want a real crowd pleaser, six layers of fresh, colorful Mexican flavors will do the trick. When you have the time, make your own low-fat chips.

Prep time: 25 minutes
Baking time: 10 minutes per batch

DIRECTIONS

1. Line a 12-inch platter with the shredded lettuce. In a small bowl stir together the black beans, sweet pepper, and jalapeño peppers or chili peppers. Spoon over the lettuce, leaving a lettuce border. Spoon sour cream over bean mixture; gently spread in a smooth layer, leaving a border of bean mixture.

2. Drain excess liquid from salsa. Spoon salsa over sour cream layer, leaving a border of sour cream. Sprinkle cheese over salsa. Top with olives. Serve immediately. (Or, cover and chill for up to 6 hours.) Serve with Homemade Tortilla Chips. Makes 24 servings.

Homemade Tortilla Chips: Cut sixteen 7- to 8-inch flour tortillas into 6 wedges each. Arrange wedges in a single layer on ungreased baking sheets. Bake in a 350° oven for 10 to 15 minutes or until dry and crisp. Makes 96 chips.

NUTRITION FACTS PER SERVING:

80 calories
2 g total fat
1 g saturated fat
2 mg cholesterol
178 mg sodium
12 g carbohydrate
1 g fiber
3 g protein

fruit kabobs

Kabobs offer a fun way to serve fruit for parties, and a cool dip adds extra pizzazz. Seasonal substitutes, such as fresh peaches, nectarines, and plums or mangoes, add flavorful variety.

INGREDIENTS

- ¾ cup cantaloupe chunks
- ¾ cup honeydew melon chunks
- ¾ cup small strawberries
- ¾ cup fresh or canned pineapple chunks
- 2 small bananas, cut into 1-inch slices
- 1 cup orange juice
- ¼ cup lime juice
- 1 8-ounce carton vanilla low-fat or fat-free yogurt
- 2 tablespoons frozen orange juice concentrate, thawed
- Ground nutmeg or cinnamon (optional)

Prep time: 20 minutes
Chilling time: 30 minutes

DIRECTIONS

1. On eight 6-inch or four 10-inch skewers, alternately thread the cantaloupe, honeydew melon, strawberries, pineapple, and bananas. Place kabobs in a glass baking dish.

2. In a small bowl combine the orange juice and lime juice; pour evenly over kabobs. Cover and chill kabobs for 30 to 60 minutes, turning occasionally.

3. Meanwhile, for dip, in a small bowl stir together the yogurt and orange juice concentrate. Cover and chill until ready to serve.

4. To serve, arrange the kabobs on a serving platter; discard juice mixture. If desired, sprinkle dip with nutmeg or cinnamon. Serve dip with kabobs. Makes 8 servings.

NUTRITION FACTS PER SERVING:

91 calories
1 g total fat
0 g saturated fat
2 mg cholesterol
20 mg sodium
21 g carbohydrate
1 g fiber
2 g protein

fruit salsa

Papaya, pineapple, and ginger lend the sweet touch and onion and sweet pepper provide the savory tones that make this eye-grabbing salsa a perfect match for chicken, fish, or seafood.

INGREDIENTS

- 1 cup chopped papaya or mango
- 1 cup finely chopped fresh pineapple
- ¼ cup finely slivered red onion
- ¼ cup slivered yellow, orange, and/or green sweet pepper
- 3 tablespoons snipped fresh cilantro
- 1 teaspoon finely shredded lime or lemon peel
- 2 tablespoons lime or lemon juice
- 2 to 4 teaspoons finely chopped fresh jalapeño pepper (see tip)
- 1 teaspoon grated fresh ginger

Prep time: 30 minutes
Chilling time: 8 hours

DIRECTIONS

1. In a medium mixing bowl stir together the papaya or mango, pineapple, red onion, sweet pepper, cilantro, lime or lemon peel, lime or lemon juice, jalapeño pepper, and ginger.

2. Cover and chill for 8 to 24 hours. Makes about 18 (2-tablespoon) servings.

Because hot peppers contain oils that can burn your eyes and skin, wear plastic bags or plastic or rubber gloves when working with them. Be sure to wash hands thoroughly before touching your eyes or face.

NUTRITION FACTS PER SERVING:

11 calories
0 g total fat
0 g saturated fat
0 mg cholesterol
1 mg sodium
3 g carbohydrate
0 g fiber
0 g protein

gingered shrimp appetizers

Lightly steamed pea pods dress up tangy marinated shrimp in this elegant appetizer.

INGREDIENTS

1	pound fresh or frozen large shrimp in shells
1½	cups water
4½	teaspoons white wine vinegar
1	teaspoon toasted sesame oil or olive oil
¼	teaspoon finely shredded lemon peel
1	teaspoon lemon juice
1	teaspoon grated fresh ginger or ½ teaspoon ground ginger
1	clove garlic, minced
¼	teaspoon sugar
	Dash salt
	Dash ground red pepper
18	to 24 fresh pea pods
6	to 8 small pieces lemon

Freeze any leftover fresh ginger;

then grate or cut off what you need from the unpeeled frozen root.

Prep time: 40 minutes
Marinating time: 1 hour

DIRECTIONS

1. Thaw shrimp, if frozen. Peel and devein shrimp, leaving the last few sections before the tails and the tails intact. In a large saucepan bring the water to boiling.

Add the shrimp. Cover and simmer for 1 to 3 minutes or until the shrimp are opaque. Drain. Rinse shrimp with cold water; drain.

2. Place shrimp in a plastic bag set in a shallow bowl. For marinade, in a small bowl combine the vinegar, oil, lemon peel, lemon juice, ginger, garlic, sugar, salt, and red pepper. Pour over shrimp; close bag. Marinate in the refrigerator for 1 to 2 hours, turning once.

3. Meanwhile, place the pea pods in a steamer basket over simmering water. Steam, covered, for 2 to 3 minutes or until the pea pods are just tender. Rinse with cold water; drain.

4. Drain shrimp, discarding marinade. Wrap each shrimp with a pea pod. On each of six to eight 6-inch skewers, thread a piece of lemon and the wrapped shrimp. Makes 6 to 8 servings.

NUTRITION FACTS PER SERVING:

60 calories
1 g total fat
0 g saturated fat
87 mg cholesterol
123 mg sodium
2 g carbohydrate
1 g fiber
10 g protein

gorgonzola & onion tart

A lower-fat oil pastry and fat-free milk rather than cream move this scrumptious tart off the list of the forbidden and onto the list of low-fat and luscious.

INGREDIENTS

Nonstick spray coating
1¼ cups all-purpose flour
½ teaspoon dried thyme, chervil, or marjoram, crushed
¼ teaspoon salt
¼ cup fat-free milk
3 tablespoons cooking oil
1 cup thinly sliced onion
½ cup shredded zucchini

½ cup crumbled Gorgonzola or blue cheese (2 ounces)
2 egg whites
1 egg
¼ teaspoon pepper
½ cup fat-free milk
Fresh thyme, chervil, or marjoram (optional)
Apple or pear slices (optional)

Prep time: 20 minutes
Baking time: 30 minutes
Cooling time: 15 minutes

DIRECTIONS

1. Spray a 9-inch tart pan with removable side with nonstick coating. Set aside.

2. For pastry, in a medium bowl stir together the flour, desired dried herb, and salt. In a 1-cup measure combine ¼ cup milk and oil. Add all at once to flour mixture. Stir lightly with a fork. On lightly floured surface, roll dough from center to edge into an 11-inch circle. Ease into prepared tart pan. Trim even with edge of pan. Do not prick pastry. Line with a double thickness of heavy foil. Press down firmly but gently. Bake in a 425° oven for 5 minutes. Remove foil. Bake for 5 to 7 minutes more or until pastry is nearly done. Remove from the oven and place on a wire rack. Reduce oven temperature to 375°.

3. For filling, cook onion and zucchini in a small amount of boiling water about 5 minutes or until onion is tender. Drain well. In a medium bowl beat the cheese, egg whites, whole egg, and pepper with an electric mixer on low speed until combined. (Cheese will be lumpy.) Stir in onion mixture and the ½ cup milk.

4. Spoon the filling into prebaked tart shell. Bake in a 375° oven about 20 minutes or until a knife inserted near the center comes out clean. Cool on a wire rack for 15 minutes. Carefully remove side of tart pan. Serve warm. If desired, garnish with fresh herb and apple or pear slices. Makes 16 servings.

NUTRITION FACTS PER SERVING:

85 calories
4 g total fat
1 g saturated fat
17 mg cholesterol
109 mg sodium
9 g carbohydrate
0 g fiber
3 g protein

23

maryland crab cakes with horseradish sauce

For a terrific start to any party, serve this bite-size version of an East Coast classic.

INGREDIENTS

- 1 6-ounce package frozen cooked crabmeat, thawed and drained
- ½ cup fine dry bread crumbs
- 2 tablespoons finely chopped green onion
- 2 tablespoons finely chopped green sweet pepper
- 2 tablespoons fat-free mayonnaise dressing or salad dressing
- 1 egg white
- ½ teaspoon dry mustard
- ½ teaspoon finely shredded lemon or lime peel
- ⅛ teaspoon black pepper
  Nonstick spray coating
- 1 recipe Horseradish Sauce

Prep time: 15 minutes
Baking time: 15 minutes

DIRECTIONS

1. In a medium mixing bowl combine the crabmeat, bread crumbs, green onion, sweet pepper, mayonnaise or salad dressing, egg white, mustard, lemon or lime peel, and black pepper. Mix well. (If mixture seems dry, stir in 1 tablespoon milk.)

2. Gently shape mixture into 18 small patties. Spray a shallow baking pan with nonstick coating. Place patties in pan. Bake in a 350° oven about 15 minutes or until the patties are a light golden brown.

3. Meanwhile, prepare Horseradish Sauce. Pass sauce with hot crab cakes. Makes 9 servings.

Horseradish Sauce: In a small bowl stir together ¼ cup plain fat-free yogurt, 2 tablespoons fat-free mayonnaise dressing or salad dressing, 2 tablespoons finely chopped green onion, 1½ teaspoons prepared horseradish, and 1 teaspoon snipped fresh parsley.

NUTRITION FACTS PER SERVING:

43 calories
1 g total fat
0 g saturated fat
19 mg cholesterol
178 mg sodium
4 g carbohydrate
0 g fiber
5 g protein

cheese-stuffed baby vegetables

An herb-spiked ricotta- and cream-cheese mixture fills these colorful vegetable snacks.

INGREDIENTS

- ⅓ cup light ricotta cheese
- 2 tablespoons fat-free cream cheese (tub style)
- 2 tablespoons finely shredded radish
- 1 tablespoon snipped fresh chives
- 2 teaspoons snipped fresh thyme, basil, dill, or marjoram or ½ teaspoon dried thyme, basil, dillweed, or marjoram, crushed
- ⅛ teaspoon onion salt
- 20 to 24 cherry tomatoes and/or 10 to 12 baby summer squash (such as zucchini or pattypan squash)
- Fresh thyme, basil, dill, or marjoram (optional)

Prep time: 30 minutes

DIRECTIONS

1. For filling, in a small mixing bowl stir together the ricotta cheese, cream cheese, radish, chives, desired snipped fresh or dried herb, and onion salt. Mix well. Set aside.

2. Slice a thin layer off the top of each tomato. Using a small spoon, carefully scoop out and discard pulp. Invert tomatoes onto paper towels to drain. (If using squash, cut in half lengthwise for zucchini or horizontally for pattypan; scoop out pulp and invert as for the cherry tomatoes.)

3. Stuff the tomatoes and/or squash with filling. Serve immediately or chill until serving time. If desired, garnish with additional desired fresh herb. Makes 10 to 12 servings.

To stuff the vegetables, place the filling in a plastic sandwich bag. Snip off one corner of the bag and squeeze some filling into each vegetable. Or put the filling in a decorating bag fitted with a large round tip and fill.

NUTRITION FACTS PER SERVING:

22 calories
1 g total fat
0 g saturated fat
3 mg cholesterol
45 mg sodium
3 g carbohydrate
1 g fiber
1 g protein

25

vegetable spring rolls

Spring rolls are the Vietnamese version of Chinese egg rolls. Instead of a dough wrapper, however, spring rolls are made with thin, translucent rice papers. Look for these papers in Asian markets or in many large supermarkets.

INGREDIENTS

- ½ cup shredded daikon (Oriental white radish) or radishes
- 2 green onions, thinly sliced
- 2 tablespoons rice vinegar
- 1 teaspoon sugar
- 1 small fresh jalapeño or serrano pepper, seeded and finely chopped (see tip, page 21)
- ½ teaspoon toasted sesame oil
- ½ cup shredded carrot
- ½ cup short thin strips cucumber
- 2 tablespoons snipped fresh cilantro
- 1 tablespoon reduced-sodium soy sauce
- 6 8½-inch-diameter rice papers
- 1½ cups shredded Boston or curly leaf lettuce
- Fresh cilantro (optional)
- Shredded carrot (optional)

Prep time: 30 minutes
Chilling time: 3 hours

DIRECTIONS

1. In a small mixing bowl combine daikon or radishes, green onions, rice vinegar, sugar, jalapeño pepper, and sesame oil. In another small bowl combine the ½ cup carrot, the cucumber, snipped cilantro, and soy sauce. Cover both mixtures; chill for 2 to 24 hours, stirring once. Drain both mixtures.

2. Pour 1 cup warm water into a pie plate. Carefully dip rice papers into water, one at a time. Place papers, not touching, on clean dry kitchen towels. Let soften for a few minutes until pliable.

3. Place ¼ cup shredded lettuce on each rice paper near 1 edge. Place about 1 rounded tablespoon of each vegetable mixture on the lettuce. Fold in the ends. Beginning at that edge, tightly roll up the rice paper. Place, seam side down, on a plate. Cover with a damp towel. Repeat with remaining

filling and papers. Cover and chill for 1 to 2 hours. Diagonally cut each roll in half crosswise. If desired, garnish with additional cilantro and shredded carrot. Makes 12 servings.

NUTRITION FACTS PER SERVING:

31 calories
0 g total fat
0 g saturated fat
0 mg cholesterol
48 mg sodium
7 g carbohydrate
0 g fiber
0 g protein

polenta with tomato-mushroom sauce

Asiago cheese, a semifirm Italian cheese, lends a rich nutty flavor to dishes. Look for it in Italian food markets or in the specialty cheese section of your supermarket. Parmesan cheese makes a comparable substitute.

INGREDIENTS

- 2 cups water
- ¾ cup cornmeal
- ¾ cup cold water
- ¼ teaspoon salt
- ¼ cup grated Asiago or Parmesan cheese (2 ounces)
- 1 recipe Tomato-Mushroom Sauce
  Finely shredded Asiago or Parmesan cheese (optional)
  Fresh basil (optional)

Prep time: 30 minutes
Chilling time: 30 minutes
Baking time: 20 minutes

DIRECTIONS

1. For polenta, in a medium saucepan bring the 2 cups water to boiling. Combine the cornmeal, the ¾ cup cold water, and salt. Slowly add cornmeal mixture to boiling water, stirring constantly. Cook and stir until mixture returns to boiling. Reduce heat to low. Cook, uncovered, for 10 to 15 minutes or until thick, stirring frequently. Stir in the ¼ cup grated cheese.

2. Spread in an ungreased 2-quart square baking dish. Cool slightly. Cover and chill about 30 minutes or until firm. Bake, uncovered, in a 350° oven about 20 minutes or until heated through. Cut into 6 rectangles; cut each rectangle in half diagonally to form 12 triangles. Serve immediately with Tomato-Mushroom Sauce. If desired, sprinkle with additional cheese and garnish with fresh basil. Makes 12 servings.

Tomato-Mushroom Sauce: In a medium saucepan cook 2 cups sliced fresh mushrooms; 1 small onion, chopped; and 1 clove garlic, minced, in 1 tablespoon hot cooking oil until tender. Cook and stir over medium-high heat for 10 minutes. Meanwhile, place one 16-ounce can whole Italian-style tomatoes in a blender container. Cover and blend until smooth. Stir blended tomatoes and 1 teaspoon sugar into mushroom mixture. Simmer, uncovered, for 15 to 20 minutes or until desired consistency. Stir in 1 tablespoon snipped fresh basil or 1 teaspoon dried basil, crushed; ⅛ teaspoon salt; and dash pepper. Heat through.

NUTRITION FACTS PER SERVING:

63 calories
2 g total fat
1 g saturated fat
2 mg cholesterol
142 mg sodium
9 g carbohydrate
1 g fiber
2 g protein

27

garden quesadillas

Most quesadillas send your calorie budget through the roof because of all of the cheese. This vegetable-stuffed version uses fat-free cream cheese and sweet peppers, saving you calories and fat.

INGREDIENTS

- **2 small green and/or red sweet peppers, cut into thin strips**
- **1 small red onion, cut into thin, 1-inch-long strips**
- **2 teaspoons olive oil or cooking oil**
- **½ teaspoon ground cumin**
- **½ teaspoon chili powder**
- **2 tablespoons snipped fresh cilantro**
- **⅓ cup fat-free cream cheese (tub style)**
- **5 6- to 7-inch flour tortillas**
- **Salsa (optional)**

The pungent taste and lively fragrance of fresh cilantro lend a wonderfully distinctive flavor to Mexican, Caribbean, and Asian dishes; however, you may use fresh parsley if you prefer a milder seasoning.

Prep time: 20 minutes
Baking time: 5 minutes

DIRECTIONS

1. In a large nonstick skillet cook sweet peppers and onion in 1 teaspoon of the oil for 3 to 5 minutes or until crisp-tender. Stir in cumin and chili powder. Cook and stir for 1 minute more. Stir in cilantro. Set vegetables aside.

2. Spread cream cheese over half of 1 side of each tortilla. Top with pepper mixture. Fold tortilla in half over peppers, pressing gently.

3. Place tortillas on an ungreased large baking sheet.

Brush tortillas with the remaining oil. Bake in a 425° oven for 5 minutes. Cut each quesadilla into 4 wedges. Serve warm. If desired, pass the salsa. Makes 10 servings.

NUTRITION FACTS PER SERVING:

60 calories
2 g fat
0 g saturated fat
1 mg cholesterol
102 mg sodium
9 g carbohydrate
1 g fiber
3 g protein

curried snack mix

Do you crave salty, high-fat snacks, such as potato chips? Bake a batch of this snack mix and you'll save yourself about half the calories and more than half the fat of a similar serving of fat-laden chips.

INGREDIENTS

- 3 plain rice cakes, broken into bite-size pieces
- 1 cup bite-size corn square cereal or oyster crackers
- ¾ cup pretzel sticks, halved (1 ounce)
- 1 tablespoon margarine or butter, melted
- 1 teaspoon Worcestershire sauce
- ½ to ¾ teaspoon curry powder

Prep time: 10 minutes
Baking time: 20 minutes
Cooling time: 30 minutes

DIRECTIONS

1. In a 13×9×2-inch baking pan stir together broken rice cakes, corn cereal or oyster crackers, and pretzels.

2. In a custard cup stir together the melted margarine or butter, Worcestershire sauce, and curry powder. Drizzle the margarine mixture over cereal mixture. Toss until coated.

3. Bake in a 300° oven for 20 minutes, stirring twice. Cool about 30 minutes before serving. Store leftovers in a tightly covered container. Makes six to eight ½-cup servings.

NUTRITION FACTS PER SERVING:

76 calories
2 g total fat
1 g saturated fat
0 mg cholesterol
175 mg sodium
12 g carbohydrate
0 g fiber
1 g protein

berry banana smoothie

Don't know what to do with all of your ripe bananas? Peel, cut up, and freeze them in a covered freezer container or sealed plastic bag. Then use the frozen, unthawed banana pieces for this fruity shake.

INGREDIENTS

- 1 small banana, cut up and frozen
- 1 cup orange juice
- ¼ cup fresh or frozen assorted berries (such as raspberries, blackberries, and/or strawberries)
- 3 tablespoons vanilla low-fat yogurt
- Fresh mint (optional)
- Fresh berries (optional)

Try your hand at creating a new flavor of smoothie. Just substitute another fresh fruit, such as peeled and cut-up peaches, mango, or papaya, for the berries.

Prep time: 10 minutes

DIRECTIONS

1. In a blender container combine the frozen banana pieces, orange juice, desired fresh or frozen berries, and yogurt. Cover and blend until smooth.

2. To serve, pour mixture into 2 glasses. If desired, garnish with fresh mint and additional fresh berries. Makes two 8-ounce servings.

NUTRITION FACTS PER SERVING:

132 calories
0 g total fat
0 g saturated fat
1 mg cholesterol
14 mg sodium
29 g carbohydrate
2 g fiber
2 g protein

iced espresso

This refreshing coffee drink becomes an elegant beverage for a summer party or a flavorful pick-me-up in the afternoon. And, keep it in mind as the perfect ending to a light lunch or dinner in place of dessert.

INGREDIENTS

½ cup ground espresso coffee or French roast coffee

1 teaspoon finely shredded orange peel

4 cups water

1½ cups fat-free milk

3 tablespoons sugar

Ice cubes

Orange peel strips (optional)

1 teaspoon grated semisweet chocolate (optional)

Prep time: 15 minutes

DIRECTIONS

1. Prepare coffee with shredded orange peel and water in a drip coffeemaker or percolator according to manufacturer's directions. Pour into a heatproof pitcher; stir in the milk and sugar. Chill until serving time.

2. To serve, fill 6 glasses with ice cubes; pour coffee mixture over ice. If desired, garnish with orange peel strips and grated chocolate. Makes six 6-ounce servings.

Make this delightful coffee

doubly delicious by serving it over coffee ice cubes. To make them, simply pour cooled coffee into ice cube trays and freeze until solid. The ice cubes won't dilute the flavor of the coffee.

NUTRITION FACTS PER SERVING:

54 calories
0 g fat
0 g saturated fat
1 mg cholesterol
35 mg sodium
11 g carbohydrate
0 g fiber
2 g protein

31

Blueberry Pancakes with Orange Sauce
Recipe, page 45

breakfasts &breads

asparagus-potato scramble

If you use fresh asparagus, rinse it thoroughly in cold water and snap off the woody ends. By gently bending them, you can find the spot where the stalks break easily.

INGREDIENTS

Nonstick spray coating

2 cups frozen loose-pack diced hash brown potatoes with onions and peppers, thawed

2 tablespoons sliced green onion

6 beaten egg whites

3 beaten eggs

3 tablespoons fat-free milk

1 tablespoon snipped fresh basil or ½ teaspoon dried basil, crushed

⅛ teaspoon salt

⅛ teaspoon pepper

1 pound asparagus, cut into 1-inch pieces (1½ cups), or one 10-ounce package frozen cut asparagus, thawed and well drained

¼ cup shredded reduced-fat sharp cheddar cheese (1 ounce)

Watching fat and cholesterol

closely? Use 1½ cups refrigerated or frozen egg product (thawed) instead of the egg whites and whole eggs.

Start to finish: 18 minutes

DIRECTIONS

1. Generously spray an unheated large nonstick skillet with nonstick coating. Preheat over medium heat. Add potatoes and onion. Cook and stir 4 to 5 minutes or until potatoes begin to brown.

2. In a large mixing bowl beat together the egg whites, whole eggs, milk, basil, salt, and pepper. Stir in asparagus. Pour egg mixture over potatoes and green onion.

3. Cook, without stirring, until mixture begins to set on the bottom and around the edge. Using a spatula or a large spoon, lift and fold the partially cooked mixture so the uncooked portion flows underneath. Continue cooking and folding about 4 minutes or until eggs are cooked through, but are still glossy and moist.

4. Remove skillet from heat; sprinkle with cheese. Cover and let stand about 1 minute or until cheese is melted. Makes 5 servings.

NUTRITION FACTS PER SERVING:

184 calories
9 g total fat
3 g saturated fat
132 mg cholesterol
217 mg sodium
132 g carbohydrate
2 g fiber
12 g protein

34

INGREDIENTS

1 cup water
1 cup broccoli flowerets
½ cup finely chopped carrot
¼ cup sliced green onions
   Nonstick spray coating
¾ cup shredded reduced-fat
   cheddar or Swiss cheese
   (3 ounces)
2 8-ounce cartons refrigerated or
   frozen egg product, thawed

1 tablespoon snipped fresh basil
   or 1 teaspoon dried basil,
   crushed
1 tablespoon Dijon-style mustard
¼ teaspoon pepper
   Tomato slices (optional)
   Fresh tarragon (optional)

vegetable frittata

When you need a spur-of-the-moment meal, this egg dish saves the day. Serve it with sliced cucumbers or fresh tomatoes topped with a light vinaigrette and a hearty bread.

Start to finish: 25 minutes

DIRECTIONS

1. In a medium saucepan combine the water, broccoli, carrot, and green onions. Bring to boiling; reduce heat. Simmer, covered, for 6 to 8 minutes or until vegetables are crisp-tender. Drain well.

2. Spray an unheated large nonstick skillet with nonstick coating. Spread the cooked vegetables in the bottom of the skillet. Sprinkle with half of the cheese. In a medium mixing bowl stir together the egg product, basil, mustard, and pepper. Pour over vegetables and cheese in skillet. Cook over medium heat. As mixture sets, run a spatula around edge of skillet, lifting egg mixture so the uncooked portion flows underneath. Continue cooking and lifting the edges until egg mixture is almost set (the surface will be moist). Remove from heat.

3. Cover and let stand for 3 to 4 minutes or until top is set. To serve, cut the frittata into wedges. Sprinkle with the remaining cheese. If desired, garnish with tomato slices and tarragon. Makes 8 servings.

NUTRITION FACTS PER SERVING:

101 calories
3 g total fat
1 g saturated fat
6 mg cholesterol
287 mg sodium
6 g carbohydrate
0 g fiber
11 g protein

puffy omelet squares

Topped with a savory zucchini and tomato sauce, these fluffy, puffy squares provide a delicious, quick choice for any meal of the day.

INGREDIENTS

　　Nonstick spray coating
6　egg yolks
½　teaspoon onion powder
¼　teaspoon salt
⅛　teaspoon pepper
6　egg whites
1　14½-ounce can pasta-style stewed tomatoes, undrained and cut up if necessary
1　medium zucchini, quartered lengthwise and sliced (about 1 cup)
⅛　teaspoon pepper

Start to finish: 40 minutes

DIRECTIONS

1. Spray a 2-quart square baking dish with nonstick coating; set aside. For omelet, in a medium bowl beat the egg yolks, onion powder, salt, and ⅛ teaspoon pepper with an electric mixer on medium speed about 4 minutes or until thick and lemon colored; set aside. Wash beaters thoroughly. In a large bowl beat egg whites until soft peaks form (tips curl). Gently fold yolk mixture into beaten egg whites.

2. Spread the egg mixture evenly into prepared dish. Bake in a 350° oven for 22 to 25 minutes or until a knife inserted near the center comes out clean.

3. Meanwhile, for sauce, in a medium saucepan combine undrained tomatoes, zucchini, and ⅛ teaspoon pepper. Bring to boiling; reduce heat. Simmer, covered, about 5 minutes or until zucchini is tender. Simmer, uncovered, for 10 to 12 minutes more or until sauce is of desired consistency. To serve, cut omelet into quarters; top with sauce. Makes 4 servings.

NUTRITION FACTS PER SERVING:

152 calories
8 g total fat
2 g saturated fat
320 mg cholesterol
549 mg sodium
10 g carbohydrate
0 g fiber
11 g protein

savory brunch strudel

INGREDIENTS

1 cup fat-free or light ricotta cheese

¼ cup freshly shredded Asiago or Parmesan cheese

1 ounce chopped lower-fat cooked ham

1 2-ounce jar diced pimiento, drained

2 tablespoons thinly sliced green onion

2 tablespoons snipped fresh dill or 1 teaspoon dried dillweed

1 slightly beaten egg white

¼ teaspoon salt

¼ teaspoon pepper

8 ounces asparagus, cut into ½-inch pieces, or ½ of a 10-ounce package frozen cut asparagus

Butter-flavor nonstick spray coating

10 sheets frozen phyllo dough, thawed

¼ cup fine dry bread crumbs

Score the phyllo before baking so it doesn't shatter when you slice the strudel.

Prep time: 20 minutes
Baking time: 30 minutes
Standing time: 10 minutes

DIRECTIONS

1. For filling, in a large bowl combine ricotta cheese, Asiago or Parmesan cheese, ham, pimiento, green onion, dill, egg white, salt, and pepper. Set aside.

2. In a covered small saucepan cook the asparagus in a small amount of boiling water for 4 to 5 minutes or just until crisp-tender (don't overcook). Drain. Rinse with cold water; drain. Stir into the ricotta mixture.

3. Spray a large baking sheet with nonstick coating; set aside. Place 1 sheet of phyllo on a dry kitchen towel (keep remaining phyllo cov-ered with a damp kitchen towel to prevent drying out). Spray with nonstick coating. Top with another sheet of phyllo. Spray with nonstick coating. Sprinkle with one-fourth of the bread crumbs. Repeat with remaining phyllo and remaining bread crumbs. Spray the last layer with non-stick coating.

4. Spoon the filling length-wise onto half of the top layer of phyllo, leaving about a 1½-inch border on all sides. Fold in the short sides over filling. Starting from a long side, roll up into a spiral.

5. Place strudel, seam side down, on the prepared baking sheet. Spray top with non-stick coating. Using a sharp knife, score into 12 slices, cutting through the top layer only. If desired, sprinkle with additional bread crumbs.

6. Bake in a 375° oven about 30 minutes or until light brown. Let stand for 10 minutes before serving. To serve, cut along scored lines into slices. Makes 6 servings.

NUTRITION FACTS PER SERVING:

175 calories
4 g total fat
0 g saturated fat
9 mg cholesterol
413 mg sodium
24 g carbohydrate
1 g fiber
12 g protein

37

vegetable quiches

Using tortillas for the crust and fat-free egg product, reduced-fat cheese, and evaporated fat-free milk for the filling cuts the fat to just 4 grams per serving in these mini quiches. A traditional quiche has more than 20 grams of fat per serving.

INGREDIENTS

Nonstick spray coating

3 7- or 8-inch flour tortillas

½ cup shredded reduced-fat Swiss, cheddar, or mozzarella cheese (2 ounces)

1 cup broccoli flowerets

½ of a small red sweet pepper, cut into thin strips (½ cup)

2 green onions, sliced

1 8-ounce carton refrigerated or frozen egg product, thawed

¾ cup evaporated fat-free milk

¼ teaspoon dried thyme, crushed

⅛ teaspoon salt

⅛ teaspoon black pepper

Thin strips red sweet pepper (optional)

Vary the look

of the crust by cutting each tortilla into 6 wedges. Press 3 tortilla wedges, points toward center, into each of six 6-ounce custard cups sprayed with nonstick coating. The tortillas do not have to cover the cups completely.

Prep time: 25 minutes
Baking time: 25 minutes
Standing time: 5 minutes

DIRECTIONS

1. Spray three 6- to 7-inch individual round baking dishes or pans with nonstick coating. Carefully press tortillas into dishes or pans. Sprinkle with cheese.

2. In a covered small saucepan cook the broccoli, the ½ cup sweet pepper strips, and the green onions in a small amount of boiling water about 3 minutes or until crisp-tender. Drain well. Sprinkle cooked vegetables over cheese in baking dishes.

3. In a medium bowl stir together the egg product, evaporated fat-free milk, thyme, salt, and black pepper. Pour over the vegetables in baking dishes. Place on a baking sheet.

4. Bake in a 375° oven for 25 to 30 minutes or until puffed and a knife inserted near the centers comes out clean. Let stand for 5 minutes before serving. If desired, garnish quiches with additional sweet pepper strips. Makes 6 servings.

NUTRITION FACTS PER SERVING:

133 calories
4 g total fat
1 g saturated fat
6 mg cholesterol
333 mg sodium
14 g carbohydrate
1 g fiber
10 g protein

INGREDIENTS

Nonstick spray coating

1½ cups frozen loose-pack diced
hash brown potatoes or
country-style hash brown
potatoes with skin, thawed

1 cup sliced fresh mushrooms

½ cup shredded carrot

½ cup shredded zucchini

¼ cup chopped onion

1 cup refrigerated or frozen egg
product, thawed, or 4 eggs

¼ cup fat-free milk

1 12-inch Italian bread
shell (Boboli)

½ cup shredded reduced-fat
mozzarella cheese (2 ounces)

½ cup chopped tomato

vegetable breakfast pizza

America's favorite food just took the a.m. shift. Count on frozen hash browns and an Italian bread shell to get breakfast on the table in short order.

Prep time: 20 minutes
Baking time: 8 minutes

DIRECTIONS

1. Spray an unheated large skillet with nonstick coating. Preheat over medium heat. Add the potatoes, mushrooms, carrot, zucchini, and onion. Cook and stir about 3 minutes or until vegetables are tender.

2. In a small mixing bowl stir together egg product or eggs and milk. Pour over vegetables. Cook, without stirring, until mixture begins to set on the bottom and around the edge. Using a spatula or a large spoon, lift and fold the partially cooked egg mixture so the uncooked portion flows underneath. Continue cooking and folding about 4 minutes or until egg product is cooked through but is still glossy and moist. Remove from heat.

3. To assemble pizza, place the Italian bread shell on a baking sheet or in a 12-inch pizza pan. Sprinkle with half of the cheese. Top with the egg mixture, tomato, and remaining cheese. Bake in a 375° oven for 8 to 10 minutes or until cheese is melted. Makes 8 servings.

NUTRITION FACTS PER SERVING:

251 calories
7 g total fat
1 g saturated fat
7 mg cholesterol
559 mg sodium
34 g carbohydrate
3 g fiber
14 g protein

breakfast couscous with fruit

Take a break from the usual bowl of flakes and try this tart-sweet couscous-and-fruit medley. It's like having a bowl of rice pudding for breakfast.

INGREDIENTS

- 1 cup fat-free milk
- ¼ teaspoon ground cinnamon
  Dash ground nutmeg
- 1 cup couscous
- ⅓ cup orange juice
- ¾ cup cranberries
- 2 tablespoons water
- 2 tablespoons honey
- 1 11-ounce can mandarin orange sections, drained
- 2 tablespoons slivered almonds, toasted (see tip, page 108)

Start to finish: 15 minutes

DIRECTIONS

1. In a medium saucepan combine the milk, cinnamon, and nutmeg. Bring to boiling over medium heat. Stir in couscous. Cover and remove from heat. Let stand for 5 minutes. Stir in orange juice. Fluff with a fork.

2. Meanwhile, in a small saucepan combine cranberries, water, and honey. Cook over low heat for 4 to 5 minutes or until the cranberry skins begin to pop. Remove from heat. Gently stir in mandarin oranges.

3. To serve, spoon the couscous mixture into serving bowls. Top with the warm cranberry-orange mixture and sprinkle with almonds. Makes 4 servings.

NUTRITION FACTS PER SERVING:

312 calories
3 g total fat
0 g saturated fat
0 mg cholesterol
11 mg sodium
66 g carbohydrate
8 g fiber
8 g protein

INGREDIENTS

- **3** cups regular rolled oats
- **1** cup coarsely shredded unpeeled apple
- **½** cup toasted wheat germ
- **¼** cup water
- **¼** cup honey
- **1½** teaspoons ground cinnamon
- **1** teaspoon vanilla or ½ teaspoon almond extract
- Nonstick spray coating
- Fat-free milk

granola

Shredded apple adds flavor and texture to this honey-sweetened granola. Sprinkle the granola over low-fat yogurt for a quick snack or breakfast on the go.

Prep time: 12 minutes
Baking time: 45 minutes
Cooling time: 30 minutes

DIRECTIONS

1. In a large bowl combine rolled oats, apple, and wheat germ; mix well. In a small saucepan stir together water, honey, and cinnamon. Bring to boiling; remove from heat. Stir in the vanilla or almond extract. Pour over the oat mixture; toss to coat.

2. Spray a 15×10×1-inch baking pan with nonstick coating. Spread oat mixture evenly in pan. Bake in a 325° oven about 45 minutes or until golden brown, stirring occasionally. Spread onto foil and cool about 30 minutes before serving. Store leftovers in an airtight container in the refrigerator for up to 2 weeks. Serve the granola with milk. Makes 8 (½-cup) servings.

NUTRITION FACTS PER SERVING:

216 calories
3 g total fat
1 g saturated fat
1 mg cholesterol
44 mg sodium
39 g carbohydrate
0 g fiber
10 g protein

breakfast blintzes

You can make crepes up to two days in advance. Layer the cooled crepes between waxed paper and store in an airtight container in the refrigerator. Fill with the ricotta filling and bake just before serving for a special brunch.

INGREDIENTS

1	beaten egg
1½	cups fat-free milk
1	cup all-purpose flour
	Nonstick spray coating
1	15-ounce carton light ricotta cheese
2	tablespoons orange marmalade
1	tablespoon sugar
⅛	teaspoon ground cinnamon
⅔	cup light dairy sour cream
5	tablespoons orange marmalade
½	cup fresh raspberries or blueberries

Prep time: 30 minutes
Baking time: 15 minutes

DIRECTIONS

1. For crepes, in a medium bowl combine egg, milk, and flour. Beat with a rotary beater until well mixed. Spray an unheated 6-inch skillet or crepe pan with nonstick coating. Preheat over medium heat. Remove from heat and pour in about 2 tablespoons batter. Lift and tilt skillet to spread batter. Return skillet to heat; cook for 30 to 60 seconds or until browned on 1 side only. Remove from pan. Repeat with remaining batter to make 15 crepes, greasing skillet occasionally.

2. Spray a shallow baking pan with nonstick coating. Set aside. For filling, in a bowl combine ricotta cheese, the 2 tablespoons orange marmalade, the sugar, and cinnamon. Spoon about 2 tablespoons filling onto the unbrowned side of a crepe; spread out slightly. Fold in half. Fold in half again, forming a wedge. Arrange in prepared pan. Repeat with remaining filling and crepes.

3. Bake in a 350° oven for 15 to 20 minutes or until heated through. To serve, spoon 2 teaspoons of sour cream and 1 teaspoon of marmalade onto each blintz. Sprinkle with berries. Makes 15 blintzes.

NUTRITION FACTS PER BLINTZ:

111 calories
2 g total fat
1 g saturated fat
21 mg cholesterol
51 mg sodium
17 g carbohydrate
1 g fiber
6 g protein

INGREDIENTS

½ cup fat-free cream cheese (block style) (about 5 ounces)

2 tablespoons apricot or strawberry spreadable fruit

8 1-inch-thick slices French bread

2 slightly beaten egg whites

1 beaten egg

¾ cup fat-free milk

½ teaspoon vanilla

⅛ teaspoon apple pie spice

Nonstick spray coating

½ cup apricot or strawberry spreadable fruit

Sliced fresh apricots or strawberries (optional)

stuffed french toast

For a change of taste, top fruit-and-cream cheese-filled French toast with a drizzle of maple syrup or a dusting of powdered sugar instead of the spreadable fruit.

Start to finish: 20 minutes

DIRECTIONS

1. In a bowl stir together cream cheese and the 2 tablespoons spreadable fruit. Using a serrated knife, cut a pocket in each of the bread slices by making a cut in the center of each slice from the top almost to the bottom. Fill each pocket with some of the cream cheese mixture.

2. In a shallow bowl beat together egg whites, whole egg, milk, vanilla, and apple pie spice. Spray a nonstick griddle with nonstick coating. Preheat over medium heat.

3. Dip bread slices into egg white mixture, coating both sides. Cook bread slices about 3 minutes or until golden brown, turning once.

4 Meanwhile, in a small saucepan heat the ½ cup spreadable fruit until melted, stirring frequently. Serve over warm French toast. If desired, garnish with fresh apricots or strawberries. Makes 8 servings.

NUTRITION FACTS PER SERVING:

150 calories
1 g total fat
0 g saturated fat
30 mg cholesterol
163 mg sodium
29 g carbohydrate
0 g fiber
7 g protein

streusel french toast

Crushed, shredded wheat biscuit adds a slightly crunchy topping to this make-ahead, nutrition-packed breakfast. Fresh strawberries make it even more special.

INGREDIENTS

Nonstick spray coating

¾ cup refrigerated or frozen egg product, thawed, or 3 eggs

1 cup evaporated fat-free milk

3 tablespoons sugar

2 teaspoons vanilla

½ teaspoon ground cinnamon

¼ teaspoon ground nutmeg

6 1-inch-thick slices Italian bread (3 to 4 inches in diameter)

1 large shredded wheat biscuit, crushed (⅔ cup)

1 tablespoon butter or margarine, melted

2 cups sliced strawberries

3 tablespoons sugar

½ teaspoon ground cinnamon

Prep time: 20 minutes
Chilling time: 2 hours
Baking time: 30 minutes

DIRECTIONS

1. Spray a 2-quart rectangular baking dish with nonstick coating; set aside. In a medium bowl beat together the egg product or eggs, evaporated milk, 3 tablespoons sugar, the vanilla, ½ teaspoon cinnamon, and the nutmeg. Arrange the bread slices in a single layer in prepared baking dish. Pour egg mixture evenly over bread slices. Cover and chill for 2 to 24 hours, turning bread once with a wide spatula.

2. In a small bowl combine the crushed biscuit and melted butter or margarine; sprinkle evenly over the bread slices.

3. Bake, uncovered, in a 375° oven about 30 minutes until lightly browned.

4. Meanwhile, in a small bowl combine the strawberries, 3 tablespoons sugar, and ½ teaspoon cinnamon. Serve with French toast. Makes 6 servings.

NUTRITION FACTS PER SERVING:

244 calories
5 g total fat
2 g saturated fat
7 mg cholesterol
300 mg sodium
41 g carbohydrate
1 g fiber
10 g protein

blueberry pancakes with orange sauce

Soak up every bit of the tangy citrus sauce with these berry-stuffed, low-fat pancakes. The easy orange sauce provides a refreshing change from regular pancake syrup. (Recipe also pictured on pages 32 and 33.)

INGREDIENTS

- 1 cup all-purpose flour
- 1 tablespoon sugar
- 1 teaspoon baking powder
- ½ teaspoon baking soda
- ⅛ teaspoon salt
- 1 slightly beaten egg white
- 1 cup buttermilk
- 2 teaspoons cooking oil
- 1 teaspoon vanilla
- ¾ cup fresh or frozen blueberries
- 1 recipe Orange Sauce
  Orange wedges and/or fresh blueberries (optional)

Prep time: 20 minutes
Cooking time: 4 minutes per batch

DIRECTIONS

1. For pancakes, in a medium mixing bowl stir together the flour, sugar, baking powder, baking soda, and salt.

2. In another mixing bowl stir together the egg white, buttermilk, cooking oil, and vanilla. Add all at once to the flour mixture. Stir just until combined but still slightly lumpy. Gently fold in the blueberries.

3. For each pancake, pour about ¼ cup of the batter onto a hot nonstick griddle. Cook over medium heat about 4 minutes or until pancakes are golden brown, turning to cook second sides when pancakes have bubbly surfaces and slightly dry edges. Serve with Orange Sauce. If desired, garnish with orange wedges and/or additional blueberries. Cover and chill any remaining sauce. Makes 4 or 5 servings.

Orange Sauce: In a small saucepan stir together ¼ cup orange juice concentrate, 1 tablespoon sugar, and 1 tablespoon cornstarch. Add 1 cup water. Cook and stir over medium heat until thickened and bubbly. Cook and stir for 2 minutes more.

NUTRITION FACTS PER SERVING:

204 calories
3 g total fat
1 g saturated fat
2 mg cholesterol
396 mg sodium
37 g carbohydrate
2 g fiber
6 g protein

45

fruit-filled puff pancakes

These puff pancakes deflate after baking to form a "bowl" just right for filling with colorful fresh fruit.

INGREDIENTS

Nonstick spray coating
½   cup refrigerated or frozen egg product, thawed, or 1 whole egg plus 1 egg white
¼   cup all-purpose flour
¼   cup fat-free milk
1   tablespoon cooking oil
¼   teaspoon salt

2   cups fresh fruit (choose from sliced strawberries, peeled and sliced kiwifruit, blackberries, raspberries, blueberries, seedless grapes, peeled and sliced peaches, sliced nectarines, sliced apricots, and/or pitted and halved sweet cherries)
2   tablespoons orange marmalade, warmed

Prep time: 10 minutes
Baking time: 25 minutes
Standing time: 5 minutes

DIRECTIONS

1. For pancakes, spray four 4¼-inch pie plates or 4½-inch foil tart pans with nonstick coating. Set aside.

2. In a large mixing bowl use a rotary beater or wire whisk to beat egg product or whole egg plus egg white, flour, milk, oil, and salt until smooth. Divide batter among prepared pans. Bake in a 400° oven about 25 minutes or until brown and puffy. Turn off oven; let stand in oven for 5 minutes.

3. To serve, immediately after removing the pancakes from oven, transfer to 4 plates. Spoon some of the fruit into center of each pancake. Drizzle fruit with warmed orange marmalade. Makes 4 servings.

NUTRITION FACTS PER SERVING:

126 calories
5 g total fat
1 g saturated fat
1 mg cholesterol
198 mg sodium
16 g carbohydrate
2 g fiber
5 g protein

INGREDIENTS

Nonstick spray coating

⅓ cup dried shiitake or porcini
    mushrooms

½ teaspoon salt

¼ teaspoon dried thyme, crushed

⅛ teaspoon pepper

1 cup milk

2 beaten eggs

1 tablespoon cooking oil

1 cup all-purpose flour

Prep time: 15 minutes
Baking time: 35 minutes

DIRECTIONS

1. Spray the cups of a popover pan or six 6-ounce custard cups with nonstick coating. Place the custard cups on a 15×10×1-inch baking pan; set side. In a small bowl pour enough boiling water over the dried mushrooms to cover. Soak for 5 minutes. Drain, pressing out the excess liquid. Finely chop mushrooms.

mostly mushrooms popovers

Towers of light, crisp-shelled popovers burst with mushroom and herb flavors.

2. In a medium mixing bowl combine the chopped mushrooms, salt, thyme, and pepper. Add milk, eggs, and oil. Beat with a rotary beater or wire whisk until well mixed. Add flour. Beat just until mixture is smooth.

3. Fill the cups about half full with batter. Bake in a 400° oven for 35 to 40 minutes or until popovers are very firm. Remove from oven. Immediately prick each popover with a fork to let steam escape. Loosen edges. Remove the popovers from cups. Serve immediately. Makes 6 popovers.

The key to airy popovers is not overbeating the batter. To prevent overbrowning, place the oven rack in the lower position of the oven so the top of the popover pan or custard cups is in the center.

NUTRITION FACTS PER POPOVER:

150 calories
5 g total fat
1 g saturated fat
74 mg cholesterol
219 mg sodium
20 g carbohydrate
1 g fiber
6 g protein

47

raspberry and cheese coffee cake

With fruit and a cheesecake-like topping, you'll never miss the fat in this calorie-reduced coffee cake.

INGREDIENTS

Nonstick spray coating
1¼ cups all-purpose flour
1¼ teaspoons baking powder
1 teaspoon finely shredded lemon or orange peel
¼ teaspoon baking soda
¼ teaspoon salt
¾ cup granulated sugar
3 tablespoons margarine or butter, softened
¼ cup refrigerated or frozen egg product, thawed
1 teaspoon vanilla
½ cup buttermilk

2 ounces reduced-fat cream cheese (Neufchâtel)
¼ cup granulated sugar
2 tablespoons refrigerated or frozen egg product, thawed
1 cup raspberries or thinly sliced apricots or nectarines
Raspberries or thinly sliced apricots or nectarines (optional)
Sifted powdered sugar

Prep time: 20 minutes
Baking time: 30 minutes

DIRECTIONS

1. Spray a 9×1½-inch round baking pan with nonstick coating. Set aside. In a medium mixing bowl stir together the flour, baking powder, lemon or orange peel, baking soda, and salt. Set aside.

2. In a medium mixing bowl beat the ¾ cup granulated sugar and margarine or butter with an electric mixer on medium to high speed until combined. Add the ¼ cup egg product and vanilla. Beat on low to medium speed for 1 minute. Alternately add the flour mixture and buttermilk to egg mixture, beating just until combined after each addition. Pour into prepared pan.

3. In a small mixing bowl beat the cream cheese and the ¼ cup granulated sugar on medium to high speed until combined. Add the 2 tablespoons egg product. Beat until combined. Arrange the 1 cup raspberries, apricots, or nectarines over batter in the pan. Pour cream cheese mixture over all.

4. Bake in a 375° oven for 30 to 35 minutes or until a wooden toothpick inserted near center comes out clean. Cool slightly on wire rack. Serve warm. If desired, top with additional fruit. Dust with powdered sugar. Makes 10 servings.

NUTRITION FACTS PER SERVING:

195 calories
5 g total fat
2 g saturated fat
5 mg cholesterol
223 mg sodium
33 g carbohydrate
1 g fiber
4 g protein

INGREDIENTS

- 1¼ cups all-purpose flour
- ½ cup sugar
- ½ teaspoon baking powder
- ½ teaspoon baking soda
- ¼ teaspoon salt
- ¼ teaspoon ground nutmeg
- 1 beaten egg
- ⅔ cup plain fat-free yogurt
- 2 tablespoons cooking oil
- ½ teaspoon vanilla
- 1 medium mango, peeled, seeded, and finely chopped (about 1 cup)
- 1 tablespoon all-purpose flour
- 2 tablespoons flaked coconut

tropical coffee cake

Mango and coconut give this delicious coffee cake an island flair. Yogurt and a small amount of oil help keep the cake moist. If you can't find fresh mangoes, substitute nectarines or peaches. (To seed a mango, see tip page 266.)

Prep time: 25 minutes
Baking time: 35 minutes

DIRECTIONS

1. Lightly grease and flour a 9×1½-inch round baking pan; set aside. In a large bowl stir together the 1¼ cups flour, the sugar, baking powder, baking soda, salt, and nutmeg. Make a well in the center of the flour mixture; set aside.

2. In a small mixing bowl stir together the egg, yogurt, oil, and vanilla. Add the egg mixture all at once to flour mixture. Stir just until moistened (batter should be slightly lumpy). Toss the chopped mango with the 1 tablespoon flour; gently fold into batter. Spread batter into prepared pan.

3. Sprinkle the coconut over the batter in pan. Bake in a 350° oven about 35 minutes or until a wooden toothpick inserted near the center comes out clean. Serve warm. Makes 8 servings.

Tossing the mango
with a small amount of the flour may seem like an extra step, but it's an important one. It helps separate the pieces of fruit so they don't clump together.

NUTRITION FACTS PER SERVING:

193 calories
5 g total fat
1 g saturated fat
27 mg cholesterol
194 mg sodium
34 g carbohydrate
1 g fiber
4 g protein

easy apricot bread

Prepare these impressive loaves with frozen bread dough and a filling of low-calorie fruit spread. Varying the filling to fit your taste is as simple as changing the flavor of the spread and the type of fruit.

INGREDIENTS

Nonstick spray coating

1 16-ounce loaf frozen white or whole wheat bread dough, thawed (see tip, page 57)

½ cup low-calorie apricot, strawberry, or raspberry spread

½ cup chopped apricots, peeled and chopped peaches, blueberries, or raspberries

1 recipe Powdered Sugar Icing

Prep time: 30 minutes
Rising time: 40 minutes
Baking time: 20 minutes

DIRECTIONS

1. Spray 2 baking sheets with nonstick coating. Turn the dough out onto a lightly floured surface. Divide dough in half. Roll each half into a 12×7-inch rectangle. Carefully transfer each rectangle of dough to a prepared baking sheet.

2. Cut up any large pieces of fruit in the fruit spread. For each loaf, spoon ¼ cup of the fruit spread down the center third of the dough rectangle to within 1 inch of the ends. Sprinkle ¼ cup of the fresh fruit over the spread. On the long sides, make 2-inch-long cuts from the edges toward the center at 1-inch intervals. Starting at one end, alternately fold opposite strips of dough, at an angle, across fruit filling. Slightly press the ends together in the center to seal. Cover and let rise in a warm place until nearly double in size (about 40 minutes).

3. Bake in a 350° oven about 20 minutes or until golden. Remove loaves from baking sheets; cool slightly on wire racks. Drizzle with Powdered Sugar Icing. Serve warm. Makes 2 loaves (24 servings).

Powdered Sugar Icing: In a small bowl stir together ½ cup sifted powdered sugar, 1 teaspoon lemon juice, and 1 to 2 teaspoons fat-free milk. Stir in enough additional fat-free milk, 1 teaspoon at a time, to make icing of drizzling consistency.

NUTRITION FACTS PER SERVING:

61 calories
0 g total fat
0 g saturated fat
0 mg cholesterol
5 mg sodium
13 g carbohydrate
0 g fiber
1 g protein

pepper-cheese bread

To boost fiber, you can replace up to half of the all-purpose flour with whole wheat flour. The loaf will be denser and coarser in texture.

INGREDIENTS

- 2¾ to 3¼ cups all-purpose flour
- 1 package active dry yeast
- 1½ to 2 teaspoons cracked black pepper
- ½ teaspoon salt
- 1 cup warm water (120° to 130°)
- 2 tablespoons olive oil or cooking oil
- ½ cup shredded provolone cheese (2 ounces)
- ¼ grated Parmesan or Romano cheese (1 ounce)
- 1 slightly beaten egg white
- 1 tablespoon water

Prep time: 40 minutes
Rising time: 1½ hours
Baking time: 35 minutes

DIRECTIONS

1. In a large mixing bowl stir together 1 cup of the flour, the yeast, pepper, and salt. Add 1 cup warm water and oil. Beat with an electric mixer on low to medium speed for 30 seconds, scraping the sides of the bowl. Beat on high speed for 3 minutes. Using a wooden spoon, stir in as much of the remaining flour as you can.

2. On a lightly floured surface, knead in enough of the remaining flour to make a stiff dough that is smooth and elastic (8 to 10 minutes total). Shape into a ball. Place in a lightly greased bowl; turn once. Cover and let rise in a warm place until double in size (1 to 1¼ hours).

3. Punch dough down. Turn out onto a lightly floured surface. Cover; let dough rest 10 minutes. Lightly grease a large baking sheet.

4. Roll the dough into a 12×10-inch rectangle. Sprinkle with the provolone cheese and Parmesan or Romano cheese. Starting from a long side, roll into a spiral. Moisten edge with water; seal. Taper ends. Place, seam side down, on prepared baking sheet. Cover; let dough rise until nearly double in size (30 to 45 minutes).

5. With a sharp knife, make 3 or 4 diagonal cuts about ¼ inch deep across the top of the loaf. Combine egg white and the 1 tablespoon water; brush over loaf. Bake in a 375° oven for 15 minutes. Brush again with egg white mixture. Bake 20 to 25 minutes more or until bread sounds hollow when tapped. Remove from baking sheet and cool on a wire rack. Makes 1 loaf (16 servings).

NUTRITION FACTS PER SERVING:

- 118 calories
- 3 g total fat
- 1 g saturated fat
- 4 mg cholesterol
- 136 mg sodium
- 17 g carbohydrate
- 1 g fiber
- 4 g protein

apple-cinnamon bread

Have this bread ready for your busy mornings when time is at a premium. Warm up a slice or two in the microwave and spread with apple butter for a real treat.

INGREDIENTS

- 2½ to 3 cups all-purpose flour
- 1 package active dry yeast
- ⅔ cup fat-free milk
- 2 tablespoons granulated sugar
- 1 tablespoon cooking oil
- ⅛ teaspoon salt
- ¼ cup refrigerated or frozen egg product, thawed

  Nonstick spray coating

- ¼ cup packed brown sugar
- 1 teaspoon ground cinnamon
- 1 medium cooking apple, finely chopped (1 cup)
- ⅓ cup sifted powdered sugar (optional)
- 1 to 1½ teaspoons apple juice or fat-free milk (optional)

Prep time: 30 minutes
Rising time: 1½ hours
Baking time: 25 minutes

DIRECTIONS

1. In a large mixing bowl combine 1 cup of the flour and the yeast. In a small saucepan heat and stir the milk, granulated sugar, oil, and salt just until warm (120° to 130°). Add to flour mixture along with egg product. Beat with an electric mixer on low to medium speed for 30 seconds, scraping bowl constantly. Beat on high speed for 3 minutes. Using a wooden spoon, stir in as much of the remaining flour as you can.

2. On a lightly floured surface, knead in enough of the remaining flour to make a moderately stiff dough that is smooth and elastic (6 to 8 minutes total). Shape into a ball. Place in a lightly greased bowl; turn once to grease surface. Cover and let rise in a warm place until double in size (about 1 hour).

3. Punch dough down. Turn out onto a lightly floured surface. Cover and let rest for 10 minutes. Spray an 8×4×2-inch loaf pan with nonstick coating. Set aside. In a small mixing bowl stir together brown sugar and cinnamon. Set aside. Roll dough into a 12×8-inch rectangle. Brush lightly with water. Sprinkle with the cinnamon mixture. Top with apple.

4. Starting from a short side, roll into a spiral. Seal edge and ends. Place, seam down, in prepared pan. Cover and let rise until nearly double in size (about 30 minutes). Bake in a 375° oven for 25 to 30 minutes or until bread sounds hollow when tapped. (If necessary, cover loosely with foil during the last 10 to 15 minutes of baking to prevent overbrowning.) Remove from pan; cool on a wire rack.

5. If desired, stir together powdered sugar and enough apple juice or milk to make of drizzling consistency. Drizzle over top of loaf. Makes 1 loaf (16 servings).

NUTRITION FACTS PER SERVING:

101 calories
1 g total fat
0 g saturated fat
0 mg cholesterol
29 mg sodium
20 g carbohydrate
1 g fiber
3 g protein

INGREDIENTS

Nonstick spray coating
1½ cups all-purpose flour
1¼ teaspoons baking powder
½ teaspoon baking soda
½ teaspoon ground cinnamon
⅛ teaspoon salt
2 slightly beaten egg whites
1 cup mashed banana
¾ cup sugar
¼ cup cooking oil

banana bread

The secret to a great-tasting banana bread is to use fully ripe bananas. Let bananas ripen at room temperature until the fruit is soft and the skins are well flecked with brown.

Prep time: 20 minutes
Baking time: 45 minutes

DIRECTIONS

1. Spray an 8×4×2-inch loaf pan with nonstick coating. Set aside. In a medium bowl stir together the flour, baking powder, baking soda, cinnamon, and salt. Set aside.

2. In a large mixing bowl stir together the egg whites, banana, sugar, and oil. Add flour mixture all at once to banana mixture. Stir just until moistened.

3. Spread batter in prepared pan. Bake in a 350° oven for 45 to 50 minutes or until a toothpick inserted near the center comes out clean.

4. Cool the bread in the pan on a wire rack for 10 minutes. Remove from pan; cool completely on rack. Wrap bread in foil or plastic wrap; store overnight. Makes 1 loaf (16 servings).

NUTRITION FACTS PER SERVING:

128 calories
4 g total fat
1 g saturated fat
0 mg cholesterol
92 mg sodium
23 g carbohydrate
1 g fiber
2 g protein

pepper and fennel batter bread

This batter bread needs only one rising time and saves on elbow grease because there's no kneading required. For maximum flavor, use freshly ground black peppercorns.

INGREDIENTS

2 cups all-purpose flour
1 package active dry yeast
½ cup cream-style cottage cheese
½ cup water
1 tablespoon sugar
1 tablespoon margarine or butter
1 to 2 teaspoons fennel seed, crushed
1 to 1½ teaspoons coarsely ground pepper
1 teaspoon dried minced onion
½ teaspoon salt
1 egg
½ cup toasted wheat germ

Working with yeast can be tricky. If it gets too hot or too cold, the bread won't rise. Use a thermometer to make sure you heat the liquid mixture to just the right temperature.

Prep time: 15 minutes
Rising time: 50 minutes
Baking time: 25 minutes

DIRECTIONS

1. In a large mixing bowl stir together 1 cup of the flour and the yeast. In a medium saucepan heat and stir cottage cheese, water, sugar, margarine or butter, fennel seed, pepper, onion, and salt just until warm (120° to 130°) and margarine almost melts. Add to flour mixture along with egg. Beat with an electric mixer on low to medium speed for 30 seconds, scraping bowl constantly. Beat on high speed for 3 minutes.

2. Using a wooden spoon, stir in the wheat germ and the remaining flour (batter will be stiff). Spoon batter into a well-greased 1-quart casserole or a 9×1½-inch round baking pan. Cover and let dough rise in a warm place until nearly double in size (50 to 60 minutes).

3. Bake in a 375° oven for 25 to 30 minutes or until bread sounds hollow when tapped. (If necessary, cover loosely with foil during the last 10 minutes of baking to prevent overbrowning.) Remove from casserole or pan; cool on a wire rack. Makes 1 loaf (8 servings).

NUTRITION FACTS PER SERVING:

187 calories
4 g total fat
1 g saturated fat
29 mg cholesterol
208 mg sodium
30 g carbohydrate
2 g fiber
8 g protein

easy herb focaccia

Focaccia (foh-COT-see-uh) is an Italian yeast bread usually topped with onions, herbs, olives, or cheese. Our easy version uses a hot roll mix. Serve focaccia warm with pasta or as a snack.

INGREDIENTS

1	16-ounce package hot roll mix
1	egg
2	tablespoons olive oil
⅔	cup finely chopped onion
1	teaspoon dried rosemary, crushed
2	teaspoons olive oil

Prep time: 20 minutes
Rising time: 30 minutes
Baking time: 15 minutes

DIRECTIONS

1. Lightly grease a 15×10×1-inch baking pan, a 12- to 14-inch pizza pan, or two 9×1½-inch round baking pans. Set aside.

2. Prepare the hot roll mix according to package directions for basic dough, using the 1 egg and substituting the 2 tablespoons oil for the margarine. Knead dough; allow to rest as directed. If using large baking pan, roll dough into a 15×10-inch rectangle. If using a pizza pan, roll dough into a 12- to 14-inch round. If using round baking pans, divide dough in half; roll into two 9-inch rounds. Carefully transfer to prepared pan(s).

3. In a skillet cook the onion and rosemary in the 2 teaspoons hot oil until tender. With fingertips, press indentations every inch or so in the dough. Top dough evenly with onion mixture. Cover; let rise in a warm place until nearly double in size (about 30 minutes).

4. Bake in a 375° oven for 15 to 20 minutes or until golden. Cool 10 minutes on a wire rack(s). Remove from pan(s) and cool completely. Makes 24 servings.

Lemon and Savory Focaccia: Prepare Easy Herb Focaccia as directed, except omit the onion, rosemary, and the 2 teaspoons oil. Add ¼ cup coarsely chopped pitted ripe olives, 3 tablespoons snipped fresh savory, and 1 teaspoon finely shredded lemon peel to the dough along with the 2 tablespoons oil. Continue as directed.

Parmesan and Pine Nut Focaccia: Prepare Easy Herb Focaccia as directed, except omit the onion, rosemary, and the 2 teaspoons oil. After making indentations, brush the dough with a mixture of 1 egg white and 1 tablespoon water. Sprinkle with ¼ cup pine nuts, pressing lightly into dough. Sprinkle with 2 tablespoons freshly grated Parmesan cheese. Bake as directed in step 4.

NUTRITION FACTS PER SERVING:

85 calories
2 g total fat
0 g saturated fat
9 mg cholesterol
133 mg sodium
14 g carbohydrate
0 g fiber
2 g protein

nutmeg-apricot rolls

Flexibility is mixed right into these rolls. Either bake them right away or refrigerate overnight before baking.

Prep time: 45 minutes
Rising time: 1½ hours
Baking time: 20 minutes

INGREDIENTS

4 to 4⅓ cups all-purpose flour
2 packages active dry yeast
1 cup fat-free milk
⅓ cup granulated sugar
3 tablespoons margarine or butter
½ teaspoon salt
2 eggs
   Nonstick spray coating
½ cup applesauce
3 tablespoons granulated sugar
½ teaspoon ground nutmeg
⅔ cup snipped dried apricots, raisins, or dried cherries

1 cup sifted powdered sugar
1 teaspoon vanilla
2 to 3 teaspoons apricot nectar or orange juice

NUTRITION FACTS PER ROLL:

141 calories
2 g total fat
0 g saturated fat
18 mg cholesterol
73 mg sodium
27 g carbohydrate
1 g fiber
3 g protein

DIRECTIONS

1. In a large mixing bowl stir together 1½ cups of the flour and the yeast. In a medium saucepan heat and stir the milk, the ⅓ cup granulated sugar, the margarine or butter, and salt just until warm (120° to 130°) and margarine almost melts. Add to flour mixture along with eggs. Beat with an electric mixer on low to medium speed for 30 seconds, scraping bowl constantly. Beat on high speed for 3 minutes. Using a wooden spoon, stir in as much of the remaining flour as you can.

2. On a lightly floured surface, knead in enough of the remaining flour to make a moderately soft dough that is smooth and elastic (3 to 5 minutes total). Shape into a ball. Place in a lightly greased bowl, turning once. Cover and let rise in a warm place until double in size (about 1 hour).

3. Punch dough down. Turn out onto a lightly floured surface. Divide in half. Cover and let rest for 10 minutes. Meanwhile, spray two 9×1½-inch round baking pans with nonstick coating. Set aside.

4. Roll each half of dough into a 12×8-inch rectangle. Spread with applesauce. Combine the 3 tablespoons granulated sugar and the nutmeg; sprinkle over applesauce. Sprinkle with the apricots, raisins, or cherries. Starting from a long side, roll up each rectangle into a spiral. Seal edges. Cut each into 12 pieces. Place, cut sides down, in prepared pans. Cover; let rise until nearly double in size (about 30 minutes). Or, cover with oiled waxed paper, then with plastic wrap; refrigerate for 2 to 24 hours.

5. If chilled, let stand, covered, for 20 minutes at room temperature. Puncture any surface bubbles with a greased wooden toothpick. Bake in a 375° oven for 20 to 25 minutes or until golden brown. Cool in pans on wire racks for 5 minutes. Remove from pans. Cool completely.

6. Meanwhile, in a bowl stir together powdered sugar and vanilla. Stir in enough apricot nectar to make of drizzling consistency. Drizzle over rolls. Makes 24 rolls.

peach butter sweet rolls

Frozen sweet roll dough makes these peach butter- or apple butter-filled rolls more convenient to make. Serve them along with fresh fruit for a satisfying weekend brunch.

INGREDIENTS

Nonstick spray coating

1   16-ounce loaf frozen sweet roll
     dough, thawed

⅓   cup peach butter or apple butter

2   tablespoons dried currants
     or raisins

⅓   cup sifted powdered sugar

½   teaspoon finely shredded
     orange peel

1   to 2 teaspoons orange juice or
     apple juice

Prep time: 20 minutes
Rising time: 15 minutes
Baking time: 20 minutes

DIRECTIONS

1. Spray twelve 2½-inch muffin cups with nonstick coating. Set aside.

2. On a lightly floured surface, roll the dough into a 12×8-inch rectangle. Spread peach or apple butter evenly over dough. Sprinkle with currants or raisins. Starting from a long side, roll up into a spiral. Seal edge. Cut into 12 pieces. Place, cut sides down, in prepared muffin cups. Cover and let rise in a warm place for 15 minutes.

3. Bake in a 350° oven about 20 minutes or until golden brown. Remove from pan. Place on a wire rack.

4. For icing, in a small bowl stir together the powdered sugar, orange peel, and enough of the orange or apple juice to make of drizzling consistency. Drizzle icing over rolls. Serve warm. Makes 12 rolls.

To quick thaw

frozen bread dough in your microwave oven, remove it from the wrapper and place dough in a microwave-safe bowl. Cover and cook on 10% power (low) for 15 to 17 minutes or until thawed, rotating dough frequently.

NUTRITION FACTS PER ROLL:

140 calories
3 g total fat
1 g saturated fat
22 mg cholesterol
68 mg sodium
26 g carbohydrate
1 g fiber
3 g protein

57

whole wheat pear spirals

A sister to the cinnamon roll, these bran-and-wheat spirals boast a luscious pear-cinnamon filling but not the usual sweet roll calories.

INGREDIENTS

½ cup whole bran cereal
⅔ cup pear nectar or white grape juice
¾ cup all-purpose flour
½ cup whole wheat flour
2 tablespoons granulated sugar
1 teaspoon baking powder
⅛ teaspoon salt
3 tablespoons margarine or butter
¾ cup chopped peeled pear
2 tablespoons granulated sugar
⅛ teaspoon ground cinnamon
    Nonstick spray coating

½ cup sifted powdered sugar
2 to 3 teaspoons pear nectar or white grape juice

Prep time: 18 minutes
Baking time: 25 minutes

DIRECTIONS

1. In a small bowl combine the whole bran cereal and pear nectar or white grape juice. Let stand for 5 minutes.

2. Meanwhile, in a medium mixing bowl stir together the all-purpose flour, whole wheat flour, 2 tablespoons granulated sugar, baking powder, and salt. Using a pastry blender, cut in the margarine or butter until the mixture resembles coarse crumbs. Add the bran cereal mixture all at once. Stir just until dough clings together. Let dough rest while preparing the filling.

3. For filling, in a small bowl stir together chopped pear, the 2 tablespoons granulated sugar, and the cinnamon. Spray a 9×1½-inch round baking pan with nonstick coating. Set aside.

4. On well-floured surface, knead dough gently for 10 to 12 strokes (dough will be slightly sticky). Roll dough into a 12×8-inch rectangle. Spread filling evenly over dough. Starting from a long side, roll up into a spiral. Seal edge. Cut into 12 pieces

5. Place, cut sides down, in the prepared pan. Bake in a 400° oven about 25 minutes or until golden. Cool in pan on a rack for 10 minutes. Remove from pan.

6. Meanwhile, for glaze, combine powdered sugar and enough of the pear nectar or grape juice to make of drizzling consistency. Drizzle over rolls. Makes 12 rolls.

NUTRITION FACTS PER ROLL:

121 calories
3 g total fat
1 g saturated fat
0 mg cholesterol
106 mg sodium
24 g carbohydrate
2 g fiber
2 g protein

pumpkin crescent rolls

These biscuit-like rolls will remind you of pumpkin pie. Make them the star of a special meal featuring roast chicken, rice pilaf, and steamed carrots.

INGREDIENTS

1¾   cups all-purpose flour
1   teaspoon baking powder
¼   teaspoon baking soda
¼   teaspoon ground nutmeg
⅛   teaspoon salt
¾   cup canned pumpkin
3   tablespoons cooking oil
2   tablespoons brown sugar
2   teaspoons granulated sugar
¼   teaspoon ground cinnamon

Prep time: 20 minutes
Baking time: 9 minutes

DIRECTIONS

1. In a medium mixing bowl combine the flour, baking powder, baking soda, nutmeg, and salt.

2. In a small mixing bowl combine pumpkin, oil, and brown sugar. Add pumpkin mixture to flour mixture, stirring with a fork until combined. Form into a ball.

3. Line a large baking sheet with foil. On a lightly floured surface, knead the dough gently for 10 to 12 strokes. Divide the dough in half. Roll each half into a 10-inch circle. Cut each circle into 8 wedges. Starting at the wide end of each wedge, loosely roll toward the point. Place, point sides down, about 2 inches apart on the prepared baking sheet. Curve ends of rolls slightly.

4. Combine the granulated sugar and cinnamon; sprinkle over crescents. Bake in a 400° oven for 9 to 11 minutes or until golden brown. Serve warm. Makes 16 rolls.

Try not to overknead the roll dough. Folding and pressing the dough *gently* for 10 to 12 strokes is enough to distribute the moisture for a flaky product.

NUTRITION FACTS PER ROLL:

80 calories
3 g total fat
0 g saturated fat
0 mg cholesterol
60 mg sodium
13 g carbohydrate
1 g fiber
1 g protein

59

dill batter rolls

Yeast breads rise best in a draft-free area that's 80° to 85°F. Turn your oven into just that spot. Place the bowl of dough in the unheated oven and set a large pan of hot water on the oven's lower rack. Close the oven door.

INGREDIENTS

1½	cups all-purpose flour
1	package active dry yeast
1	cup low-fat cottage cheese
¼	cup water
1	tablespoon sugar
2	teaspoons dillseed or caraway seed
½	teaspoon salt
1	egg
	Nonstick spray coating

Freeze leftover rolls in a freezer container or bag for up to 3 months. To warm rolls, wrap in foil and heat in a 300° oven about 25 minutes.

Prep time: 30 minutes
Rising time: 1 hour
Baking time: 15 minutes

DIRECTIONS

1. In a large mixing bowl combine 1 cup of the flour and the yeast. Set aside.

2. In a small saucepan heat and stir cottage cheese, water, sugar, dillseed or caraway seed, and salt just until warm (120° to 130°). Add cottage cheese mixture to flour mixture along with egg. Beat with an electric mixer on low to medium speed 30 seconds, scraping bowl constantly. Beat on high speed for 3 minutes. Using a wooden spoon, stir in remaining flour until nearly smooth.

3. Cover and let rise in a warm place until double in size (about 45 minutes). Stir batter down with a wooden spoon. Let rest for 5 minutes.

4. Spray twelve 2½-inch muffin cups with nonstick coating. Spoon batter evenly into cups. Cover loosely with plastic wrap; let batter rise until nearly double in size (15 to 20 minutes).

5. Bake in a 375° oven for 15 to 18 minutes or until golden brown. Serve warm. Makes 12 rolls.

NUTRITION FACTS PER ROLL:

82 calories
1 g total fat
0 g saturated fat
19 mg cholesterol
171 mg sodium
13 g carbohydrate
1 g fiber
5 g protein

INGREDIENTS

Nonstick spray coating

1 cup yellow cornmeal

¾ cup all-purpose flour

2 tablespoons sugar

1½ teaspoons baking powder

¼ teaspoon baking soda

¼ teaspoon salt

¼ teaspoon ground red pepper

¾ cup buttermilk

¼ cup refrigerated or frozen egg product, thawed

1 tablespoon cooking oil

1 11-ounce can whole kernel corn with sweet peppers, drained

¼ cup shredded reduced-fat sharp cheddar cheese (1 ounce)

Yellow cornmeal (optional)

pepper corn bread

Get a double corn flavor from the cornmeal and kernel corn. Serve this spunky bread with chili or stew.

Prep time: 10 minutes
Baking time: 20 minutes

DIRECTIONS

1. Spray a 9×1½-inch round baking pan with nonstick coating. Set aside.

2. In a large bowl stir together the 1 cup cornmeal, the flour, sugar, baking powder, baking soda, salt, and red pepper. In a medium bowl stir together buttermilk, egg product, and oil.

3. Add buttermilk mixture all at once to flour mixture. Stir just until moistened. Stir in corn and cheese. Spread into prepared pan. If desired, sprinkle with additional cornmeal. Bake in a 425° oven about 20 minutes or until golden. Serve warm or cool. Makes 10 servings.

After adding the liquid mixture

to the dry mixture, stir ingredients just until they are moistened. If you stir out all the lumps, your quick breads and muffins will have peaks, tunnels, and a tough texture.

NUTRITION FACTS PER SERVING:

149 calories
3 g total fat
1 g saturated fat
3 mg cholesterol
298 mg sodium
27 g carbohydrate
2 g fiber
5 g protein

61

lemon-blueberry muffins

Mix a batch of these easy muffins for dinner tonight. They'll be ready in about half an hour.

INGREDIENTS

Nonstick spray coating

2 cups all-purpose flour

3 tablespoons sugar

1½ teaspoons baking powder

½ teaspoon baking soda

1 8-ounce carton plain fat-free yogurt

¼ cup refrigerated or frozen egg product, thawed

2 tablespoons milk

2 tablespoons cooking oil

1 teaspoon finely shredded lemon peel

1 cup fresh or frozen blueberries, thawed

Prep time: 15 minutes
Baking time: 20 minutes

DIRECTIONS

1. Spray twelve 2½-inch muffin cups with nonstick coating; set aside.

2. In a large mixing bowl stir together the flour, sugar, baking powder, and baking soda. Make a well in the center of flour mixture.

3. In a medium mixing bowl combine the yogurt, egg product, milk, oil, and lemon peel. Add the yogurt mixture all at once to flour mixture. Stir just until moistened (batter should be lumpy).

Fold in blueberries. Spoon batter into prepared muffin cups, filling each ⅔ full.

4. Bake in a 400° oven for 20 to 25 minutes or until a toothpick inserted in center comes out clean.

5. Cool in muffin cups on a rack for 5 minutes. Remove from muffin cups. Serve warm. Makes 12 muffins.

NUTRITION FACTS PER MUFFIN:

119 calories
3 g total fat
0 g saturated fat
0 mg cholesterol
68 mg sodium
20 g carbohydrate
1 g fiber
3 g protein

INGREDIENTS

Nonstick spray coating

1⅓ cups all-purpose flour

¾ cup buckwheat flour

⅓ cup sugar

1½ teaspoons baking powder

1 teaspoon ground cinnamon

½ teaspoon baking soda

½ teaspoon salt

2 slightly beaten eggs

1 cup canned pumpkin

½ cup fat-free milk

2 tablespoons cooking oil

½ teaspoon finely shredded orange peel

¼ cup orange juice

pumpkin muffins

The secret to these enticing muffins lies in the combination of moist, rich pumpkin and flavorful buckwheat. Though often thought of as a cereal, buckwheat actually comes from the seeds of the buckwheat herb.

Prep time: 15 minutes
Baking time: 15 minutes

DIRECTIONS

1. Spray twelve 2½-inch muffin cups with nonstick coating; set aside. In a large mixing bowl stir together the all-purpose flour, buckwheat flour, sugar, baking powder, cinnamon, baking soda, and salt. Make a well in the center of flour mixture.

2. In a medium mixing bowl combine the eggs, pumpkin, milk, oil, orange peel, and orange juice. Add the egg mixture all at once to flour mixture. Stir just until moistened (batter should be lumpy).

3. Spoon the batter into the prepared muffin cups, dividing the batter evenly. Bake in a 400° oven for 15 to 20 minutes or until the muffins are light brown. Cool in muffin cups on a wire rack for 5 minutes. Remove from muffin cups. Serve warm. Makes 12 muffins.

Once the batter is mixed, pop the muffins or quick bread into the preheated oven right away. Batters with baking powder or baking soda need to be baked immediately so that the leavening power is not lost.

NUTRITION FACTS PER MUFFIN:

138 calories
4 g total fat
1 g saturated fat
36 mg cholesterol
204 mg sodium
23 g carbohydrate
2 g fiber
4 g protein

scones with currants

Scones are best eaten warm on the day they are made. For variety, stir in dried cherries or cranberries in place of the currants or raisins.

INGREDIENTS

Nonstick spray coating

2½ cups all-purpose flour

¼ cup sugar

2 teaspoons baking powder

⅛ teaspoon ground nutmeg

2 tablespoons margarine or butter, chilled

⅓ cup dried currants or raisins

⅔ cup fat-free milk

1 beaten egg

1 egg white

2 teaspoons fat-free milk

1 recipe Strawberry Cream Cheese (optional)

When baking, use a margarine

or stick spread that contains at least 60-percent vegetable oil. Do not use an extra-light spread that contains less oil.

Prep time: 15 minutes
Baking time: 12 minutes

DIRECTIONS

1. Spray a baking sheet with nonstick coating. Set aside. In a large mixing bowl stir together the flour, sugar, baking powder, and nutmeg. With a pastry blender, cut in margarine or butter until mixture resembles coarse crumbs. Stir in currants or raisins. Make a well in the center of flour mixture.

2. In a medium mixing bowl stir together the ⅔ cup milk, egg, and egg white. Add milk mixture all at once to flour mixture. Stir just until moistened. On a lightly floured surface, knead the dough gently for 10 to 12 strokes or until smooth.

3. Roll or pat into a 9-inch circle; cut into 10 wedges. Place wedges on prepared baking sheet. Brush with the 2 teaspoons milk. Bake in a 450° oven about 12 minutes or until light golden brown. Serve warm. If desired, serve with Strawberry Cream Cheese. Makes 10 scones.

Strawberry Cream Cheese: In a food processor bowl or blender container combine ½ of an 8-ounce tub fat-free cream cheese and 3 tablespoons low-calorie strawberry spread. Cover and process or blend until smooth. Makes about ½ cup.

NUTRITION FACTS PER SCONE:

174 calories
1 g total fat
1 g saturated fat
0 g saturated fat
22 mg cholesterol
121 mg sodium
32 g carbohydrate
1 g fiber
5 g protein

INGREDIENTS

- 1 **cup all-purpose flour**
- 1 **green onion, thinly sliced**
- 1½ **teaspoons baking powder**
- 1 **teaspoon sugar**
- ¾ **teaspoon snipped fresh basil or**
  - ¼ **teaspoon dried basil, crushed**
  - **Dash salt**
- ⅓ **cup fat-free milk**
- 2 **tablespoons cooking oil**
  - **Fat-free cream cheese (optional)**

green onion and basil biscuits

Even though these biscuits have only a small amount of oil, they bake up tender and delicious.

Prep time: 18 minutes
Baking time: 10 minutes

DIRECTIONS

1. In a mixing bowl stir together flour, green onion, baking powder, sugar, basil, and salt. Make a well in the center of the flour mixture.

2. In a small mixing bowl combine the milk and oil. Add the milk mixture all at once to flour mixture. Stir just until moistened.

3. On a lightly floured surface, knead the dough gently for 10 to 12 strokes. Roll or pat dough to ½-inch thickness. Cut with a 2-inch biscuit cutter, dipping cutter into additional flour between cuts. Transfer biscuits to an ungreased baking sheet.

4. Bake in a 450° oven for 10 to 12 minutes or until golden brown. Serve warm. If desired, serve with cream cheese. Makes 8 biscuits.

NUTRITION FACTS PER BISCUIT:

88 calories
4 g total fat
1 g saturated fat
0 mg cholesterol
90 mg sodium
12 g carbohydrate
0 g fiber
2 g protein

Peppered Steak with Mushroom Sauce
Recipe, page 72

meats

peppered chutney roast

This marinated beef tenderloin is a great choice for a special-occasion or holiday dinner because all of the preparations are done ahead of time. Just before dinner, the only work involves putting the tenderloin in the oven.

INGREDIENTS

- ¾ cup unsweetened pineapple juice
- ½ cup steak sauce
- ⅓ cup port wine
- ⅓ cup Worcestershire sauce
- ¼ cup lemon juice
- 1 teaspoon seasoned salt
- 1 teaspoon lemon-pepper seasoning
- 1 teaspoon dry mustard
- 1 teaspoon ground black pepper
- 1 2½- to 3-pound beef tenderloin
- 1 teaspoon cracked black pepper
- 3 slices bacon, cooked and drained
- ½ cup chutney
  Chutney

Prep time: 15 minutes
Marinating time: 4 hours
Roasting time: 35 minutes
Standing time: 15 minutes

DIRECTIONS

1. For marinade, in a medium mixing bowl stir together the pineapple juice, steak sauce, port wine, Worcestershire sauce, lemon juice, seasoned salt, lemon-pepper seasoning, dry mustard, and ground pepper.

2. To score the meat, make shallow cuts at 1-inch intervals diagonally across top of meat in a diamond pattern. Repeat on other side. Place meat in a large plastic bag; set in a large, deep bowl. Pour marinade over meat; seal bag. Marinate in the refrigerator for 4 to 8 hours, turning bag occasionally. Drain meat, reserving the marinade.

3. Rub meat with the cracked pepper. Place on a rack in a shallow roasting pan. Insert meat thermometer. Roast, uncovered, in a 425° oven for 30 to 45 minutes or until meat thermometer registers 135°, basting twice with marinade up to the last 5 minutes of roasting.

4. Arrange bacon strips along top of meat. Cut up any large pieces in the ½ cup chutney; spoon evenly over meat. Return to oven for 5 to 10 minutes more or until thermometer registers 140°. Transfer the meat to serving platter. Let stand, covered, about 15 minutes before slicing. Serve with additional chutney. Makes 12 servings.

NUTRITION FACTS PER SERVING:

203 calories
7 g total fat
3 g saturated fat
55 mg cholesterol
507 mg sodium
13 g carbohydrate
0 g fiber
19 g protein

spinach-stuffed flank steak

Dried tomatoes add a burst of flavor to sauces, salads, soups, and many other dishes. They are vine-ripened tomatoes picked at their peak of freshness, cut in half, sometimes salted, then dried. The result is a chewy, meaty tomato with a concentrated flavor.

INGREDIENTS

- ¼ cup dried tomatoes (not oil-packed)
- 1 1-pound beef flank steak or top round steak, trimmed of separable fat
- ⅛ teaspoon salt
- ⅛ teaspoon pepper
- 1 10-ounce package frozen chopped spinach, thawed and well drained
- 2 tablespoons grated Parmesan cheese
- 2 tablespoons snipped fresh basil

Prep time: 20 minutes
Broiling time: 10 minutes

DIRECTIONS

1. In a small bowl pour enough boiling water over the dried tomatoes to cover. Soak for 10 minutes. Drain. Snip into small pieces.

2. Score meat by making shallow diagonal cuts at 1-inch intervals in a diamond pattern on both sides of meat. Place meat between 2 pieces of plastic wrap. Working from center to edges, pound with flat side of a meat mallet into 12×8-inch rectangle.

Remove plastic wrap. Sprinkle with salt and pepper.

3. Spread the spinach over the meat. Sprinkle with the softened tomatoes, Parmesan cheese, and basil. Starting from a short side, roll up the meat into a spiral. Secure with wooden toothpicks at 1-inch intervals, starting ½ inch from one end. Cut between the toothpicks into eight 1-inch-thick slices.

4. Place slices, cut sides down, on the unheated rack of a broiler pan. Broil 3 to 4 inches from heat to desired doneness, turning once. (Allow 10 to 12 minutes for medium-rare or 12 to 16 minutes for medium.) Before serving, remove the toothpicks. Makes 4 servings.

Store dried tomatoes in an airtight container out of direct light or in a refrigerator or freezer for up to 1 year.

NUTRITION FACTS PER SERVING:

202 calories
9 g total fat
4 g saturated fat
56 mg cholesterol
303 mg sodium
5 g carbohydrate
0 g fiber
25 g protein

beer-braised rump roast with cabbage

Beer, onion, brown sugar, and thyme give this tender roast a robust, well-rounded flavor.

INGREDIENTS

1 3-pound boneless beef round rump roast
Nonstick spray coating
1½ cups light beer (12 ounces)
1 cup water
1 medium onion, sliced
1 tablespoon brown sugar
1 teaspoon instant beef bouillon granules
1 bay leaf
½ teaspoon dried thyme, crushed
½ teaspoon salt-free seasoning blend
½ teaspoon pepper

1 medium head cabbage, cored
8 medium carrots, bias-sliced into 1-inch pieces

Prep time: 20 minutes
Cooking time: 2 hours and 5 minutes

DIRECTIONS

1. Trim fat from meat. Spray a 4-quart Dutch oven with nonstick coating. Preheat over medium-high heat. Brown the meat on all sides.

2. Add the beer, water, onion, brown sugar, bouillon granules, bay leaf, thyme, seasoning blend, and pepper. Bring to boiling; reduce heat. Simmer, covered, about 1¾ hours or until meat is nearly tender. Cut cabbage into 10 wedges.

3. Add cabbage and carrots to meat. Cook, covered, about 20 minutes more or until cabbage and carrots are crisp-tender and meat is very tender. Remove bay leaf.

4. Transfer the meat and vegetables to a serving platter; cover and keep warm. Skim fat from pan juices. Thinly slice meat; pass meat and vegetables with pan juices. Makes 10 servings.

NUTRITION FACTS PER SERVING:

243 calories
7 g total fat
2 g saturated fat
86 mg cholesterol
180 mg sodium
9 g carbohydrate
2 g fiber
34 g protein

cranberry pot roast

Although poultry most often comes to mind when you think of cranberries, the tart berry flavor also blends well with beef. Here, both cranberry juice and fresh berries flavor the gravy.

INGREDIENTS

- 1 2- to 2½-pound beef bottom round roast, trimmed of separable fat
- 2 teaspoons cooking oil
- 1 cup cranberry juice
- ½ cup beef broth
- ½ teaspoon dried thyme, crushed
- 1 16-ounce package frozen small whole onions
- ¼ cup packed brown sugar
- 2 cups cranberries
- 3 tablespoons cold water
- 2 tablespoons cornstarch

Prep time: 20 minutes
Baking time: 2 hours

DIRECTIONS

1. In a Dutch oven quickly brown meat in hot oil over medium-high heat, turning to brown on all sides. Remove from heat.

2. Pour cranberry juice and beef broth over the meat. Add the thyme. Bake, covered, in a 325° oven for 1 hour. Stir onions and brown sugar into the pan juices. Bake meat, covered, 1 to 1¼ hours more or until meat and onions are tender. Transfer the meat to a serving platter, reserving pan juices. Cover meat and keep warm.

3. Strain pan juices, reserving onions. Measure pan juices. If necessary, add enough water to measure 2 cups liquid. Return to Dutch oven. Stir in cranberries and onions. Bring to boiling. Stir together cold water and cornstarch. Stir into mixture in Dutch oven. Cook and stir until thickened and bubbly. Cook and stir for 2 minutes more. Serve over meat. Makes 10 servings.

NUTRITION FACTS PER SERVING:

205 calories
5 g total fat
2 g saturated fat
58 mg cholesterol
85 mg sodium
16 g carbohydrate
2 g fiber
22 g protein

peppered steak with mushroom sauce

Tenderloin is one of the leanest cuts of beef. To keep the steaks at their moist and juicy best, don't overcook them. (Recipe also pictured on pages 66 and 67.)

INGREDIENTS

- 6 beef tenderloin steaks or 3 beef top loin steaks, cut 1 inch thick (about 1½ pounds total)
- 1½ teaspoons dried whole green peppercorns, crushed, or ½ teaspoon coarsely ground black pepper
- ½ teaspoon dried thyme, crushed
- ½ teaspoon dried oregano, crushed
- ¼ teaspoon salt
  Nonstick spray coating
- ⅓ cup water
- ½ teaspoon instant beef bouillon granules
- ¾ cup sliced fresh shiitake mushrooms or other fresh mushrooms
- ¾ cup fat-free milk
- 2 tablespoons all-purpose flour
- ½ teaspoon dried thyme, crushed
- ⅔ cup fat-free or light dairy sour cream
- 1 tablespoon snipped chives (optional)

To crush peppercorns, use a mortar and pestle. Just place the peppercorns in the mortar and crush them against the side and bottom of the bowl with the pestle. For a more uniform size, crush only a small amount at a time.

Prep time: 10 minutes
Cooking time: 20 minutes

DIRECTIONS

1. Trim any fat from the meat. Combine peppercorns or pepper, ½ teaspoon thyme, the oregano, and salt. Sprinkle both sides of meat with the mixture, pressing into meat.

2. Spray an unheated large nonstick skillet with nonstick coating. Preheat skillet over medium heat. Cook the meat for 10 to 12 minutes for medium doneness, turning once. Remove from skillet. Cover and keep warm.

3. Add water and bouillon granules to skillet. Bring to boiling. Add mushrooms. Cook about 2 minutes or until tender. Stir together the milk, flour, and ½ teaspoon thyme. Add to skillet. Cook and stir until thickened and bubbly. Stir in sour cream; heat through, but do not boil. To serve, spoon sauce over meat. If desired, garnish with chives. Makes 6 servings.

NUTRITION FACTS PER SERVING:

206 calories
7 g total fat
3 g saturated fat
64 mg cholesterol
243 mg sodium
9 g carbohydrate
0 g fiber
25 g protein

INGREDIENTS

- 12 dried tomato halves (not oil-packed)
- 1 to 3 dried chipotle chili peppers
- 1 cup boiling water
- 1 cup dry red or white wine, or 1 cup water plus ½ teaspoon instant beef bouillon granules
- ½ cup chopped onion
- 1 tablespoon brown sugar
- 1 tablespoon lime or lemon juice
- 2 cloves garlic, quartered
- ¼ teaspoon black pepper
- 12 ounces boneless beef top sirloin steak, cut 1 inch thick

grilled sirloin with smoky pepper sauce

Chipotle chili peppers are actually smoked jalapeños; they have a smoky, slightly sweet, spicy flavor.

Prep time: 40 minutes
Marinating time: 2 hours
Grilling time: 12 minutes

DIRECTIONS

1. For marinade, in a medium mixing bowl place dried tomatoes and chili peppers; add boiling water. Let stand about 30 minutes or until vegetables are softened. Drain, reserving liquid.

2. Cut up tomatoes; place in a food processor bowl or blender container. Wearing disposable plastic gloves, trim stems from chilies; scrape out seeds. Cut up chili peppers; add to tomatoes along with ¼ cup reserved soaking liquid, the wine or water and bouillon granules, onion, brown sugar, lime or lemon juice, garlic, and black pepper. Cover and process or blend until nearly smooth.

Place meat in a shallow glass bowl; pour marinade over meat. Cover and marinate in the refrigerator for 2 to 8 hours. Drain, reserving the marinade.

3. Grill meat on the rack of an uncovered grill directly over medium coals for 12 to 15 minutes for medium doneness, turning and brushing once with marinade halfway through grilling. (Or, spray the unheated rack of a broiler pan with nonstick coating. Place meat on rack and broil 4 inches from heat for 12 to 15 minutes, turning and brushing once with marinade halfway through.)

4. Bring the remaining marinade to boiling. Boil gently, uncovered, for 1 minute. Pass with meat. Makes 4 servings.

NUTRITION FACTS PER SERVING:

240 calories
8 g total fat
3 g saturated fat
57 mg cholesterol
105 mg sodium
12 g carbohydrate
1 g fiber
21 g protein

73

italian beef skillet

For an alternative, serve the saucy beef mixture over baked polenta (see page 27) instead of pasta.

INGREDIENTS

1 pound boneless beef round steak, trimmed of separable fat
Nonstick spray coating
2 cups sliced fresh mushrooms
1 cup chopped onion
1 cup coarsely chopped green sweet pepper
½ cup chopped celery
2 cloves garlic, minced
1 14½-ounce can tomatoes, undrained and cut up
½ teaspoon dried basil, crushed
¼ teaspoon dried oregano, crushed
¼ teaspoon crushed red pepper
8 ounces packaged dried spaghetti
2 tablespoons grated Parmesan cheese

Prep time: 35 minutes
Cooking time: 1¼ hours

DIRECTIONS

1. Cut meat into 5 serving-size pieces. Spray an unheated large skillet with nonstick coating. Preheat over medium heat. Add meat to skillet; cook each piece on both sides until browned. Remove from skillet.

2. Add mushrooms, onion, sweet pepper, celery, and garlic to the skillet. Cook until vegetables are nearly tender. Stir in undrained tomatoes, basil, oregano, and crushed red pepper. Add meat to skillet, spooning vegetable mixture over the meat. Simmer, covered, about 1¼ hours or until meat is tender, stirring occasionally.

Meanwhile, cook spaghetti according to package directions, except omit any oil and salt.

3. Transfer meat to a serving platter. Spoon vegetable mixture over meat. Serve with spaghetti. Sprinkle with Parmesan cheese. Makes 5 servings.

NUTRITION FACTS PER SERVING:

354 calories
6 g total fat
2 g saturated fat
60 mg cholesterol
255 mg sodium
43 g carbohydrate
2 g fiber
31 g protein

INGREDIENTS

12 ounces boneless beef sirloin, cut 1 inch thick and trimmed of separable fat

2 teaspoons finely shredded lemon peel

⅓ cup lemon juice

3 tablespoons olive oil or cooking oil

1 tablespoon honey

1½ teaspoons snipped fresh basil or ½ teaspoon dried basil, crushed

1 teaspoon coarsely cracked black pepper

¼ teaspoon garlic salt

8 ounces baby carrots, peeled, or packaged, peeled baby carrots

1 medium zucchini

Hot cooked couscous or rice (optional)

summer vegetables and beef kabobs

A light lemon-basil marinade flavors the grilled steak and complements the summer vegetables.

Prep time: 20 minutes
Marinating time: 2 hours
Grilling time: 12 minutes

DIRECTIONS

1. Cut meat into 1-inch cubes. Place in a plastic bag set in a shallow bowl.

2. For marinade, stir together lemon peel, lemon juice, oil, honey, basil, pepper, and garlic salt. Pour half of marinade over meat in bag. Close bag. Marinate in refrigerator for 2 to 4 hours, turning bag occasionally. Cover and refrigerate remaining marinade.

3. Meanwhile, in a medium covered saucepan cook the carrots in a small amount of boiling water for 3 minutes. Drain. Cut zucchini in half lengthwise; cut into ½-inch-thick slices.

4. Drain meat, discarding marinade. On 8 long metal skewers, alternately thread meat, carrots, and zucchini slices.

5. Grill kabobs on the rack of an uncovered grill directly over medium coals for 12 to 14 minutes or until meat is of desired doneness, turning once and brushing often with reserved marinade. If desired, serve with hot couscous or rice. Makes 4 servings.

When threading the meat and vegetables onto the skewers, leave about ¼ inch between pieces. This allows the food to cook evenly.

NUTRITION FACTS PER SERVING:

264 calories
15 g total fat
4 g saturated fat
57 mg cholesterol
170 mg sodium
12 g carbohydrate
2 g fiber
20 g protein

ginger beef stir-fry

When you crave steak, but don't want high fat and calories, try this stir-fry. Lean beef and crispy spring vegetables combine for a full-flavored dinner you can toss together in 30 minutes.

INGREDIENTS

- 8 ounces beef top round steak, trimmed of separable fat
- ½ cup beef broth
- 3 tablespoons reduced-sodium soy sauce
- 2½ teaspoons cornstarch
- 1 teaspoon sugar
- ½ teaspoon grated fresh ginger
  Nonstick spray coating
- 12 ounces asparagus spears, trimmed and cut into 1-inch pieces (2 cups)
- 1½ cups sliced fresh mushrooms
- 1 cup small broccoli flowerets
- 4 green onions, bias-sliced into 1-inch lengths (½ cup)
- 1 tablespoon cooking oil
- 2 cups hot cooked rice

Assemble and prepare all of the ingredients before you start to stir-fry. If you like, you can even do this up to 24 hours ahead and chill each ingredient separately.

Start to finish: 30 minutes

DIRECTIONS

1. If desired, partially freeze meat. Thinly slice meat across the grain into bite-size strips. Set aside. For the sauce, in a small bowl stir together the beef broth, soy sauce, cornstarch, sugar, and ginger. Set aside.

2. Spray an unheated wok or large skillet with nonstick coating. Preheat over medium-high heat. Add asparagus, mushrooms, broccoli, and green onions. Stir-fry for 3 to 4 minutes or until vegetables are crisp-tender. Remove from wok.

3. Add oil to hot wok. Add the meat; stir-fry for 2 to 3 minutes or until desired doneness. Push meat from center of wok. Stir sauce; add to center of wok. Cook and stir until thickened and bubbly.

4. Return vegetables to the wok. Stir all ingredients together to coat with sauce; heat through. Serve immediately with hot cooked rice. Makes 4 servings.

NUTRITION FACTS PER SERVING:

270 calories
7 g total fat
2 g saturated fat
36 mg cholesterol
541 mg sodium
32 g carbohydrate
4 g fiber
21 g protein

INGREDIENTS

- 12 ounces beef top round steak, trimmed of separable fat
- 1 8-ounce can pineapple slices (juice pack)
- 2 tablespoons reduced-sodium soy sauce
- ½ teaspoon grated fresh ginger or ⅛ teaspoon ground ginger
- ¼ teaspoon crushed red pepper
- 1 tablespoon cornstarch
  Nonstick spray coating
- 4 green onions, cut into ½-inch pieces
- 1 6-ounce package frozen pea pods
- 1 medium tomato, cut into wedges
- 2 cups hot cooked rice

pineapple beef

Fresh ginger gives a pleasant pungency and crushed red pepper lends a hint of hotness to this bright, fresh-tasting stir-fry.

Prep time: 15 minutes
Marinating time: 15 minutes
Cooking time: 5 minutes

DIRECTIONS

1. If desired, partially freeze meat. Thinly slice meat across the grain into bite-size strips. Drain pineapple, reserving juice. Cut pineapple slices into quarters. Set aside.

2. In a bowl stir together reserved pineapple juice, soy sauce, ginger, and crushed red pepper. Add the meat; stir until coated. Cover and marinate meat at room temperature for 15 minutes. Drain, reserving marinade. For sauce, stir cornstarch into reserved marinade. Set aside.

3. Spray an unheated large nonstick skillet or wok with nonstick coating. Preheat over medium heat. Add meat and green onions. Stir-fry for 2 to 3 minutes or until meat is desired doneness. Push from center of skillet.

4. Stir sauce; add to center of skillet. Cook and stir until thickened and bubbly. Add pineapple, pea pods, and tomato. Cook and stir for 2 minutes more. Serve immediately over hot cooked rice. Makes 4 servings.

NUTRITION FACTS PER SERVING:

304 calories
5 g total fat
1 g saturated fat
54 mg cholesterol
311 mg sodium
40 g carbohydrate
2 g fiber
25 g protein

hot-and-sour beef with broccoli

Partially freezing the round steak for about 30 minutes makes it easy to cut the meat into strips.

INGREDIENTS

- 12 ounces boneless beef top round steak, trimmed of separable fat
- ⅓ cup water
- 2 tablespoons light soy sauce
- 2 tablespoons rice wine vinegar or white wine vinegar
- 4 teaspoons cornstarch
- 1 teaspoon sugar
- ¼ teaspoon black pepper
  Several dashes bottled hot pepper sauce
- 8 fresh shiitake or medium brown mushrooms
  Nonstick spray coating

- 2 cloves garlic, minced
- ½ cup reduced-sodium chicken broth
- 2 cups broccoli flowerets
- 1 medium red or green sweet pepper, cut into thin strips
- 1 cup fresh pea pods, strings removed and halved
- 2 cups cooked cellophane noodles

To cut veggies

into strips, first cut them it into thin, matchlike sticks about 2 inches long. Speed up cutting by first slicing the food into pieces about 2 inches long and ¼ inch thick. Then stack the slices and cut them lengthwise into thinner strips about ⅛ to ¼ inch wide.

Start to finish: 35 minutes

DIRECTIONS

1. If desired, partially freeze meat. Thinly slice meat across the grain into bite-size strips. For sauce, stir together water, soy sauce, vinegar, cornstarch, sugar, black pepper, and hot pepper sauce; set aside.

2. Trim stems from mushrooms; discard. Slice mushroom caps; set aside.

3. Spray an unheated large wok or skillet with nonstick coating. Preheat over medium-high heat. Add meat and garlic. Stir-fry for 2 to 3 minutes or until meat is desired doneness. Remove from wok.

4. Reduce heat to medium. Carefully add broth; bring to boiling. Add broccoli; reduce heat. Simmer, covered, for 3 minutes. Add sweet pepper and mushrooms. Simmer, covered, for 2 minutes. Add pea pods. Simmer, covered, for 1 minute more. Push vegetables from center of wok. Stir sauce; add to center of wok. Cook and stir until thickened and bubbly. Cook and stir for 2 minutes more.

5. Return meat mixture to wok. Stir ingredients to coat with sauce; heat through. Serve immediately over noodles. Makes 4 servings.

NUTRITION FACTS PER SERVING:

437 calories
5 g total fat
1 g saturated fat
54 mg cholesterol
390 mg sodium
75 g carbohydrate
4 g fiber
25 g protein

INGREDIENTS

- 1 12-ounce can light beer
- ½ cup reduced-sodium chicken broth
- 1 bay leaf
- 1 tablespoon snipped fresh thyme or 1 teaspoon dried thyme, crushed
- ¼ teaspoon salt
- ⅛ teaspoon black pepper
- 12 ounces boneless beef round steak, trimmed of separable fat and cut into 1-inch pieces
- 2 small onions, cut into wedges
- 2 medium green and/or red sweet peppers, cut into thin strips
- 2 tablespoons cold water
- 4 teaspoons cornstarch
- 3 cups hot cooked noodles

beef and brew with noodles

Beer subtly flavors and tenderizes the beef as it slowly simmers. Accompany the beef with hearty Italian bread or a small fresh salad for a well-rounded meal.

Prep time: 25 minutes
Cooking time: 1 hour

NUTRITION FACTS PER SERVING:

340 calories
6 g total fat
2 g saturated fat
94 mg cholesterol
265 mg sodium
38 g carbohydrate
3 g fiber
27 g protein

DIRECTIONS

1. In a large saucepan stir together beer, chicken broth, bay leaf, thyme, salt, and black pepper. Stir in meat. Bring to boiling; reduce heat. Simmer, covered, for 50 minutes. Add onions and sweet peppers. Simmer about 10 minutes more or until meat and vegetables are tender. Discard bay leaf.

2. Stir together the cold water and cornstarch; stir into meat mixture. Cook and stir until thickened and bubbly. Cook and stir 2 minutes more. Serve over noodles. Makes 4 servings.

beef curry and potatoes

This stir-fry pleases the family that loves meat and potatoes. Add as much or as little curry powder as you like, depending on your tastes.

INGREDIENTS

- 12 ounces beef top round steak, trimmed of separable fat
- 2 medium potatoes, halved and thinly sliced
- ½ cup beef broth
- 2 teaspoons cornstarch
- ¼ teaspoon salt
  Nonstick spray coating
- ¾ cup chopped onion
- ¾ cup chopped green or red sweet pepper
- 1 tablespoon cooking oil
- 1 to 3 teaspoons curry powder
- 1 medium tomato, chopped

Start to finish: 30 minutes

DIRECTIONS

1. If desired, partially freeze meat. Thinly slice meat across the grain into bite-size strips. Set aside.

2. In a saucepan cook the potatoes in lightly salted boiling water about 5 minutes or until tender. Drain and set aside.

3. Meanwhile, for the sauce, stir together beef broth, cornstarch, and salt. Set aside.

4. Spray an unheated wok or large skillet with nonstick coating. Preheat over medium-high heat. Add onion and stir-fry for 2 minutes. Add sweet pepper and stir-fry about 2 minutes more or until vegetables are crisp-tender. Remove from wok. Add the oil to hot wok. Add meat and curry powder. Stir-fry for 2 to 3 minutes or until meat is desired doneness. Push the meat from center of wok.

6. Stir the sauce; add to the center of wok. Cook and stir until thickened and bubbly. Stir in the onion mixture, potatoes, and tomato. Cook and stir for 2 minutes more. Serve immediately. Makes 4 servings.

NUTRITION FACTS PER SERVING:

268 calories
8 g total fat
2 g saturated fat
54 mg cholesterol
282 mg sodium
26 g carbohydrate
2 g fiber
24 g protein

INGREDIENTS

- 12 ounces boneless beef sirloin steak, trimmed of separable fat
- Nonstick spray coating
- ½ cup chopped onion
- 1 clove garlic, minced
- 1½ cups low-sodium vegetable juice
- 1 10-ounce package frozen mixed vegetables
- ¾ cup beef broth
- 1 teaspoon dried basil, crushed
- ½ teaspoon dried marjoram, crushed
- ¼ teaspoon pepper
- 1 cup all-purpose flour
- 3 tablespoons cornmeal
- 2 teaspoons sugar
- 1½ teaspoons baking powder
- ⅛ teaspoon salt
- 3 tablespoons shortening
- ⅓ cup fat-free milk
- ¼ cup plain fat-free yogurt

beef pot pie

You can enjoy pot pies again. This lean version uses a modest amount of meat and lots of vegetables to make up for it. A made-from-scratch biscuit topper becomes the golden-brown crust.

Prep time: 45 minutes
Baking time: 15 minutes

DIRECTIONS

1. Cut meat into ¾-inch cubes. Spray an unheated large Dutch oven with non-stick coating. Preheat over medium-high heat. Add meat and cook until brown. Remove meat from pan.

2. Add onion and garlic to pan. Cook and stir until onion is tender. Stir in vegetable juice, frozen vegetables, beef broth, basil, marjoram, and pepper. Stir in meat. Bring to boiling; reduce heat. Simmer, covered, for 20 to 25 minutes or until vegetables are tender.

3. For topper, in a medium mixing bowl stir together flour, cornmeal, sugar, baking powder, and salt. Cut in shortening until mixture resembles coarse crumbs. Stir together the milk and yogurt. Add to flour mixture. Stir just until moistened.

4. Spoon hot meat mixture into a 2-quart casserole. Immediately drop the topper in small mounds onto hot mixture. Bake in a 450° oven for 15 to 20 minutes or until topper is golden brown. Makes 5 servings.

Be sure the meat mixture in the casserole is hot before adding the biscuit topper. This ensures that the topper will cook through completely.

NUTRITION FACTS PER SERVING:

368 calories
14 g total fat
5 g saturated fat
46 mg cholesterol
368 mg sodium
38 g carbohydrate
2 g fiber
22 g protein

mustard-pepper steak sandwiches

Save calories by serving this sandwich open-face. Use a knife and fork for easier eating.

INGREDIENTS

- 2 tablespoons Dijon-style mustard
- 1 teaspoon brown sugar
- 1 clove garlic, minced
- ½ teaspoon coarsely cracked pepper
- 1 pound beef flank steak, trimmed of separable fat
- 3 hoagie rolls, split and toasted
- 1 cup shredded lettuce
  Thinly sliced tomato
  Dijon-style mustard (optional)

To mince garlic,

use a utility knife to cut the peeled clove into very tiny, irregularly shaped pieces. Or save time by substituting ½ teaspoon of bottled minced garlic.

Prep time: 10 minutes
Broiling time: 12 minutes

DIRECTIONS

1. In a small bowl stir together the 2 tablespoons mustard, the brown sugar, garlic, and pepper. Set aside.

2. Place the meat on the unheated rack of a broiler pan. Brush with some of the mustard mixture. Broil 4 to 5 inches from the heat for 12 to 14 minutes for medium doneness, turning and brushing once with the remaining mustard mixture halfway through broiling.

3. To serve, thinly slice meat diagonally across the grain. Fill each hoagie roll with some of the lettuce and sliced tomato. Layer meat slices on each sandwich. If desired, serve with additional mustard. Makes 6 servings.

NUTRITION FACTS PER SERVING:

320 calories
8 g total fat
3 g saturated fat
35 mg cholesterol
554 mg sodium
40 g carbohydrate
2 g fiber
21 g protein

barbecue-sauced beef sandwiches

Serve half of these saucy sandwiches now and freeze the rest for later. When you're short on time or the shelves are bare, you'll have a ready-to-heat meal in the freezer.

INGREDIENTS

- 1 2-pound boneless beef round steak, cut ¾ to 1 inch thick and trimmed of separable fat
- Nonstick spray coating
- 1 14½-ounce can tomatoes, undrained and cut up
- 1 cup chopped onion
- 1 cup chopped carrot
- 2 tablespoons Worcestershire sauce
- 2 tablespoons vinegar
- 1 tablespoon brown sugar
- 1 bay leaf
- 1 clove garlic, minced
- 2 teaspoons chili powder
- 1 teaspoon dried oregano, crushed
- ⅛ teaspoon pepper
- 8 hamburger buns, split and toasted

Prep time: 40 minutes
Cooking time: 2 hours

DIRECTIONS

1. Cut the meat into 4 to 6 pieces. Spray an unheated Dutch oven with nonstick coating. Preheat over medium heat. Add half of the meat; cook each piece on both sides until browned. Remove meat. Repeat to brown remaining meat. Drain off fat. Return all meat to Dutch oven.

2. Add undrained tomatoes, onion, carrot, Worcestershire sauce, vinegar, brown sugar, bay leaf, garlic, chili powder, oregano, and pepper. Bring to boiling; reduce heat. Simmer, covered, for 2 to 2½ hours or until meat is tender.

3. Remove meat from sauce; shred meat. Return meat to sauce. If necessary, simmer, uncovered, for 5 to 10 minutes or until slightly thickened. Discard bay leaf. Serve on buns. Makes 8 servings.

NUTRITION FACTS PER SERVING:

319 calories
8 g total fat
2 g saturated fat
72 mg cholesterol
393 mg sodium
30 g carbohydrate
2 g fiber
31 g protein

Stash any leftover meat in the freezer for up to 6 months. To reheat, transfer the mixture to a saucepan; add 1 tablespoon water. Cook, covered, over medium-low heat until heated through, stirring occasionally to break up. (Allow 8 to 10 minutes for 1 or 2 servings; 25 to 30 minutes for 4 servings.)

festive taco burgers

A flour tortilla has about the same number of calories as a hamburger bun, and it's twice the fun with these burgers.

INGREDIENTS

- 1 cup finely chopped tomato
- ¼ cup green or red taco sauce
- 2 tablespoons snipped fresh cilantro
- 5 7-inch flour tortillas
- 1 4-ounce can diced mild green chili peppers, drained
- ¼ cup fine dry bread crumbs
- ¼ cup finely chopped green onions
- 2 tablespoons fat-free milk
- 1 teaspoon dried oregano, crushed
- ½ teaspoon ground cumin
- ¼ teaspoon black pepper
- ⅛ teaspoon salt
- 1 pound extra-lean ground beef
- Nonstick spray coating
- 1 cup shredded lettuce or red cabbage

For safety's sake, cook ground meat patties and meat loaves with added ingredients to 170° or until no pink remains. Ground meat patties with no other ingredients added, however, may be cooked just until their centers are brownish pink (medium doneness).

Prep time: 20 minutes
Broiling time: 10 minutes

DIRECTIONS

1. In a medium mixing bowl stir together tomato, taco sauce, and cilantro. Cover and set aside. Wrap the tortillas in foil; heat in a 350° oven for 15 minutes. Remove from oven; do not open foil packet.

2. Meanwhile, in a large bowl stir together the chili peppers, bread crumbs, green onions, milk, oregano, cumin, pepper, and salt. Add meat; mix well. Shape mixture into 5 oval patties 4½ to 5 inches long and ½ inch thick.

3. Spray the unheated rack of a broiler pan with nonstick coating; arrange patties on broiler pan. Broil patties 4 inches from heat for 10 to 12 minutes or until no longer pink, turning once halfway through broiling.

4. To serve, place a patty on each warm tortilla; spoon some of the shredded lettuce and tomato mixture over the patty. Wrap tortillas around patties. Makes 5 servings.

NUTRITION FACTS PER SERVING:

303 calories
12 g total fat
4 g saturated fat
57 mg cholesterol
456 mg sodium
27 g carbohydrate
1 g fiber
21 g protein

INGREDIENTS

- 10 ounces extra-lean ground beef
- 1 teaspoon chili powder
- ¼ teaspoon ground cumin
- ½ cup loose-pack frozen whole kernel corn, thawed
- ¼ cup salsa
- ¾ cup all-purpose flour
- ¾ cup cornmeal
- 2 tablespoons sugar
- 2 teaspoons baking powder
- ½ teaspoon salt
- 2 beaten eggs
- ¾ cup fat-free milk
- 2 tablespoons cooking oil
- Nonstick spray coating

- ½ cup shredded reduced-fat cheddar cheese (2 ounces)
- ⅓ cup salsa, heated
- Fresh cilantro (optional)
- Jalapeño pepper slices (optional)

beefy corn bread

This meat pie with a Mexican flair boasts a ground beef-and-corn filling topped with corn bread, cheese, and salsa. Serve with a mixed greens salad.

Prep time: 25 minutes
Baking time: 20 minutes
Standing time: 5 minutes

DIRECTIONS

1. In a large skillet cook the ground beef, chili powder, and cumin until meat is brown. Drain off fat. Stir the corn and the ¼ cup salsa into the meat.

2. In a medium bowl stir together the flour, cornmeal, sugar, baking powder, and salt. In a small bowl combine the eggs, milk, and oil; add to the flour mixture, stirring just until moistened.

3. Spray a 2-quart rectangular baking dish with nonstick coating. Spread half of the cornmeal mixture in dish. Spoon meat mixture over batter and sprinkle with half of the cheese. Spoon the remaining cornmeal mixture over cheese; spread to cover the meat layer.

4. Bake, uncovered, in a 375° oven about 20 minutes or until a wooden toothpick inserted near the center comes out clean. Sprinkle with remaining cheese. Let stand for 5 minutes. Serve with the ⅓ cup heated salsa. If desired, garnish with fresh cilantro and jalapeño pepper slices. Makes 6 servings.

NUTRITION FACTS PER SERVING:

335 calories
14 g total fat
4 g saturated fat
108 mg cholesterol
512 mg sodium
35 g carbohydrate
1 g fiber
18 g protein

greek town pizza

Be sure to drain all liquid from the spinach so it doesn't cause the crust to become soggy.

INGREDIENTS

Nonstick spray coating
1 16-ounce loaf frozen honey wheat bread dough, thawed
2 10-ounce packages frozen chopped spinach, thawed
1 pound extra-lean ground beef
1 cup chopped onion
2 cloves garlic, minced
1 cup lower-calorie, lower-sodium, and lower-fat spaghetti sauce

2 cups chopped tomato
1 cup shredded reduced-fat Monterey Jack or mozzarella cheese (4 ounces)
½ cup crumbled feta cheese (2 ounces)
Fresh oregano (optional)

Look for 90-percent lean

ground beef to use in dishes such as chili, tacos, and meat casseroles. In some parts of the country, you can buy 95-percent lean ground beef.

Prep time: 25 minutes
Baking time: 30 minutes
Standing time: 5 minutes

DIRECTIONS

1. Spray a 12-inch pizza pan or 13×9×2-inch baking pan with nonstick coating. Press bread dough into pan, forming a 1-inch-thick edge. Using the tines of a fork, prick the dough several times. Bake in a 375° oven for 10 minutes. Remove the crust from oven.

2. Meanwhile, squeeze all of the liquid from thawed spinach. Sprinkle the spinach over prebaked crust. In a large skillet cook the ground beef, onion, and garlic about 5 minutes or until meat is brown. Drain off excess fat. Stir in the spaghetti sauce. Spoon meat mixture over the spinach layer. Sprinkle with chopped tomato and cheeses.

3. Bake pizza for 30 to 35 minutes or until cheese is golden brown. Let stand for 5 minutes. Cut into wedges or squares. If desired, garnish with fresh oregano. Makes 8 servings.

NUTRITION FACTS PER SERVING:

341 calories
12 g total fat
5 g saturated fat
52 mg cholesterol
288 mg sodium
37 g carbohydrate
3 g fiber
23 g protein

INGREDIENTS

- 6 to 8 whole tiny new potatoes
- 4 cups torn mixed salad greens
- 1 medium cucumber, halved lengthwise and sliced
- 4 radishes, sliced
- 4 ounces very thinly sliced cooked roast beef or turkey
- 2 small tomatoes, cut into wedges
- ½ cup low-calorie creamy cucumber or ranch salad dressing
- 1 teaspoon snipped fresh dill or ¼ teaspoon dried dillweed

beef and new potato salad

No need to peel the potatoes. Leaving the skin on the potatoes hastens preparation, adds color, and provides a little extra fiber to these salads.

Start to finish: 30 minutes

DIRECTIONS

1. Scrub the new potatoes; cut into quarters.

2. In a medium saucepan cook the potatoes in a small amount of lightly salted boiling water for 10 to 15 minutes or until tender. Drain. Rinse with cold water. Drain.

3. In a mixing bowl gently toss together greens, cucumber, and radishes. Add potatoes. Gently toss. Arrange on 4 plates. Roll up the beef or turkey slices and arrange on top of greens mixture. Place a few tomato wedges to the side of each salad.

4. Combine salad dressing and dill. Drizzle over salads. Makes 4 servings.

Give the cucumber slices

a ruffled edge if you like. Before halving and slicing, draw the tines of a fork lengthwise down the cucumber. Repeat scoring all around the vegetable.

NUTRITION FACTS PER SERVING:

197 calories
7 g total fat
1 g saturated fat
25 mg cholesterol
494 mg sodium
20 g carbohydrate
3 g fiber
12 g protein

beef and fruit salad

For an exotic presentation, serve the fruit mixture in a kiwano (kee-WAH-noh) shell. Also called "horned melon," the kiwano has a jellylike pulp with a tart, yet sweet flavor likened to a combination of banana and cucumber.

INGREDIENTS

12 ounces boneless beef sirloin steak, cut 1 inch thick
⅓ cup reduced-sodium teriyaki sauce or soy sauce
¼ cup lemon juice
¼ cup water
2 teaspoons toasted sesame oil
⅛ teaspoon bottled hot pepper sauce
3 cups shredded napa cabbage
1 cup torn or shredded sorrel or spinach
2 cups fresh fruit (choose from sliced plums, nectarines, or kiwi fruit; halved seedless grapes or strawberries; raspberries; and/or blueberries)
2 kiwanos (optional)

To serve the fruit in kiwano shells, cut each kiwano in half crosswise. Scoop out the pulp.

Prep time: 20 minutes
Marinating time: 30 minutes
Grilling time: 14 minutes

DIRECTIONS

1. Trim fat from meat. Place meat in a plastic bag set in a shallow dish. For marinade, combine the teriyaki sauce, lemon juice, water, sesame oil, and hot pepper sauce. Reserve ⅓ cup for dressing. Pour remaining marinade over meat; close bag. Marinate at room temperature up to 30 minutes, turning bag occasionally. (Or, marinate in the refrigerator for up to 8 hours.)

2. Drain meat, reserving marinade. Grill meat on the rack of an uncovered grill directly over medium coals to desired doneness, turning once and brushing occasionally with marinade up to the last 5 minutes of grilling. (Allow 14 to 18 minutes for medium-rare and 18 to 22 minutes for medium.) Discard any remaining marinade.

3. To serve, divide the cabbage and sorrel among 4 dinner plates. Thinly slice meat diagonally. Arrange meat and fruit on top of greens. (Or, if desired, serve the fruit in kiwano shells.) Drizzle with the dressing (and, if desired, the pulp of kiwano fruit). Makes 4 servings.

NUTRITION FACTS PER SERVING:

248 calories
10 g total fat
3 g saturated fat
57 mg cholesterol
307 mg sodium
19 g carbohydrate
2 g fiber
22 g protein

INGREDIENTS

1	large tomato, chopped
½	of a medium yellow sweet pepper, cut into thin strips
¼	cup snipped fresh basil
2	tablespoons balsamic vinegar
1	tablespoon olive oil
1	clove garlic, minced
8	ounces beef flank steak or lean beef top loin steak
6	cups torn mixed salad greens
	Nonstick spray coating
1	clove garlic, minced
¼	teaspoon black pepper
⅛	teaspoon salt

beef and basil salad

When you cook with lively-tasting ingredients, you don't have to rely on adding a lot of fat or sodium for flavor. Fresh herbs, spices, and vinegar are three such flavor boosters.

Prep time: 25 minutes
Marinating time: 4 hours
Cooking time: 2 minutes

DIRECTIONS

1. In a medium mixing bowl stir together the tomato, sweet pepper, and basil. In a screw-top jar combine vinegar, olive oil, and 1 clove garlic. Cover and shake well. Pour over vegetable mixture, tossing to coat. Cover and marinate in the refrigerator for 4 to 24 hours.

2. Meanwhile, partially freeze meat. Trim any fat from meat. Cut meat into thin bite-size strips. Arrange mixed greens on 4 salad plates.

3. Spray an unheated large skillet with nonstick coating. Preheat over medium-high heat. Add meat and 1 clove garlic. Cook and stir for 2 to 3 minutes or until desired doneness. Sprinkle with black pepper and salt.

4. Stir in tomato mixture. Heat through. Top each salad with some of the hot meat mixture. Serve immediately. Makes 4 servings.

NUTRITION FACTS PER SERVING:

153 calories
8 g total fat
2 g saturated fat
27 mg cholesterol
114 mg sodium
8 g carbohydrate
2 g fiber
13 g protein

89

veal roast with herb crust

A tasty mustard- and lemon-seasoned crust adorns this succulent roast. You may need to order the meat from your butcher ahead of time.

INGREDIENTS

- 1 3-pound boneless veal leg round roast
- ¼ cup fine dry bread crumbs
- 2 tablespoons water
- 1 tablespoon Dijon-style mustard
- 1 tablespoon lemon juice
- 1 teaspoon dried basil, crushed
- 1 teaspoon dried thyme, crushed
- ½ teaspoon coarsely ground pepper
- 1 cup beef broth
- 2 tablespoons all-purpose flour
- ¼ cup light dairy sour cream

For an accurate reading, insert the meat thermometer into the center of the largest muscle or thickest portion of the meat. It should not touch any fat or bone.

Prep time: 15 minutes
Roasting time: 2½ hours

DIRECTIONS

1. Place meat on a rack in a shallow roasting pan. In a small mixing bowl stir together bread crumbs, water, mustard, lemon juice, basil, thyme, and pepper. Spread mixture over surface of meat.

2. Insert meat thermometer. Roast meat in a 325° oven for 2½ to 3 hours or until thermometer registers 160°. (If crust becomes too dry, cover meat loosely with foil after 1½ to 2 hours.) Transfer meat to a warm platter; cover and keep warm.

3. For sauce, skim fat from pan drippings. In a small saucepan stir beef broth into flour; add meat drippings.

Cook and stir until thickened and bubbly. Cook and stir for 1 minute more. Stir in the sour cream; heat through, but do not boil. Pass the sauce with meat. Makes 10 to 12 servings.

NUTRITION FACTS PER SERVING:

200 calories
6 g total fat
2 g saturated fat
111 mg cholesterol
214 mg sodium
4 g carbohydrate
0 g fiber
31 g protein

INGREDIENTS

Nonstick spray coating

12 ounces veal scaloppine or
boneless veal leg round steak
or beef top round steak, cut
¼ inch thick and trimmed of
separable fat

1 apple, thinly sliced

1 clove garlic, minced

½ cup dry Marsala

⅓ cup reduced-sodium
chicken broth

1 tablespoon snipped fresh parsley

veal with apple-marsala sauce

Veal may be labeled "scaloppine" in your supermarket meat section. Scaloppine technically describes a thin scallop of meat that is quickly sautéed. It is generally cut about ⅛ inch thick and needs no pounding.

time, for 4 to 5 minutes or until no longer pink, turning once. Transfer the meat to a serving platter. Cover and keep warm.

2. Add the sliced apple and garlic to skillet. Stir in the Marsala and chicken broth. Bring to boiling; reduce heat. Boil gently, uncovered, for 4 to 5 minutes or until mixture is reduced by half. Spoon the apple mixture over meat. Sprinkle with parsley. Makes 4 servings.

If using veal round or beef steak, cut meat into 8 pieces. Place 1 piece of meat between 2 pieces of plastic wrap. Working from center to edges, pound with flat side of meat mallet to about ⅛-inch thickness. Remove plastic wrap. Repeat with remaining meat.

Prep time: 10 minutes
Cooking time: 12 minutes

DIRECTIONS

1. Spray an unheated large skillet with nonstick coating. Preheat over medium-high heat. Cook meat, half at a

NUTRITION FACTS PER SERVING:

167 calories
4 g total fat
1 g saturated fat
68 mg cholesterol
100 mg sodium
7 g carbohydrate
1 g fiber
19 g protein

veal scaloppine

Serve this fat- and calorie-trimmed classic with hot cooked broccoli and whole-wheat dinner rolls.

INGREDIENTS

12 ounces boneless veal leg round steak, veal leg sirloin steak, or beef top round steak, cut ¼ inch thick and trimmed of separable fat
Salt and pepper
½ cup chopped onion
¼ cup water
2 cloves garlic, minced
1 14½-ounce can tomatoes, undrained and cut up
3 tablespoons dry white wine
1 tablespoon snipped fresh oregano or 1 teaspoon dried oregano, crushed
1 tablespoon capers, drained (optional)
⅛ teaspoon pepper
Nonstick spray coating
2 cups hot cooked noodles

Start to finish: 30 minutes

DIRECTIONS

1. Cut meat into 8 pieces. Place each piece of meat between 2 pieces of plastic wrap. Working from center to edges, pound with flat side of a meat mallet to about ⅛-inch thickness. Remove plastic wrap. Sprinkle meat lightly with salt and pepper. Set aside.

2. For sauce, in a medium covered saucepan combine the onion, water, and garlic. Cook until onion is tender. Stir in undrained tomatoes, wine, oregano, capers (if desired), and pepper. Bring to boiling; reduce heat. Simmer, uncovered, about 15 minutes or until desired consistency. Keep warm.

3. Meanwhile, spray an unheated large skillet with nonstick coating. Preheat over medium-high heat. Cook meat, half at a time, for 2 to 4 minutes or until desired doneness, turning once. Transfer meat to a serving platter. Keep warm.

4. To serve, spoon the sauce over meat. Serve with hot cooked noodles. Makes 4 servings.

NUTRITION FACTS PER SERVING:

246 calories
5 g total fat
1 g saturated fat
94 mg cholesterol
216 mg sodium
25 g carbohydrate
3 g fiber
23 g protein

apple-stuffed pork roast

Serve pinwheel slices of this spicy fruit-stuffed roast on a bed of steamed white or brown rice.

INGREDIENTS

- 1 3- to 3½-pound boneless pork single-loin roast
- ½ cup chunky-style applesauce
- ½ cup finely chopped celery
- 2 tablespoons raisins
- 1 teaspoon ground cinnamon
- ½ teaspoon ground sage
- ¼ teaspoon pepper
   Dash salt
- ¼ cup finely chopped red apple
- 1¼ cups apple cider or apple juice
- 4 teaspoons cornstarch

Prep time: 30 minutes
Roasting time: 1¾ hours

DIRECTIONS

1. To butterfly the meat, make a single lengthwise cut down the center of the meat, cutting to within ½ inch of the other side. Starting at the center of the meat, make 1 horizontal slit to the right and 1 horizontal slit to the left of the center cut. Spread the meat open. Cover meat with plastic wrap. Pound with a meat mallet to about 10 inches wide. Remove plastic wrap. Set meat aside.

2. In a small mixing bowl stir together the applesauce, celery, raisins, cinnamon, sage, pepper, and salt. Spread the mixture over the meat to within ½ inch of edges.

3. Starting from a long side, roll up the meat into a spiral. Secure the roll with 100% cotton string, tying the meat crosswise at several places to prevent it from unrolling during cooking.

4. Place on a rack in a shallow roasting pan. Insert a meat thermometer. Roast, uncovered, in a 325° oven for 1¾ to 2½ hours or until meat thermometer registers 160°. Transfer to a warm platter; cover and keep warm.

5. For sauce, in a small saucepan cook the apple in ½ cup of the apple cider or juice for 3 to 5 minutes or until tender. In a small bowl stir remaining cider or juice into cornstarch; add to saucepan. Cook and stir until thickened and bubbly. Cook and stir for 2 minutes more. Untie meat; thinly slice. Serve sauce with meat. Makes 10 to 12 servings.

NUTRITION FACTS PER SERVING:

201 calories
9 g total fat
3 g saturated fat
61 mg cholesterol
72 mg sodium
10 g carbohydrate
1 g fiber
20 g protein

mustard-orange pork tenderloin

Roast a mixture of vegetables, such as cut-up red onions, baby carrots, and chunks of zucchini, alongside the meat. Just spray the vegetables with olive oil-flavored nonstick coating before placing them in the pan around the meat.

INGREDIENTS

- 12 ounces pork tenderloin
- ½ cup apricot preserves or orange marmalade
- 3 tablespoons Dijon-style mustard
  Nonstick spray coating
- 2 cups sliced fresh mushrooms
- ½ cup sliced green onions
- 2 tablespoons orange juice

Prep time: 10 minutes
Cooking time: 25 minutes

DIRECTIONS

1. Trim any fat from meat. Place the meat in a shallow roasting pan. Insert a meat thermometer. Roast, uncovered, in a 425° oven for 10 minutes.

2. Meanwhile in a small mixing bowl stir together the preserves and mustard. Spoon half of the mustard mixture over the meat; set remaining mixture aside. Roast for 15 to 25 minutes more or until thermometer registers 160°. Cover meat with foil and let stand for 10 minutes before carving.

3. Spray a medium saucepan with nonstick coating. Preheat over medium heat. Add mushrooms and green onions. Cook and stir for 2 to 3 minutes or until mushrooms are tender. Stir in remaining mustard mixture and orange juice. Cook and stir until heated through. To serve, thinly slice meat. Spoon mushroom mixture over meat. Makes 4 servings.

NUTRITION FACTS PER SERVING:

240 calories
4 g total fat
1 g saturated fat
60 mg cholesterol
334 mg sodium
32 g carbohydrate
3 g fiber
21 g protein

pork with apple-sour cream sauce

Apple slices and a hint of sage complement these medallions of pork. Apple juice adds a light sweetness.

INGREDIENTS

- 12 ounces pork tenderloin
  Nonstick spray coating
- 1 medium apple, cored and thinly sliced
- ¾ cup apple juice or apple cider
- 1 small onion, chopped
- ¼ teaspoon salt
- ¼ teaspoon dried sage, crushed
- 1 8-ounce carton fat-free dairy sour cream
- 2 tablespoons all-purpose flour

- 1 9-ounce package refrigerated spinach fettuccine or
  4 ounces packaged dried spinach fettuccine, cooked and drained
  Cracked black pepper (optional)

Start to finish: 30 minutes

DIRECTIONS

1. Trim fat from meat. Cut meat crosswise into 4 slices. Place a slice of meat between 2 pieces of plastic wrap. Working from the center to the edges, pound lightly with the flat side of a meat mallet to ½-inch thickness. Remove plastic wrap. Repeat with remaining slices.

2. Spray an unheated large skillet with nonstick coating. Preheat the skillet over medium-high heat. Cook the meat slices, half at a time, for 3½ to 4 minutes or until meat is slightly pink in center, turning once. Remove the meat from skillet. Cover and keep warm.

3. For sauce, add apple slices, apple juice or cider, onion, salt, and sage to skillet. Bring just to boiling; reduce heat. Simmer, covered, for 4 to 5 minutes or until apple is just tender. Using a slotted spoon, carefully remove apple slices and set aside.

4. In a small bowl stir together sour cream and flour. Add sour cream mixture to skillet. Cook and stir until thickened and bubbly. Cook and stir for 1 minute more.

5. Arrange the meat and apple slices over fettuccine. Spoon sauce over meat, apple slices, and pasta. If desired, sprinkle with pepper. Makes 4 servings.

NUTRITION FACTS PER SERVING:

373 calories
4 g total fat
1 g saturated fat
60 mg cholesterol
231 mg sodium
54 g carbohydrate
1 g fiber
28 g protein

peach-sauced pork

Serve these tender pork and peach slices over rice for an extra-special dinner. Steamed broccoli or asparagus adds an attractive green contrast to the yellow peaches.

INGREDIENTS

12 ounces pork tenderloin
    Nonstick spray coating
1 16-ounce can peach slices in light syrup
¼ cup cold water
1½ teaspoons cornstarch
¼ teaspoon salt
⅛ teaspoon ground allspice
    Hot cooked rice (optional)

Start to finish: 30 minutes

DIRECTIONS

1. Trim fat from meat. Cut meat crosswise into about sixteen ½-inch-thick slices. Place each slice of meat between 2 pieces of plastic wrap. Working from the center to the edges, pound lightly with flat side of a meat mallet to ¼-inch thickness. Remove plastic wrap.

2. Spray an unheated large skillet with nonstick coating. Preheat skillet over medium heat. Cook meat slices, half at a time, about 4 minutes or until meat is slightly pink in center, turning once. Remove meat from skillet. Cover and keep warm. Carefully wipe skillet with a paper towel.

3. Drain peaches, reserving ½ cup syrup. Set peaches aside. In a small bowl stir together the reserved syrup, water, cornstarch, salt, and allspice. Add mixture to skillet. Cook and stir until thickened and bubbly. Cook and stir for 2 minutes more. Add the meat and peaches to skillet; heat through. If desired, serve with rice.

NUTRITION FACTS PER SERVING:

174 calories
3 g total fat
1 g saturated fat
60 mg cholesterol
183 mg sodium
17 g carbohydrate
1 g fiber
19 g protein

roast pork and cabbage

INGREDIENTS

- 12 ounces pork tenderloin
- ⅛ teaspoon pepper
- 6 cups shredded cabbage
- 1 large onion, sliced
- ⅔ cup shredded carrot
- ⅓ cup water
- 2 tablespoons vinegar
- 1 teaspoon dillseed, crushed
- ¼ teaspoon salt
- ⅛ teaspoon pepper

Dillseed refers to the small, hard, dried seeds of the dill plant. Compared to the leaves from the plant, the seeds have a stronger, slightly pungent flavor.

Prep time: 15 minutes
Roasting time: 25 minutes
Standing time: 10 minutes

DIRECTIONS

1. Trim fat from meat. Sprinkle meat with ⅛ teaspoon pepper. Place meat on a rack in a shallow roasting pan. Insert a meat thermometer. Roast, uncovered, in a 425° oven for 25 to 35 minutes or until the thermometer registers 160°. Cover meat with foil; let stand for 10 minutes before carving.

2. Meanwhile, in a large saucepan combine cabbage, onion, carrot, water, vinegar, dillseed, salt, and ⅛ teaspoon pepper. Bring to boiling; reduce heat. Simmer, covered, for 8 to 10 minutes or just until the vegetables are tender.

3. Slice the meat and serve with the vegetables. Makes 4 servings.

Remove roasted meat from the oven when the thermometer reaches the temperature specified in the recipe. The temperature will rise 5° during the standing time to reach the proper doneness.

NUTRITION FACTS PER SERVING:

166 calories
4 g total fat
1 g saturated fat
60 mg cholesterol
224 mg sodium
14 g carbohydrate
7 g fiber
21 g protein

sweet-and-sour pork kabobs

Try pork tenderloin or loin chops for these kabobs. They're both boneless, lean cuts. Serve the kabobs with couscous, which adds 57 calories per ½ cup serving.

INGREDIENTS

2 medium carrots, bias-sliced into 1-inch pieces

1 8-ounce can pineapple slices (juice pack)

⅓ cup wine vinegar

2 tablespoons reduced-sodium soy sauce

1 tablespoon cooking oil

2 teaspoons cornstarch

1 teaspoon sugar

1 clove garlic, minced

2 small green and/or red sweet peppers, cut into 1-inch squares

12 ounces lean boneless pork, cut into 1-inch pieces

Hot cooked couscous (optional)

Prep time: 35 minutes
Grilling time: 12 minutes

DIRECTIONS

1. In a covered saucepan cook carrots in a small amount of boiling water for 8 minutes; drain well. Drain pineapple, reserving juice. Cut pineapple slices into quarters; set aside.

2. For sauce, in a saucepan combine reserved pineapple juice, vinegar, soy sauce, oil, cornstarch, sugar, and garlic. Cook and stir until thickened and bubbly. Cook and stir for 2 minutes more.

3. On 8 short or 4 long metal skewers, alternately thread the carrots, pineapple, sweet peppers, and meat, leaving about ¼ inch between pieces. Brush with the sauce.

4. Grill kabobs on the rack of an uncovered grill directly over medium coals for 12 to 14 minutes or until meat is slightly pink in center and juices run clear, turning once and brushing often with sauce during first half of grilling. (Or, broil on the unheated rack of a broiler pan 4 to 5 inches from the heat for 12 to 14 minutes, turning once and brushing often with sauce during first half of broiling.) If desired, serve over hot cooked couscous. Makes 4 servings.

NUTRITION FACTS PER SERVING:

203 calories
9 g total fat
2 g saturated fat
38 mg cholesterol
318 mg sodium
19 g carbohydrate
2 g fiber
14 g protein

INGREDIENTS

- 12 ounces pork tenderloin
- ⅓ cup light soy sauce
- 2 tablespoons lemon juice
- 1½ teaspoons chili powder
- 1 recipe Peanut Sauce
- 8 green onions, cut into 1-inch pieces

- Green onion brushes (optional)
- Hot cooked brown or white rice (optional)

spicy pork satay with peanut sauce

Marinate the meat, make the sauce, and thread the skewers all ahead of time. When dinnertime comes, the kabobs take only 10 minutes to grill.

Prep time: 20 minutes
Marinating time: 1 hour
Grilling time: 10 minutes

DIRECTIONS

1. Trim fat from meat. Cut meat diagonally into strips about 3 inches long and ¼ inch thick. In a shallow glass dish stir together soy sauce, lemon juice, and chili powder; add the meat strips. Cover and marinate meat in the refrigerator for 1 to 2 hours, stirring occasionally. Meanwhile, prepare the Peanut Sauce.

2. Drain the meat strips, reserving marinade. On 8 long metal skewers, alternately thread meat strips and green onions, leaving about ¼ inch between pieces.

3. Grill skewers on the rack of an uncovered grill directly over medium coals for 10 to 12 minutes or until meat is slightly pink in center, turning and brushing once with marinade halfway through grilling. (Or, spray the unheated rack of a broiler pan with nonstick spray coating. Place skewers on rack and broil 4 to 5 inches from the heat for 8 to 10 minutes, turning and brushing once with marinade halfway through broiling.)

4. Serve meat skewers with Peanut Sauce for dipping. If desired, garnish with green onion brushes and serve with rice. Makes 4 servings.

Peanut Sauce: In a small mixing bowl stir together 2 tablespoons creamy peanut butter; 2 tablespoons hot water; 4 teaspoons light soy sauce; 1 small clove garlic, minced; ½ teaspoon sugar; ½ teaspoon grated fresh ginger; and ¼ to ½ teaspoon bottled hot pepper sauce. Stir before serving.

NUTRITION FACTS PER SERVING:

- 165 calories
- 7 g total fat
- 2 g saturated fat
- 60 mg cholesterol
- 925 mg sodium
- 5 g carbohydrate
- 1 g fiber
- 22 g protein

99

southwest pork chops with corn salsa

In late summer, when corn is its sweetest and tomatoes their juiciest, these meaty pork chops—crowned with a colorful, chunky salsa—stand unsurpassed as the freshest tastes of the season.

INGREDIENTS

- ¼ cup white wine vinegar
- 3 tablespoons snipped fresh cilantro
- 1 teaspoon olive oil
- 1 cup fresh or frozen whole kernel corn
- 3 plum tomatoes, chopped
- ½ cup thinly sliced green onions
- 1 small fresh jalapeño pepper, seeded and minced (see tip, page 21)
- 4 center-cut pork loin chops, cut ¾ inch thick
- Cactus leaves (optional)

Today's pork is leaner, and therefore lower in fat and calories, than ever before. Because there is so little fat, pork requires a little extra attention when being grilled. Closely check the timings and temperatures in the recipe to ensure tender, juicy meat.

Prep time: 20 minutes
Grilling time: 8 minutes

DIRECTIONS

1. For sauce, combine 3 tablespoons of the vinegar, 1 tablespoon of the cilantro, and the olive oil.

2. For salsa, thaw corn, if frozen. In a medium bowl combine corn, tomatoes, green onions, jalapeño pepper, the remaining vinegar, and the remaining cilantro. Set aside.

3. Trim fat from chops. Grill chops on the rack of an uncovered grill directly over medium coals for 8 to 11 minutes or until chops are slightly pink in center and juices run clear, turning once and brushing occasionally with sauce up to the last 5 minutes of grilling. If desired, serve chops on cactus leaves. Serve with salsa. Makes 4 servings.

NUTRITION FACTS PER SERVING:

201 calories
9 g total fat
3 g saturated fat
51 mg cholesterol
51 mg sodium
14 g carbohydrate
2 g fiber
18 g protein

grilled apricot-stuffed pork chops

The tangy flavor of apricots pairs deliciously with the smoky taste of grilled pork.

INGREDIENTS

- ½ cup cooked brown rice or long grain rice
- ¼ cup snipped dried apricots
- ¼ cup finely chopped onion
- 1 tablespoon reduced-calorie apricot spread
- ¼ teaspoon dried thyme, crushed
- ¼ teaspoon pepper
- 4 center-cut pork loin chops, cut 1 inch thick
- ¼ cup reduced-calorie apricot spread

Prep time: 15 minutes
Grilling time: 30 minutes

DIRECTIONS

1. For stuffing, in a medium mixing bowl stir together the rice, apricots, onion, the 1 tablespoon apricot spread, the thyme, and pepper. Trim fat from meat. Make a pocket in each chop by cutting horizontally from the fat side almost to the bone. Spoon one-fourth of the stuffing into each pocket. If necessary, secure openings with toothpicks.

2. In a covered grill arrange medium-hot coals around a drip pan. Test for medium heat above the drip pan. Place chops on the grill rack over drip pan, but not over coals. Lower the grill hood. Grill for 30 to 40 minutes or until juices run clear, turning once halfway through grilling.

3. Meanwhile, in a small saucepan heat the ¼ cup apricot spread until melted. Brush over chops the last 5 minutes of grilling. (Or, spray the unheated rack of a broiler pan with nonstick spray coating. Place chops on rack and broil 4 inches from heat for 15 to 18 minutes, turning chops once halfway through broiling and brushing with the apricot spread the last 3 minutes of broiling.) Makes 4 servings.

NUTRITION FACTS PER SERVING:

208 calories
7 g total fat
2 g saturated fat
48 mg cholesterol
59 mg sodium
19 g carbohydrate
2 g fiber
16 g protein

101

pork chops in creamy vegetable sauce

This cream sauce combines reduced-fat soup and fat-free sour cream, providing a seemingly high-fat richness that won't give away its real secret.

INGREDIENTS

Nonstick spray coating
6 pork rib chops, cut ½ inch thick and trimmed of separable fat (about 1¾ pounds total)
1½ cups sliced fresh mushrooms
1 medium green or red sweet pepper, cut into thin strips
1 10¾-ounce can condensed reduced-fat and reduced-sodium cream of mushroom soup
½ cup fat-free dairy sour cream
¼ cup fat-free milk
1 teaspoon paprika

1 medium tomato, seeded and chopped
Hot cooked noodles or rice (optional)

Start to finish: 25 minutes

DIRECTIONS

1. Spray an unheated 12-inch skillet with nonstick coating. Preheat over medium heat. Add pork chops; cook for 6 minutes. Turn chops; add mushrooms and sweet pepper. Cook about 6 minutes more or until meat is slightly pink in center and juices run clear. Remove the chops and vegetables.

2. For sauce, in a small mixing bowl stir together the soup, sour cream, milk, and paprika. Stir the mixture into skillet; bring to boiling.

3. Return the chops and vegetables to skillet. Cook, covered, for 5 minutes. Add the tomato. Cook for 1 to 2 minutes more or until heated through. If desired, serve with hot cooked noodles. Makes 6 servings.

NUTRITION FACTS PER SERVING:

193 calories
9 g total fat
3 g saturated fat
50 mg cholesterol
264 mg sodium
11 g carbohydrate
1 g fiber
17 g protein

INGREDIENTS

- 12 ounces lean ground pork
- 2 cups sliced fresh mushrooms
- 1 cup shredded or biased-sliced carrot
- ½ cup red and/or green sweet pepper cut into bite-size strips
- 2 cloves garlic, minced
- 1 tablespoon cornstarch
- 1 cup reduced-sodium chicken broth
- 1 tablespoon reduced-sodium soy sauce
- 1 teaspoon grated fresh ginger
- ¼ teaspoon crushed red pepper
- ¼ teaspoon curry powder
- 4 ounces packaged dried thin spaghetti, broken, or linguine, cooked and drained (2 cups cooked)
- 1 cup fresh bean sprouts
- ½ cup sliced green onions
  Sliced green onion (optional)

pork lo mein

If you prefer, use lean boneless pork, thinly sliced into bite-size strips, instead of the ground pork. Boneless loin chops work well.

Start to finish: 35 minutes

DIRECTIONS

1. In a large skillet cook the meat, mushrooms, carrot, sweet pepper, and garlic until meat is brown and vegetables are tender. Drain off fat.

2. Stir cornstarch into meat mixture. Stir in broth, soy sauce, ginger, crushed red pepper, and curry powder. Cook and stir until thickened and bubbly. Cook and stir for 2 minutes more.

3. Stir in cooked pasta, bean sprouts, and the ½ cup green onions; heat through. If desired, garnish with additional green onion. Makes 4 servings.

NUTRITION FACTS PER SERVING:

269 calories
7 g total fat
0 g saturated fat
40 mg cholesterol
350 mg sodium
34 g carbohydrate
3 g fiber
17g protein

To cook boneless pork,

heat 1 teaspoon cooking oil in the large skillet. Add the meat strips. Stir-fry for 2 to 3 minutes or until no longer pink. Remove meat from skillet. Cook the mushrooms, carrot, sweet pepper, and garlic as directed. Return meat to skillet and continue as directed.

ham with sweet potatoes and apples

Although it's hard to beat fresh vegetables of any kind, canned vegetables help out in a pinch. By using canned sweet potatoes, you'll cut your preparation time to just 10 minutes.

INGREDIENTS

4 medium sweet potatoes or one 18-ounce can sweet potatoes, drained

2 ½-inch-thick slices lower-fat, lower-sodium cooked ham, trimmed of separable fat (about 12 ounces)

2 medium apples

1 teaspoon finely shredded orange peel

¾ cup orange juice

2 teaspoons cornstarch

1 teaspoon reduced-sodium soy sauce

1 teaspoon grated fresh ginger

1 clove garlic, minced
Snipped fresh parsley (optional)

Prep time: 30 minutes
Baking time: 25 minutes

DIRECTIONS

1. Peel and quarter fresh sweet potatoes. In a large covered saucepan cook the potatoes in a small amount of boiling water about 15 minutes or until almost tender. Drain.

2. Cut each ham slice in half. Core apples and cut each apple into 8 wedges. Arrange drained, fresh or canned sweet potatoes and the apple wedges in a 2-quart rectangular baking dish. Arrange ham slices on top of sweet potatoes and apples.

3. In a small saucepan combine orange peel, orange juice, cornstarch, soy sauce, ginger, and garlic. Cook and stir until thickened and bubbly. Pour over ham.

4. Bake, covered, in a 375° oven for 15 minutes. Uncover and bake about 10 minutes more or until potatoes and apples are just tender. If desired, sprinkle with fresh parsley. Makes 4 servings.

NUTRITION FACTS PER SERVING:

266 calories
3 g total fat
1 g saturated fat
36 mg cholesterol
986 mg sodium
44 g carbohydrate
6 g fiber
18 g protein

INGREDIENTS

- 6 packaged dried lasagna noodles (4 ounces)
- 1 10-ounce package frozen chopped spinach
- 2 cups fat-free milk
- ¼ cup chopped onion
- 3 tablespoons cornstarch
- 1½ cups diced lower-fat, lower-sodium cooked ham (about 8 ounces)
- ½ teaspoon dried Italian seasoning, crushed
- 1 cup low-fat cottage cheese
- 1 cup shredded mozzarella cheese (4 ounces)

spinach and ham lasagna

Deviate from the traditional red-sauced lasagna. This luscious lasagna is layered with spinach, ham, cheese, and a lightened "cream" sauce. Ham adds a tasty smoky flavor.

Prep time: 40 minutes
Baking time: 30 minutes
Standing time: 10 minutes

DIRECTIONS

1. Cook the lasagna noodles according to package directions, except omit oil. Drain. Rinse with cold water; drain again. Set aside.

2. Meanwhile, cook the spinach according to package directions; drain well. Set spinach aside.

3. For sauce, in a medium saucepan combine the milk, onion, and cornstarch. Cook and stir until thickened and bubbly. Cook and stir for 2 minutes more.

4. Spread 2 tablespoons of the sauce evenly on the bottom of a 2-quart rectangular baking dish. Stir ham and Italian seasoning into remaining sauce. Arrange 3 lasagna noodles in the dish. Spread with one-third of the remaining sauce. Layer the spinach on top. Layer another one-third of the sauce, the cottage cheese, and half of the mozzarella cheese over the spinach.

Place remaining noodles on top. Top with the remaining sauce and mozzarella cheese.

5. Bake, uncovered, in a 375° oven for 30 to 35 minutes or until heated through. Let stand 10 minutes before serving. Makes 6 servings.

NUTRITION FACTS PER SERVING:

241 calories
5 g total fat
2 g saturated fat
30 mg cholesterol
724 mg sodium
26 g carbohydrate
0 g fiber
22 g protein

ham and potato skillet

Fat-free sour cream becomes the base for a creamy, rich-tasting sauce in this family-style dish. For the best herb flavor, use fresh herbs when you can. You can substitute another fresh herb for the dill.

INGREDIENTS

- 1 pound small potatoes
- 1 cup water
- 8 ounces fresh green beans, cut into 1-inch pieces, or one 9-ounce package frozen cut green beans
- 1 8-ounce carton fat-free dairy sour cream
- 2 tablespoons all-purpose flour
- 2 teaspoons prepared mustard
- ¾ teaspoon snipped fresh dill or ¼ teaspoon dried dillweed
- ⅛ teaspoon pepper
- 1½ cups cubed lower-fat, lower-sodium cooked ham (about 8 ounces)
- Tomato slices (optional)
- Fresh dill (optional)

Start to finish: 30 minutes

DIRECTIONS

1. Scrub and slice potatoes; halve any large slices.

2. In a large skillet bring the water to boiling. Add the potatoes and fresh green beans (if using). Cover and cook about 15 minutes or until potatoes and beans are tender. (If using frozen beans, cook potatoes for 10 minutes; add beans. Return to boiling. Cook for 5 minutes more.) Drain well; return to skillet.

3. Meanwhile, in a small saucepan stir together sour cream, flour, mustard, the snipped or dried dill, and the pepper. Cook and stir until thickened and bubbly. Pour over vegetables in skillet. Stir in ham. Heat through. If desired, garnish with tomato slices and additional fresh dill. Makes 4 servings.

NUTRITION FACTS PER SERVING:

254 calories
2 g total fat
1 g saturated fat
24 mg cholesterol
698 mg sodium
41 g carbohydrate
3 g fiber
18 g protein

pork and mango salad

Mango chutney supplies the flavor for this exotic vinaigrette, which is a natural for complementing the flavor of pork. Look for the chutney next to the jams and jellies at your supermarket.

INGREDIENTS

- 3 tablespoons mango chutney
- 2 tablespoons white wine vinegar or rice wine vinegar
- 1 tablespoon Dijon-style mustard or brown mustard
- 1 clove garlic, minced
- ⅛ teaspoon pepper
- 1 tablespoon olive oil or salad oil
- 1 tablespoon water
- 8 ounces pork tenderloin
  Nonstick spray coating
- 6 cups torn mixed salad greens
- ½ of an 8-ounce can sliced water chestnuts, drained
- 1 medium mango, peeled, seeded, and sliced, or 2 medium nectarines, sliced
- 2 tablespoons snipped fresh chives

Start to finish: 30 minutes

DIRECTIONS

1. For vinaigrette, in a blender container or food processor bowl combine the chutney, vinegar, mustard, garlic, and pepper. Cover and blend or process until smooth. In a small bowl combine olive oil and water. With blender or food processor running, add oil mixture in a thin steady stream to chutney mixture. Cover and blend or process for 15 seconds more.

2. Trim any fat from meat. Cut meat into ¼-inch-thick slices. Spray an unheated large skillet with nonstick coating. Preheat over medium-high heat. Cook the meat slices, half at a time, in the skillet for 3 to 4 minutes or until meat is slightly pink in center, turning once. Remove all meat from skillet. Cover and keep warm.

3. In a large bowl toss together the salad greens and water chestnuts. Pour about half of the vinaigrette over greens mixture. Toss to coat.

4. To serve, divide greens mixture among 4 plates. Arrange some of the mango or nectarine slices and meat on the greens mixture. Drizzle each serving with about 1 tablespoon of the remaining vinaigrette. Sprinkle with the chives. Makes 4 servings.

NUTRITION FACTS PER SERVING:

192 calories
6 g total fat
1 g saturated fat
40 mg cholesterol
137 mg sodium
21 g carbohydrate
2 g fiber
14 g protein

balsamic pork and berry salad

Balsamic vinegar is made from white Trebbiano grape juice that's been aged in wooden barrels. Look for it at your grocery store or in specialty food stores. In this dressing, balsamic vinegar adds a delicate sweetness.

INGREDIENTS

- 6 cups torn romaine
- 2 cups sliced fresh strawberries
- ½ cup thinly sliced celery
- 1 teaspoon snipped fresh chives
- 8 ounces pork tenderloin
  Nonstick spray coating
- 1 teaspoon olive oil or salad oil
- 2 cloves garlic, minced
- ¼ cup honey
- ¼ cup balsamic vinegar
- ¼ teaspoon pepper
- 2 tablespoons chopped pecans or walnuts, toasted

To toast nuts,

spread them in a single layer in a shallow baking pan. Bake in a 350° oven for 5 to 10 minutes or until light golden brown, watching carefully and stirring once or twice so the nuts don't burn.

Start to finish: 30 minutes

DIRECTIONS

1. In a large mixing bowl toss together the romaine, strawberries, celery, and chives. Set aside.

2. Trim any fat from meat. Cut meat into ¼-inch-thick slices. Spray an unheated large skillet with nonstick coating. Preheat over medium-high heat. Cook the meat slices, half at a time, in the skillet for 3 to 4 minutes or until meat is slightly pink in center, turning once. Remove all meat from skillet. Cover and keep warm.

3. For dressing, add the oil to skillet. Add garlic; cook and stir for 15 seconds. Stir in the honey, vinegar, and pepper. Cook and stir until heated through.

4. Place romaine mixture on 4 plates. Top with the meat. Drizzle with dressing. Sprinkle with pecans or walnuts. Serve immediately. Makes 4 servings.

NUTRITION FACTS PER SERVING:

227 calories
6 g total fat
1 g saturated fat
40 mg cholesterol
54 mg sodium
30 g carbohydrate
3 g fiber
15 g protein

INGREDIENTS

- 1 cup frozen peas and carrots or frozen mixed vegetables
- ½ cup packaged dried orzo, tripolini, tiny tube macaroni, or tiny star macaroni
- 6 ounces lower-fat, lower-sodium cooked ham, cut into ½-inch cubes (about 1 cup)
- 4 green onions, sliced
- ½ cup light dairy sour cream
- 2 tablespoons reduced-calorie ranch salad dressing
- 1 teaspoon snipped fresh dill or ¼ teaspoon dried dillweed
- 2 medium tomatoes, sliced
- 1 green sweet pepper, cut into half rings
- Lettuce leaves

ham and orzo salad

Use any tiny pasta you have on hand for this salad. Orzo, shown in the photograph, looks like grains of rice; tripolini resembles tiny bow ties.

Prep time: 35 minutes
Chilling time: 4 hours

DIRECTIONS

1. In a medium saucepan bring a large amount of water to boiling. Add the frozen vegetables and the pasta. Return to boiling. Boil, uncovered, for 5 to 8 minutes or until pasta and vegetables are tender. Immediately drain mixture in a colander. Rinse with cold water. Drain.

2. In a medium mixing bowl stir together pasta mixture, ham, and green onions. In a small mixing bowl stir together sour cream, salad dressing, and dill. Pour the sour cream mixture over the pasta mixture. Toss until well coated. Cover and chill for 4 to 8 hours.

3. To serve, arrange the tomato slices and sweet pepper on 4 lettuce-lined plates. Stir the pasta mixture; spoon onto the plates. Makes 4 servings.

NUTRITION FACTS PER SERVING:

224 calories
6 g total fat
1 g saturated fat
22 mg cholesterol
597 mg sodium
31 g carbohydrate
3 g fiber
15 g protein

herbed lamb with apples

Grill the apple rings in a foil packet alongside the lamb. Be sure to turn the packet often so the apples cook evenly. To keep the apples from losing their shape and to add color, do not peel them.

INGREDIENTS

1 cup apple juice or apple cider

¼ teaspoon finely shredded lemon peel

2 tablespoons lemon juice

1 tablespoon honey

1 teaspoon dried rosemary, crushed

1 clove garlic, minced

½ teaspoon salt

¼ teaspoon pepper

2 pounds boneless leg of lamb, cut crosswise into 1-inch-thick slices and trimmed of separable fat

4 small red and/or green apples, cored and sliced crosswise into ½-inch-thick rings

3 tablespoons apple juice or apple cider

Fresh rosemary (optional)

Prep time: 20 minutes
Marinating time: 6 hours
Grilling time: 16 minutes

DIRECTIONS

1. For marinade, stir together the 1 cup apple juice or cider, the lemon peel, lemon juice, honey, dried rosemary, garlic, salt, and pepper. Place meat in a plastic bag set in a deep bowl. Pour the marinade over meat. Close bag. Marinate in the refrigerator for 6 to 24 hours. Drain meat, reserving the marinade.

2. Place apple rings on an 18-inch square piece of heavy foil. Sprinkle with the

3 tablespoons apple juice or cider. Bring up 2 opposite edges of foil and, leaving a little space for steam expansion, seal tightly with a double fold. Fold the remaining ends to seal.

3. In a covered grill arrange medium-hot coals around outside edges of grill. Test for medium heat above the center of grill (not over coals). Place meat and the apple packet on the grill rack in center, but not over the coals. Lower the grill hood. Grill meat to desired doneness and apples just until tender, brushing meat occasionally with marinade up to the last 5 minutes of grilling. (For meat, allow 16 to 18 minutes for medium-rare or 18 to 20 minutes for

medium doneness. For apples, allow 16 to 18 minutes.)

4. Serve apple rings with the meat. If desired, garnish with fresh rosemary. Makes 8 servings.

NUTRITION FACTS PER SERVING:

175 calories
5 g total fat
2 g saturated fat
57 mg cholesterol
212 mg sodium
13 g carbohydrate
1 g fiber
18 g protein

lamb chops and peppers

INGREDIENTS

4 lamb leg sirloin chops, cut
  ¾ inch thick (about
  1¼ pounds total)
  Nonstick spray coating
1 cup julienned green
  sweet pepper
1 cup julienned red or yellow
  sweet pepper
1 cup julienned zucchini
½ cup thinly sliced leek
1 clove garlic, minced
½ cup dry white wine or water
1 teaspoon instant beef
  bouillon granules

1 teaspoon dried basil, crushed
½ teaspoon dried oregano, crushed
⅛ teaspoon black pepper

Enjoy this quick-cooking skillet dish in the summertime, when sweet peppers and zucchini are at their peak. To julienne the vegetables, see the tip on page 78.

NUTRITION FACTS PER SERVING:

181 calories
6 g total fat
2 g saturated fat
58 mg cholesterol
268 mg sodium
8 g carbohydrate
2 g fiber
19 g protein

Start to finish: 30 minutes

DIRECTIONS

1. Trim fat from chops. Spray an unheated large nonstick skillet with nonstick coating. Preheat over medium-high heat. Cook the chops in the skillet about 4 minutes or until browned, turning once. Remove chops from skillet. Add the sweet peppers, zucchini, leek, and garlic to the skillet and cook for 3 minutes. Return the chops to skillet.

2. In a small mixing bowl stir together wine, bouillon granules, basil, oregano, and black pepper. Add to skillet.

When using nonstick spray coating,
hold the pan you're spraying over the sink so you don't make the floor or counter slippery. And spray only cold pans because the coating can burn or smoke if applied to hot surfaces.

Bring to boiling; reduce heat. Simmer, covered, for 6 to 8 minutes or until chops are slightly pink in the center and juices run clear. Makes 4 servings.

111

saucy lamb with vegetables

To save yourself some preparation time for this hearty dish, look for boneless lamb or ask the butcher to bone and cut it.

INGREDIENTS

1 pound lean boneless lamb, cut into 1-inch pieces
2 teaspoons olive oil or cooking oil
1 cup chopped onion
1 cup dry red wine
½ cup reduced-sodium chicken broth
½ cup water
2 cloves garlic, minced
1 teaspoon dried basil, crushed
½ teaspoon dried rosemary, crushed
½ teaspoon dried oregano, crushed
⅛ teaspoon pepper

1 medium eggplant, peeled, if desired, and cut into 1-inch cubes
1½ cups julienned carrots
1½ cups chopped tomatoes
3 cups hot cooked rice
2 tablespoons snipped fresh parsley

Whether you're making an emergency substitution or experimenting with a new flavor, you can vary the herbs to suit your taste. Try thyme, marjoram, or savory. Or save measuring steps by substituting Italian seasoning.

Prep time: 20 minutes
Cooking time: 1½ hours

DIRECTIONS

1. In a large Dutch oven or kettle cook meat, half at a time, in hot oil until browned. Drain off fat. Return all meat to Dutch oven. Add onion, wine, broth, water, garlic, basil, rosemary, oregano, and pepper. Bring to boiling; reduce heat. Simmer, covered, for 1 hour.

2. Stir in the eggplant, carrots, and tomatoes. Return to boiling; reduce heat. Simmer, covered, about 30 minutes more or until the meat and vegetables are tender. Serve over hot cooked rice. Sprinkle with parsley. Makes 6 servings.

NUTRITION FACTS PER SERVING:

314 calories
11 g total fat
4 g saturated fat
42 mg cholesterol
134 mg sodium
32 g carbohydrate
3 g fiber
14 g protein

greek-style salad

Preparation is easy—make the dressing and arrange the salad ingredients on serving plates while the meat broils.

INGREDIENTS

- 12 ounces boneless lamb leg center slice or beef top round steak, cut 1 inch thick
- 1 teaspoon finely shredded lemon peel
- ¼ cup lemon juice
- 1 tablespoon snipped fresh oregano or 1 teaspoon dried oregano, crushed
- 1 tablespoon olive oil or salad oil
- 1 tablespoon water
- 1 clove garlic, minced
- ¼ teaspoon salt
- ¼ teaspoon pepper
- 6 cups torn fresh spinach and/or romaine leaves
- 1 medium cucumber, thinly sliced
- ¼ cup chopped red onion
- 4 pitted ripe olives, halved
- 2 tablespoons crumbled feta cheese
- 2 small pita bread rounds, cut into wedges and toasted

Start to finish: 18 minutes

DIRECTIONS

1. Trim fat from meat. Place meat on the unheated rack of a broiler pan. Broil 3 to 4 inches from heat 12 to 15 minutes or until desired doneness, turning meat once.

2. Meanwhile, for the dressing, in a screw-top jar combine the lemon peel, lemon juice, oregano, oil, water, garlic, salt, and pepper. Cover jar and shake well. Set aside.

3. Divide spinach and/or romaine leaves among 4 plates. Cut the broiled meat across the grain into thin, bite-size strips. Arrange warm sliced meat, cucumber, red onion, olives, and feta cheese on top of greens. Drizzle dressing over salads. Serve with toasted pita bread wedges. Makes 4 servings.

NUTRITION FACTS PER SERVING:

269 calories
11 g total fat
4 g saturated fat
50 mg cholesterol
504 mg sodium
25 g carbohydrate
3 g fiber
21 g protein

Rosemary Chicken
Recipe, page 120

poultry

chicken with mushroom sauce

For a colorful sauce, use half of a green and half of a red sweet pepper. Then accent the dish with a colorful sprinkling of fresh edible flowers.

INGREDIENTS

- 4 small skinless, boneless chicken breast halves (about 12 ounces total)
  Nonstick spray coating
- 1 teaspoon olive oil
- 2 cups sliced fresh mushrooms
- 1 medium red or green sweet pepper, cut into ¾-inch squares
- 1 clove garlic, minced
- ½ cup reduced-sodium chicken broth
  Salt and pepper
- ½ cup fat-free dairy sour cream
- 1 tablespoon all-purpose flour
- ⅛ teaspoon black pepper
- 1 tablespoon dry sherry (optional)
- 2 cups hot cooked white or brown rice
  Snipped fresh parsley
  Fresh chives (optional)
  Edible flowers (optional)

Choose unsprayed edible flowers, such as nasturtiums, pansies, dianthus, or daylilies, from your own garden or supermarket produce section. Avoid blossoms from florist shops—they're usually treated with chemicals.

Start to finish: 30 minutes

DIRECTIONS

1. Rinse chicken; pat dry with paper towels. Spray an unheated large nonstick skillet with nonstick coating. Preheat skillet over medium heat. Cook chicken for 3 to 5 minutes or until browned, turning once. Remove chicken from skillet.

2. Add oil to hot skillet. Cook the mushrooms, sweet pepper, and garlic in hot oil until tender. Remove vegetables; keep warm. Carefully stir broth into skillet. Return chicken to skillet. Sprinkle lightly with salt and black pepper. Bring to boiling; reduce heat. Simmer, covered, for 5 to 7 minutes or until chicken is tender and no longer pink. Transfer chicken to a platter; keep warm.

3. For sauce, in a bowl stir or whisk together sour cream, flour, and the ⅛ teaspoon black pepper until smooth. If desired, stir in sherry. Stir into mixture in skillet. Cook and stir until bubbly. Cook and stir 1 minute more. Serve chicken, vegetables, and sauce over hot cooked rice tossed with parsley. If desired, garnish with chives and flowers. Makes 4 servings

NUTRITION FACTS PER SERVING:

259 calories
4 g total fat
1 g saturated fat
45 mg cholesterol
176 mg sodium
32 g carbohydrate
1 g fiber
22 g protein

INGREDIENTS

4 medium skinless, boneless
   chicken breast halves
   (about 1 pound total)
2 tablespoons lime juice
4 teaspoons teriyaki sauce
   or soy sauce
1 medium peach, peeled, pitted,
   and chopped, or ½ of a
   medium papaya, peeled,
   seeded, and chopped
   (about 1 cup)
1 small tomato, chopped
2 tablespoons sliced green onion
1 tablespoon lime juice

1 teaspoon grated ginger or
   ¼ teaspoon ground ginger
¼ teaspoon bottled minced garlic
   or ⅛ teaspoon garlic powder
   Hot cooked rice (optional)
   Fresh thyme (optional)

chicken with peach salsa

If fresh peaches or papayas aren't in season, thaw and chop 1 cup frozen peach slices.

Prep time: 20 minutes
Marinating time: 30 minutes
Broiling time: 12 minutes

DIRECTIONS

1. Rinse chicken and pat dry with paper towels. In a small bowl stir together the 2 tablespoons lime juice and the teriyaki or soy sauce. Brush chicken with lime juice mixture. Cover and marinate at room temperature for 30 minutes or in the refrigerator for up to 2 hours.

2. For salsa, in a medium mixing bowl stir together the peach or papaya, tomato, green onion, the 1 tablespoon lime juice, the ginger, and garlic or garlic powder. Cover and let stand at room temperature for 30 minutes or chill for up to 2 hours.

3. Place chicken on the unheated rack of a broiler pan. Broil 4 to 5 inches from the heat for 12 to 15 minutes or until tender and no longer pink, turning once. Serve chicken with salsa. If desired, serve over hot cooked rice and garnish with thyme. Makes 4 servings.

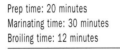

NUTRITION FACTS PER SERVING:

146 calories
3 g total fat
1 g saturated fat
59 mg cholesterol
287 mg sodium
6 g carbohydrate
1 g fiber
22 g protein

117

chicken in phyllo

Look for phyllo in the freezer case in large supermarkets, delis, and specialty food shops.

INGREDIENTS

½ of an 8-ounce package reduced-fat cream cheese (Neufchâtel), softened

¼ cup sliced green onions

1 tablespoon fat-free milk

½ teaspoon dried basil, crushed

½ teaspoon dried rosemary, crushed

4 medium skinless, boneless chicken breast halves (about 1 pound total)

6 sheets frozen phyllo dough, thawed

Nonstick spray coating

2 teaspoons margarine, melted

1 tablespoon grated Parmesan cheese

Prep time: 20 minutes
Baking time: 20 minutes

DIRECTIONS

1. For filling, in a blender container or food processor bowl combine cream cheese, green onions, milk, basil, and rosemary. Cover and blend or process until well mixed; set filling aside.

2. Rinse chicken; pat dry with paper towels. Place 1 sheet of the phyllo dough on a flat surface; spray with nonstick coating. Top with a second sheet; spray again. Repeat with a third sheet. Cut stack of phyllo in half crosswise. On each half, place a chicken breast diagonally across 1 corner of the dough.

3. Spoon one-fourth of the filling over chicken. Fold corner nearest chicken over filling; fold in sides and roll up. Repeat with remaining phyllo dough, chicken, and filling. Spray a 13×9×2-inch baking pan with nonstick coating. Place bundles, seam sides down, in pan. Brush bundles with melted margarine; sprinkle with Parmesan cheese.

4. Bake, uncovered, in a 400° oven for 20 to 30 minutes or until chicken is no longer pink and phyllo is a deep golden brown. Makes 4 servings.

NUTRITION FACTS PER SERVING:

309 calories
15 g total fat
6 g saturated fat
83 mg cholesterol
358 mg sodium
16 g carbohydrate
0 g fiber
27 g protein

chicken and pasta primavera

Here's a homespun dish that should appeal to your whole family. You can use spaghetti or any fun-shaped pasta.

INGREDIENTS

- 2 to 2½ pounds meaty chicken pieces (breasts, thighs, and drumsticks)
- 4 cups vegetables, peeled, trimmed, and cut into 1-inch pieces (carrots, celery, zucchini, and/or yellow summer squash)
- 1 medium onion, cut into wedges
- 2 tablespoons Dijon-style mustard
- 1 tablespoon olive oil
- 2 large cloves garlic, minced
- 1 teaspoon dried oregano, crushed
- ½ teaspoon dried thyme, crushed
- ½ teaspoon celery salt
- ¼ teaspoon pepper
- ⅛ teaspoon salt
- 6 ounces packaged dried spaghetti, linguine, or farfalle (bow ties)
- Freshly shredded Parmesan cheese (optional)

Prep time: 20 minutes
Baking time: 1 hour

DIRECTIONS

1. If desired, skin chicken. Rinse chicken; pat dry with paper towels. Set aside.

2. In a 13×9×2-inch baking pan combine vegetables and onion. In a bowl stir together mustard and oil. Drizzle about 2 tablespoons of the oil mixture over vegetables. Sprinkle with garlic, oregano, thyme, celery salt, pepper, and salt. Toss to coat.

3. Arrange the chicken pieces, bone sides down, on top of vegetables. Brush chicken with the remaining mustard mixture.

4. Bake, uncovered, in a 350° oven about 1 hour or until chicken is tender and no longer pink. Just before removing chicken from the oven, cook pasta according to package directions. Drain well. Transfer the chicken to a serving platter; cover and keep warm.

5. In a large serving bowl combine the pasta and the vegetables and juices from pan, tossing to combine. If desired, sprinkle with Parmesan cheese. Serve pasta and vegetable mixture with chicken. Makes 6 servings.

To retain the full flavor of pasta,

just cook it enough to maintain a firm texture. This texture is sometimes described as chewy or al dente.

NUTRITION FACTS PER SERVING:

329 calories
12 g total fat
3 g saturated fat
69 mg cholesterol
410 mg sodium
27 g carbohydrate
2 g fiber
27 g protein

119

rosemary chicken

You may have to fend off the neighbors once they get a whiff of this aromatic grilled chicken. Better yet, invite them to join your family for a backyard picnic. (Recipe also pictured on pages 114–115.)

INGREDIENTS

- 2 to 2½ pounds meaty chicken pieces (breasts, thighs, and drumsticks)
- ½ cup dry white wine
- 2 tablespoons olive oil
- 4 cloves garlic, minced
- 4 teaspoons snipped fresh rosemary
- 1 tablespoon finely shredded lemon peel
- ¼ teaspoon salt
- ¼ teaspoon pepper
- Fresh rosemary (optional)

Prep time: 15 minutes
Marinating time: 6 hours
Grilling time: 35 minutes

DIRECTIONS

1. If desired, skin chicken. Rinse chicken; pat dry with paper towels. Place chicken in a plastic bag set in a shallow dish.

2. For marinade, in a blender container or food processor bowl combine wine, oil, garlic, snipped rosemary, lemon peel, salt, and pepper. Cover and blend or process about 15 seconds or until well combined. Pour over chicken. Close bag. Marinate in the refrigerator for 6 hours or overnight, turning bag occasionally.

3. Drain chicken, reserving marinade. Place the chicken, bone side up, on the rack of an uncovered grill directly over medium coals. Grill for 35 to 45 minutes or until chicken is tender and no longer pink, turning and brushing once with marinade halfway through grilling.

4. Discard any remaining marinade. Transfer chicken to a serving platter. If desired, garnish with additional rosemary. Makes 6 servings.

NUTRITION FACTS PER SERVING:

192 calories
10 g total fat
3 g saturated fat
69 mg cholesterol
93 mg sodium
0 g carbohydrate
0 g fiber
22 g protein

INGREDIENTS

- ¼ cup water
- 3 tablespoons hoisin sauce
- 2 tablespoons peach preserves
- 1 tablespoon sugar
- 2 teaspoons soy sauce
- 4 medium tangerines or
  2 large oranges
- 3 tablespoons snipped
  fresh cilantro
- 4 medium skinless, boneless
  chicken breast halves
  (about 1 pound total)
- 1 tablespoon cooking oil
  Finely shredded tangerine or
  orange peel (optional)

fusion chicken

The watchword of '90s cooking has been "simplify," and that's what we've done with this quick main dish that's perfect for an after-work meal. Brown the chicken, then quickly glaze with an Asian-style sauce. Serve with a South American-inspired relish that has just two ingredients.

Start to finish: 30 minutes

DIRECTIONS

1. In a bowl combine the water, hoisin sauce, preserves, sugar, and soy sauce. Finely shred 1 teaspoon peel from one of the tangerines or oranges; add to hoisin mixture. Set aside. Peel and coarsely chop tangerines or oranges; remove seeds. In a bowl gently toss chopped tangerines or oranges and cilantro; set aside.

2. Rinse chicken; pat dry with paper towels. In a large skillet cook chicken in hot oil over medium heat for 3 to 5 minutes or until chicken is browned, turning once. Drain off fat. Carefully pour hoisin mixture over chicken. Bring to boiling; reduce heat. Simmer, covered, for 5 to 7 minutes or until chicken is tender and no longer pink.

3. Remove chicken from skillet. Boil sauce gently, uncovered, about 5 minutes or until reduced to ⅓ cup. Return chicken to skillet. Heat through, turning once to coat with glaze.

4. Transfer chicken to serving plates or a serving platter; spoon glaze over chicken. If desired, sprinkle with additional shredded tangerine or orange peel. Serve the tangerine mixture alongside the chicken. Makes 4 servings.

NUTRITION FACTS PER SERVING:

270 calories
8 g total fat
2 g saturated fat
59 mg cholesterol
446 mg sodium
27 g carbohydrate
2 g fiber
23 g protein

121

sautéed chicken with brandied fruit & almonds

Ground red pepper gives a slight hotness to these scaloppine-style chicken breasts. A sweet, aromatic nectarine sauce coats the mixture. Add a tossed spinach salad to create a light summertime meal.

INGREDIENTS

4 medium skinless, boneless chicken breast halves (about 1 pound total)

¼ cup all-purpose flour

¼ teaspoon salt

⅛ teaspoon ground red pepper

1 tablespoon olive oil

1 tablespoon butter or margarine

3 medium nectarines, pitted and cut into thin wedges

3 tablespoons brandy

2 tablespoons water

1 tablespoon lemon juice

2 tablespoons sliced almonds, toasted (see tip, page 108)

Fresh oregano (optional)

When you have fresh peaches, pears, or plums on hand, go ahead and substitute one of these alternates for the nectarines. The results will be just as tasty.

Start to finish: 30 minutes

DIRECTIONS

1. Rinse chicken; pat dry with paper towels. Place each chicken piece between 2 pieces of plastic wrap. Pound lightly with the flat side of a meat mallet to ¼-inch thickness. Remove plastic wrap. Combine flour, salt, and red pepper. Coat chicken pieces with flour mixture, shaking off excess.

2. In a large skillet heat olive oil and butter or margarine over medium heat. Add chicken and cook for 6 to 8 minutes or until chicken is tender and no longer pink, turning once. Remove skillet from heat. Transfer chicken to a serving platter; cover and keep warm.

3. Add the nectarines, brandy, water, and lemon juice to the skillet; return to heat. Cook for 1 minute, stirring gently. Serve fruit mixture over chicken. Sprinkle with the almonds. If desired, garnish with oregano. Makes 4 servings.

NUTRITION FACTS PER SERVING:

303 calories
12 g total fat
3 g saturated fat
67 mg cholesterol
217 mg sodium
19 g carbohydrate
2 g fiber
24 g protein

lime-sauced chicken

For the lime peel garnish, use a vegetable peeler to remove the peel from a lime. Scrape off as much of the white membrane from the peel as you can. Then with a sharp knife, cut the peel into very thin strips.

INGREDIENTS

4 small skinless, boneless chicken
    breast halves (about
    12 ounces total)
    Nonstick spray coating
½ of a medium lime
¾ cup apple juice or apple cider
2 teaspoons cornstarch
½ teaspoon instant chicken
    bouillon granules
2 cups hot cooked rice
    Lime slices (optional)

Start to finish: 20 minutes

DIRECTIONS

1. Rinse chicken; pat dry with paper towels. Spray an unheated large skillet with nonstick coating. Preheat over medium heat. Add chicken. Cook for 8 to 10 minutes or until tender and no longer pink, turning to brown evenly. Remove from skillet; keep warm.

2. If desired, remove strips of peel from lime, using a vegetable peeler. Cut peel into very thin strips; set aside. Squeeze 1 tablespoon juice from lime.

3. For sauce, in a small mixing bowl combine the 1 tablespoon lime juice, the apple juice or cider, cornstarch, and bouillon granules; carefully add to skillet. Cook and stir until thickened and bubbly. Cook and stir for 2 minutes more.

4. To serve, cut each chicken breast half diagonally into 1-inch-thick pieces; arrange on top of rice. Spoon some of the sauce over each serving. If desired, garnish with lime strips and lime slices. Pass the remaining sauce. Makes 4 servings.

NUTRITION FACTS PER SERVING:

223 calories
3 g total fat
1 g saturated fat
45 mg cholesterol
152 mg sodium
29 g carbohydrate
0 g fiber
18 g protein

123

tomato-stuffed chicken rolls

Serve these tomato- and cheese-stuffed rolls with pasta and steamed asparagus spears for a healthful yet tasty meal.

INGREDIENTS

- 4 small skinless, boneless chicken breast halves (about 12 ounces total)
- 1 medium tomato, seeded and chopped (about ½ cup)
- 2 tablespoons grated Parmesan cheese
- ¼ teaspoon dried Italian seasoning, oregano, or basil, crushed
- ⅛ teaspoon pepper
  Nonstick spray coating
- 1 beaten egg white
- 1 tablespoon water
- ⅓ cup cornflake crumbs
- ½ teaspoon dried Italian seasoning, oregano, or basil, crushed
  Reduced-sodium spaghetti sauce, warmed (optional)
  Hot cooked fettuccine or other pasta (optional)

Use the flat side

of a meat mallet when pounding chicken breasts. The ridged sides are for tenderizing tougher cuts of meat and would tear the delicate chicken. For best results, pound from the center and work out toward the edges.

Prep time: 20 minutes
Baking time: 20 minutes

DIRECTIONS

1. Rinse chicken; pat dry with paper towels. Place each chicken piece between 2 pieces of plastic wrap. Pound lightly with the flat side of a meat mallet into a rectangle about ⅛ inch thick. Remove plastic wrap.

2. Top chicken with the tomato, Parmesan cheese, the ¼ teaspoon herb, and the pepper. Fold in long sides of chicken; roll into a spiral. Secure with toothpicks.

3. Spray a 2-quart square baking dish with nonstick coating. Set aside. In a shallow dish combine the egg white and water. In another shallow dish combine the cornflake crumbs and the ½ teaspoon herb. Dip each roll into the egg mixture, then roll in crumb mixture to coat. Place rolls in prepared dish.

4. Bake in a 400° oven for 20 to 25 minutes or until chicken is tender and no longer pink. Remove toothpicks. If desired, slice rolls; serve with spaghetti sauce over pasta. Makes 4 servings.

NUTRITION FACTS PER SERVING:

131 calories
4 g total fat
1 g saturated fat
47 mg cholesterol
162 mg sodium
5 g carbohydrate
1 g fiber
19 g protein

chicken and barley bake

Replace your high-fat chicken noodle casserole with this updated one-dish meal. It's low in calories and fat, and it's economical, too. Barley supplies more fiber than noodles or rice.

INGREDIENTS

- 4 **chicken thighs, skinned (about 1½ pounds total)**
- **Nonstick spray coating**
- 1 **cup chopped onion**
- ¾ **cup chopped carrot**
- ¾ **cup water**
- ½ **cup pearl barley**
- 1 **teaspoon instant chicken bouillon granules**
- 1 **clove garlic, minced**
- ½ **teaspoon poultry seasoning**
- 2 **tablespoons snipped fresh parsley**

Prep time: 20 minutes
Baking time: 1 hour
Standing time: 10 minutes

DIRECTIONS

1. Rinse chicken; pat dry with paper towels. Spray an unheated large skillet with nonstick coating. Preheat over medium heat. Add chicken and cook for 10 minutes, turning to brown evenly. Remove from skillet.

2. In same skillet combine the onion, carrot, water, barley, bouillon granules, garlic, and poultry seasoning. Bring to boiling.

3. Pour hot barley mixture into a 1½-quart casserole. Arrange the chicken thighs on top of mixture.

4. Bake, covered, in a 350° oven about 1 hour or until barley and chicken are tender and chicken is no longer pink. Let stand, covered, for 10 minutes before serving. Sprinkle with parsley. Makes 4 servings.

NUTRITION FACTS PER SERVING:

219 calories
7 g total fat
2 g saturated fat
49 mg cholesterol
284 mg sodium
23 g carbohydrate
5 g fiber
17 g protein

Pearl barley is the most readily available form of the cereal grain barley. It has the outer hull removed and has been polished or "pearled." Pearl barley is sold in regular and quick-cooking forms; be sure to use the regular barley for this recipe.

herb roasted chicken

The best way to cut back on fat and calories with poultry is to remove the skin. However, leaving the skin on during roasting helps keep the meat moist. Simply remove the skin when carving or leave it on your plate.

INGREDIENTS

¼ cup snipped fresh herbs (such as basil, rosemary, marjoram, or sage) or 4 teaspoons dried mixed herbs, crushed

¼ teaspoon salt

¼ teaspoon pepper

1 3-pound whole broiler-fryer chicken

2 cups ½-inch-long carrot pieces

1 cup pearl onions, peeled

2 teaspoons olive oil

1 10-ounce package frozen peas, thawed

Fresh rosemary (optional)

Prep time: 20 minutes
Roasting time: 1¼ hours

DIRECTIONS

1. For herb rub, combine the herbs, salt, and pepper. Rinse chicken; pat dry with paper towels. Loosen skin on chicken breast. Using your fingers, carefully spread half of the herb rub under the skin. Skewer neck skin to back; tie legs to tail. Twist wings under back.

2. Place chicken, breast side up, on a rack in a shallow roasting pan. If desired, insert a meat thermometer into center of an inside thigh muscle. Roast, uncovered, in a 375° oven for 30 minutes.

3. In a 1½-quart casserole combine carrots and onions.

Toss with the remaining herb rub and the olive oil. Cover; place in oven. Roast about 45 minutes more or until chicken is no longer pink, juices run clear (the meat thermometer, if using, should register 180° to 185°), and vegetables are tender, adding peas to the casserole the last 15 minutes of roasting. If desired, garnish with fresh rosemary. Makes 6 servings.

NUTRITION FACTS PER SERVING:

293 calories
14 g total fat
4 g saturated fat
79 mg cholesterol
230 mg sodium
13 g carbohydrate
4 g fiber
27 g protein

INGREDIENTS

4 small skinless, boneless chicken
  breast halves (about
  12 ounces total)
Nonstick spray coating
½ cup white grape juice, apple
  juice, or apple cider
1 teaspoon instant chicken
  bouillon granules
1 teaspoon cornstarch
1 cup seedless green and/or red
  grapes, halved
Hot cooked linguine (optional)
Fresh herb, such as oregano or
  thyme (optional)

chicken with grapes

For a delicious dinner entrée, begin with fruit juice plus a few simple ingredients. Red and green grapes add a light sweetness and a pretty color too.

Start to finish: 20 minutes

DIRECTIONS

1. Rinse chicken; pat dry with paper towels. Spray an unheated large skillet with nonstick coating. Preheat over medium to medium-high heat. Add chicken. Cook chicken for 8 to 10 minutes or until tender and no longer pink, turning to brown evenly. Remove chicken from skillet; keep warm.

2. Combine the grape or apple juice or cider, bouillon granules, and cornstarch. Add to the skillet. Cook and stir until thickened and bubbly. Cook and stir for 2 minutes more. Stir in the grapes; heat through. Serve sauce over chicken. If desired, serve chicken with hot linguine and garnish with fresh herb. Makes 4 servings.

NUTRITION FACTS PER SERVING:

143 calories
3 g total fat
1 g saturated fat
45 mg cholesterol
258 mg sodium
13 g carbohydrate
0 g fiber
17 g protein

chicken with golden raisins and pine nuts

Pine nuts, also called pignoli, are frequently used in Italian pasta sauces, pesto, rice dishes, and cookies.

INGREDIENTS

- 1½ pounds meaty chicken pieces (breasts, thighs, and drumsticks), skinned
- 1 medium onion, cut into thin slivers
- 2 cloves garlic, minced
- 1 tablespoon olive oil
- ½ cup white wine vinegar
- ¼ teaspoon salt
- ⅛ teaspoon pepper
- 1 cup reduced-sodium chicken broth
- ½ cup golden raisins
- 2 teaspoons snipped fresh thyme or ½ teaspoon dried thyme, crushed
- 1 teaspoon snipped fresh rosemary or ¼ teaspoon dried rosemary, crushed
- 1 tablespoon cold water
- 1½ teaspoons cornstarch
- 2 tablespoons pine nuts, toasted (see tip, page 108)
- Fresh rosemary (optional)

To prevent pine nuts from turning rancid quickly at room temperature, refrigerate the nuts in an airtight container for up to 2 months or freeze them for up to 6 months.

Prep time: 20 minutes
Cooking time: 45 minutes

DIRECTIONS

1. Rinse chicken; pat dry with paper towels. In a large nonstick skillet cook onion and garlic in hot oil over medium heat for 1 minute. Add chicken pieces to skillet and cook for 10 to 15 minutes or until lightly browned, turning to brown evenly. Drain well.

2. Add the vinegar, salt, and pepper to skillet. Bring to boiling. Cook, uncovered, over high heat about 5 minutes or until vinegar is nearly evaporated, turning chicken once. Carefully add broth, raisins, thyme, and rosemary to the skillet. Bring to boiling; reduce heat. Simmer, covered, for 30 to 35 minutes or until chicken is tender and no longer pink.

3. To serve, transfer the chicken to a serving platter. Combine cold water and cornstarch. Add to skillet. Cook and stir until thickened and bubbly. Cook and stir for 2 minutes more. Spoon some of the sauce over chicken; pass remainder. Sprinkle chicken with pine nuts. If desired, garnish with additional fresh rosemary. Makes 4 servings.

NUTRITION FACTS PER SERVING:

269 calories
10 g total fat
2 g saturated fat
71 mg cholesterol
334 mg sodium
22 g carbohydrate
1 g fiber
24 g protein

INGREDIENTS

- 1½ to 2 pounds meaty chicken pieces (breasts, thighs, and drumsticks), skinned
- Nonstick spray coating
- 1 14½-ounce can tomatoes, undrained and cut up
- ¼ cup dry red wine
- 1 tablespoon snipped fresh basil or 1 teaspoon dried basil, crushed
- 1 teaspoon sugar
- 1 clove garlic, minced
- 1 bay leaf
- 1 tablespoon cold water
- 2 teaspoons cornstarch

- Hot cooked spaghetti (optional)
- ¼ cup sliced pimiento-stuffed green olives or pitted ripe olives

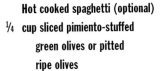
mediterranean-style chicken

Olives added to the robust sauce impart a characteristic briny or salty flavor. You can use either full-flavored pimiento-stuffed green olives or the smooth, mellow tasting black variety.

Start to finish: 1 hour

DIRECTIONS

1. Rinse chicken; pat dry with paper towels.

2. Spray an unheated large skillet with nonstick coating. Preheat skillet over medium heat. Add chicken; cook for 10 to 15 minutes or until lightly browned, turning to brown evenly.

3. Add undrained tomatoes, wine, basil, sugar, garlic, and bay leaf. Bring to boiling; reduce heat. Simmer, covered, for 30 to 35 minutes or until chicken is tender and no longer pink. Remove chicken from skillet. Cover; keep warm. Discard bay leaf.

4. In a small bowl stir together the cold water and cornstarch. Stir into tomato mixture in skillet. Cook and stir until thickened and bubbly. Cook and stir for 2 minutes more.

5. If desired, serve chicken and tomato mixture over hot spaghetti. Sprinkle with olives. Makes 4 servings.

To cut up canned tomatoes quickly, pour the tomatoes into a bowl (or leave them in the can, if desired). Using kitchen scissors, snip the canned tomatoes, cutting them into pieces.

NUTRITION FACTS PER SERVING:

194 calories
7 g total fat
2 g saturated fat
69 mg cholesterol
401 mg sodium
8 g carbohydrate
1 g fiber
23 g protein

129

chutney chicken and squash bake

Chutney is a versatile condiment that you can add to baked main dishes, stir into a sauce or salad dressing, or mix with light sour cream for a fresh-fruit dip.

INGREDIENTS

Nonstick spray coating

2 pounds meaty chicken pieces, skinned (breasts, thighs, and drumsticks)

2 small acorn squash, quartered

2 teaspoons cooking oil

¼ teaspoon salt-free seasoning blend

⅛ teaspoon pepper

¼ cup chutney, snipped

1 tablespoon snipped fresh chives or 1 teaspoon dried chives (optional)

Hot cooked pasta (optional)

Prep time: 15 minutes
Baking time: 40 minutes

DIRECTIONS

1. Spray a 3-quart rectangular baking dish with nonstick coating. Rinse chicken; pat dry with paper towels. Arrange chicken and squash, cut sides up, in dish. Brush chicken pieces with oil; sprinkle with seasoning blend and pepper. Spoon chutney over chicken and, if desired, sprinkle with chives.

2. Bake, uncovered, in a 400° oven for 40 to 45 minutes or until chicken and squash are tender and chicken is no longer pink, basting occasionally with pan drippings. Transfer chicken and squash to a serving platter. Cover; keep warm.

3. Skim fat from the pan drippings; spoon juices over chicken and squash. If desired, serve over hot cooked pasta tossed with a few vegetables. Makes 4 servings.

NUTRITION FACTS PER SERVING:

269 calories
7 g total fat
2 g saturated fat
80 mg cholesterol
82 mg sodium
25 g carbohydrate
4 g fiber
27 g protein

INGREDIENTS

- 4 small skinless, boneless chicken breast halves (about 12 ounces total)
- Nonstick spray coating
- 1 tablespoon honey
- 1 tablespoon orange juice
- ¼ teaspoon ground ginger
- ¼ teaspoon black pepper
- Dash ground red pepper (optional)
- ¾ cup cornflakes, crushed (about ⅓ cup)
- ½ teaspoon dried parsley flakes

honey-ginger crusted chicken

Honey, orange juice, and ginger give "fried" chicken an updated flavor. Best of all, the chicken has the crisp, crunchy texture of fried chicken without all the calories and fat.

Prep time: 10 minutes
Baking time: 18 minutes

DIRECTIONS

1. Rinse chicken; pat dry with paper towels. Spray a shallow baking pan with nonstick coating. Place chicken in baking pan.

2. In a small bowl combine the honey, orange juice, ginger, black pepper, and, if desired, red pepper. Brush honey mixture over chicken.

3. Combine the cornflakes and parsley flakes. Sprinkle mixture over chicken to coat.

4. Bake, uncovered, in a 350° oven for 18 to 20 minutes or until chicken is tender and no longer pink. Makes 4 servings.

NUTRITION FACTS PER SERVING:

127 calories
3 g total fat
1 g saturated fat
45 mg cholesterol
94 mg sodium
8 g carbohydrate
0 g fiber
17 g protein

mango chicken

To complement this Caribbean-style dish, cook your rice with a bit of fresh ginger and chopped mint.

INGREDIENTS

½ cup reduced-sodium chicken broth

2 teaspoons finely shredded lime peel or orange peel

2 tablespoons lime juice

2 teaspoons brown sugar

2 teaspoons curry powder

1 teaspoon cornstarch

12 ounces skinless, boneless chicken breast halves or thighs

2 teaspoons peanut oil or cooking oil

2 cloves garlic, minced

1 cup sliced red onion

2 cups chopped, peeled mango or papaya

2 cups hot cooked rice
   Lime peel strips (optional)

Start to finish: 30 minutes

DIRECTIONS

1. For sauce, in a small bowl stir together the broth, shredded lime or orange peel, lime juice, brown sugar, curry powder, and cornstarch; set aside. Rinse chicken; pat dry with paper towels. Cut chicken into bite-size strips; set aside.

2. In a large wok or 12-inch skillet heat oil over medium-high heat. Add garlic; stir-fry for 30 seconds. Add onion slices; stir-fry for 3 minutes. Remove onion mixture from wok. Add chicken; stir-fry for 2 to 3 minutes or until chicken is no longer pink. Push chicken from center of wok.

3. Stir sauce; add to center of wok. Cook and stir until thickened and bubbly. Return onion mixture to the wok. Add mango or papaya. Cook and stir about 2 minutes or until heated through. Serve immediately over rice. If desired, garnish with lime peel strips. Makes 4 servings.

NUTRITION FACTS PER SERVING:

301 calories
5 g total fat
1 g saturated fat
45 mg cholesterol
125 mg sodium
44 g carbohydrate
3 g fiber
20 g protein

INGREDIENTS

- 12 ounces skinless, boneless chicken breast halves
- 3 tablespoons reduced-sodium soy sauce
- 1 tablespoon dry sherry
- ¼ cup reduced-sodium chicken broth
- 1 teaspoon cornstarch
- ¼ teaspoon black pepper
  Nonstick spray coating
- 1 medium onion, cut into wedges
- 1 medium green sweet pepper, thinly sliced
- 1 medium red sweet pepper, thinly sliced
- 1½ cups sliced fresh mushrooms
- 2 teaspoons cooking oil
- 1 teaspoon grated fresh ginger
- ½ of an 8-ounce can bamboo shoots, drained (about ½ cup)
- 2 cups hot cooked brown rice

chicken and sweet pepper stir-fry

Dress up this simple stir-fry by using a variety of exotic mushrooms. Many kinds are available in larger grocery stores. Try chanterelle, shiitake (use only the caps), or straw mushrooms.

Prep time: 20 minutes
Marinating time: 30 minutes
Cooking time: 12 minutes

DIRECTIONS

1. Rinse chicken; pat dry with paper towels. Cut into ½-inch pieces. Place chicken in a bowl; stir in soy sauce and sherry. Cover and marinate at room temperature for 30 minutes. Drain chicken, reserving marinade. Stir broth, cornstarch, and black pepper into reserved marinade. Set aside.

2. Spray an unheated nonstick wok or large skillet with nonstick coating. Preheat over medium-high heat. Add onion; stir-fry for 2 minutes. Add sweet peppers; stir-fry for 2 minutes. Add mushrooms; stir-fry about 2 minutes more or until vegetables are crisp-tender. Remove.

3. Add the oil to hot wok. Add ginger; stir-fry for 15 seconds. Add the chicken; stir-fry for 2 to 3 minutes or until no longer pink. Push from center of wok. Stir sauce; add to center of wok. Cook and stir until slightly thickened and bubbly. Return the cooked vegetables. Add the bamboo shoots. Cook and stir for 2 minutes more. Serve immediately with rice. Makes 4 servings.

Don't overload your wok or skillet.

When too much of any item is added at once, the food stews rather than fries. Add no more than 12 ounces of poultry or meat. If your recipe calls for more, stir-fry half at a time.

NUTRITION FACTS PER SERVING:

258 calories
5 g total fat
1 g saturated fat
45 mg cholesterol
480 mg sodium
30 g carbohydrate
1 g fiber
21 g protein

thai chicken-curry stir-fry

You can make this dish as spicy as desired by adding more or less jalapeño or serrano pepper.

INGREDIENTS

⅔ cup fat-free milk

2 tablespoons snipped fresh cilantro

1 tablespoon soy sauce

2 teaspoons cornstarch

1 teaspoon curry powder

½ teaspoon coconut flavoring (optional)

¼ teaspoon crushed red pepper

⅛ teaspoon salt

12 ounces skinless, boneless chicken breast halves
Nonstick spray coating

1 large green sweet pepper, cut into 1-inch pieces

1 large red sweet pepper, cut into 1-inch pieces

1 fresh jalapeño or serrano chili pepper, seeded and finely chopped (see tip, page 21)

1 cup sliced fresh shiitake mushrooms (stems removed)

3 green onions, cut into 1-inch pieces

2 teaspoons peanut oil or cooking oil

3 cups hot cooked Chinese egg noodles or rice
Fresh cilantro (optional)

To keep stir-fries low in fat,

start with lean cuts of poultry or meat and allow 12 ounces for four servings. Tossed with vegetables and served over rice, this will make a satisfying serving for even the heartiest of eaters.

Start to finish: 30 minutes

DIRECTIONS

1. For sauce, in a small bowl stir together the milk, snipped cilantro, soy sauce, cornstarch, curry powder, coconut flavoring (if desired), crushed red pepper, and salt. Set aside.

2. Rinse chicken; pat dry with paper towels. Cut the chicken into bite-size strips; set aside.

3. Spray an unheated wok or large nonstick skillet with nonstick coating. Preheat over medium heat. Add sweet peppers and jalapeño pepper; stir-fry for 2 minutes. Add mushrooms and green onions; stir-fry about 2 minutes more or until vegetables are crisp-tender. Remove from wok.

4. Add the oil to hot wok. Add chicken; stir-fry for 2 to 3 minutes or until chicken is no longer pink. Push the chicken from center of wok. Stir sauce; add to center of wok. Cook and stir until thickened and bubbly.

5. Return vegetables to wok. Cook and stir about 1 minute more or until heated through. Serve immediately with noodles or rice. If desired, garnish with cilantro. Makes 4 servings.

NUTRITION FACTS PER SERVING:

430 calories
7 g total fat
1 g saturated fat
83 mg cholesterol
394 mg sodium
66 g carbohydrate
5 g fiber
24 g protein

INGREDIENTS

½	cup finely chopped plum tomatoes
½	cup finely chopped, peeled mango
¼	cup finely chopped red onion
¼	cup lime juice
3	tablespoons snipped fresh cilantro
2 to 3	teaspoons finely chopped, seeded jalapeño pepper (see tip, page 21)

12	ounces skinless, boneless chicken breast halves
½	cup water
¼	teaspoon salt
⅛ to ¼	teaspoon ground red pepper
8	6-inch corn tortillas
1½	cups shredded romaine or leaf lettuce
¼	cup light dairy sour cream
	Fresh cilantro (optional)

chicken burritos

Say "Con mucho gusto!" to these mango salsa-topped chicken burritos. And, if the heat index starts to climb too high, just dab them with a little palate-soothing light sour cream.

Start to finish: 1 hour

DIRECTIONS

1. For salsa, in a bowl combine tomatoes, mango, red onion, 2 tablespoons of the lime juice, cilantro, and jalapeño pepper. Cover and chill for 30 minutes.

2. Rinse chicken; pat dry with paper towels. In a large heavy skillet place the chicken and the water. Bring to boiling; reduce heat. Simmer, covered, for 12 to 14 minutes or until chicken is very tender. Drain well; let cool until easy to handle.

3. Using 2 forks, shred the chicken. Toss shredded chicken with the remaining lime juice, salt, and ground red pepper.

4. Wrap the tortillas in foil. Heat in a 350° oven for 10 minutes.

5. To serve, spoon the shredded chicken down the centers of warm tortillas. Top each with some of the salsa, the romaine or leaf lettuce, and sour cream. Roll up. Serve with the remaining salsa. If desired, garnish with additional cilantro. Makes 8 burritos.

NUTRITION FACTS PER BURRITO:

129 calories
2 g total fat
1 g saturated fat
23 mg cholesterol
138 mg sodium
17 g carbohydrate
1 g fiber
10 g protein

135

chicken with peppers and potatoes

This dish is packed with the flavor of fresh herbs and roasted sweet peppers. If you like, substitute Greek kalamata olives packed in vinegar, not oil, for the ripe olives.

INGREDIENTS

12 ounces skinless, boneless chicken breast halves
Nonstick spray coating
2 cups diced potatoes
1 7-ounce jar roasted red sweet peppers, drained and diced
½ cup reduced-sodium chicken broth
4½ teaspoons snipped fresh basil or 1½ teaspoons dried basil, crushed
4½ teaspoons snipped fresh oregano or 1½ teaspoons dried oregano, crushed
⅛ teaspoon salt
⅛ teaspoon black pepper
2 tablespoons sliced pitted ripe olives
Fresh oregano (optional)

Start to finish: 30 minutes

DIRECTIONS

1. Rinse chicken; pat dry with paper towels. Cut into 1-inch pieces. Spray an unheated large skillet with nonstick coating. Preheat over medium-high heat. Add chicken. Cook and stir for 4 to 5 minutes or until tender and no longer pink. Remove from skillet. Set aside.

2. Add uncooked potatoes, sweet peppers, chicken broth, basil, oregano, salt, and black pepper to the skillet. Bring to boiling; reduce heat. Simmer, covered, about 7 minutes or until potatoes are just tender.

3. Stir in the chicken and olives. Heat through. If desired, garnish with additional fresh oregano. Makes 4 servings.

NUTRITION FACTS PER SERVING:

183 calories
4 g total fat
1 g saturated fat
45 mg cholesterol
213 mg sodium
20 g carbohydrate
2 g fiber
19 g protein

skillet chicken paella

INGREDIENTS

- 1¼ pounds skinless, boneless chicken breast halves
- 1 tablespoon olive oil or cooking oil
- 1 medium onion, chopped
- 2 cloves garlic, minced
- 2¼ cups reduced-sodium chicken broth
- 1 cup long grain rice
- 1 teaspoon dried oregano, crushed
- ½ teaspoon paprika
- ¼ teaspoon salt
- ¼ teaspoon black pepper
- ⅛ teaspoon ground saffron or ground turmeric

- 1 14½-ounce can reduced-sodium stewed tomatoes, undrained
- 1 medium red sweet pepper, cut into strips
- ¾ cup frozen peas

Paella, a Spanish rice dish, usually contains shellfish and meat. This company-special chicken version is easier to prepare and takes less time to cook.

Start to finish: 40 minutes

DIRECTIONS

1. Rinse chicken; pat dry with paper towels. Cut chicken into bite-size strips.

2. In a 10-inch skillet cook chicken strips, half at a time, in hot oil for 2 to 3 minutes or until no longer pink. Remove from skillet. Set aside.

3. Add onion and garlic to skillet; cook until onion is tender. Add broth, uncooked rice, oregano, paprika, salt, black pepper, and saffron or turmeric. Bring to boiling; reduce heat. Simmer, covered, for 15 minutes.

4. Add the undrained tomatoes, sweet pepper, and frozen peas to skillet. Simmer, covered, about 5 minutes or until rice is tender. Stir in the cooked chicken. Cook and stir about 1 minute more or until heated through. Makes 6 servings.

NUTRITION FACTS PER SERVING:

285 calories
6 g total fat
1 g saturated fat
50 mg cholesterol
415 mg sodium
35 g carbohydrate
3 g fiber
23 g protein

chicken tacos

If you don't have any leftover chicken to use, buy frozen chopped cooked chicken at your supermarket.

INGREDIENTS

Nonstick spray coating
1 cup chopped onion
1 clove garlic, minced
2 cups chopped cooked chicken
1 8-ounce can tomato sauce
1 4-ounce can diced green chili peppers, drained
12 taco shells
2 cups shredded lettuce
1 medium tomato, seeded and chopped
½ cup finely shredded reduced-fat cheddar cheese and/or Monterey Jack cheese (2 ounces)

Start to finish: 30 minutes

DIRECTIONS

1. Spray an unheated large skillet with nonstick coating. Preheat over medium heat. Add the onion and garlic; cook until onion is tender.

2. Stir in the chicken, tomato sauce, and chili peppers. Heat through.

3. Divide chicken mixture among taco shells. Top with lettuce, tomato, and cheese. Makes 6 servings.

NUTRITION FACTS PER SERVING:

276 calories
12 g total fat
3 g saturated fat
52 mg cholesterol
502 mg sodium
23 g carbohydrate
2 g fiber
21 g protein

INGREDIENTS

12	ounces skinless, boneless chicken breast halves
2	beaten egg whites
1	tablespoon honey
2	cups cornflakes, crushed
¼	teaspoon pepper
¼	cup honey
4	teaspoons prepared mustard or Dijon-style mustard
¼	teaspoon garlic powder

chicken fingers with honey sauce

Serve your favorite barbecue sauce as a quick alternative to the honey sauce.

Prep time: 15 minutes
Baking time: 11 minutes

DIRECTIONS

1. Rinse chicken; pat dry with paper towels. Cut into strips about 3 inches long and ¾ inch wide.

2. In a small mixing bowl combine the egg whites and the 1 tablespoon honey. In a shallow bowl combine the cornflake crumbs and pepper. Dip chicken strips into the egg white mixture, then roll in the crumb mixture to coat.

3. Place in a single layer on an ungreased baking sheet.

Bake chicken in a 450° oven for 11 to 13 minutes or until no longer pink.

4. Meanwhile, for sauce, in a small bowl stir together the ¼ cup honey, the mustard, and garlic powder. Serve with chicken. Makes 4 servings.

NUTRITION FACTS PER SERVING:

230 calories
2 g total fat
1 g saturated fat
45 mg cholesterol
275 mg sodium
31 g carbohydrate
1 g fiber
19 g protein

139

stroganoff-style chicken

Chicken replaces the usual beef in this rich-tasting dish. Named after a 19th-century Russian diplomat, traditional stroganoff contains butter and sour cream. Here, low-fat sour cream helps pare down the fat and calories.

INGREDIENTS

- 12 ounces skinless, boneless chicken breast halves
- Nonstick spray coating
- 2 cups sliced fresh mushrooms
- ½ cup chopped onion
- 2 teaspoons cooking oil (optional)
- 1 8-ounce carton light dairy sour cream
- 2 tablespoons all-purpose flour
- 1 teaspoon paprika
- ¼ teaspoon salt
- ½ cup reduced-sodium chicken broth
- 3¾ cups hot cooked noodles

Start to finish: 25 minutes

DIRECTIONS

1. Rinse chicken; pat dry with paper towels. Cut into 1-inch pieces. Spray an unheated large skillet with nonstick coating. Preheat over medium heat. Add the mushrooms and onion; cook until onion is nearly tender.

2. If needed, add the oil to skillet. Add the chicken pieces and cook for 3 to 4 minutes or until chicken is tender and no longer pink.

3. In a small bowl stir together the sour cream, flour, paprika, and salt; stir in chicken broth. Add to skillet. Cook and stir until slightly thickened and bubbly. Cook and stir for 1 minute more. Serve over hot cooked noodles. Makes 5 servings.

NUTRITION FACTS PER SERVING:

308 calories
7 g total fat
2 g saturated fat
79 mg cholesterol
257 mg sodium
39 g carbohydrate
3 g fiber
23 g protein

INGREDIENTS

1 pound fresh tomatillos, husked and chopped, or one 18-ounce can tomatillos, rinsed, drained, and cut up

1½ cups chopped onion

¼ cup firmly packed fresh cilantro leaves or fresh parsley sprigs

1 4-ounce can diced green chili peppers, drained

¼ teaspoon ground cumin

¼ teaspoon pepper

1 cup chopped tomato

3 cups shredded cooked chicken or turkey (1 pound)

Nonstick spray coating

⅔ cup low-sodium tomato juice

12 6-inch corn tortillas

⅔ cup shredded reduced-fat Monterey Jack cheese

green-and-red chicken enchiladas

Although tomatillos are not related to tomatoes, their texture is like that of a firm tomato (with lots of seeds) and their flavor is rather acidic with hints of lemon and apple. Look for firm tomatillos with tight-fitting, dry husks.

Prep time: 25 minutes
Baking time: 35 minutes

DIRECTIONS

1. In a blender container or food processor bowl combine the tomatillos, 1 cup of the onion, the cilantro or parsley, chili peppers, cumin, and pepper. Cover and blend or process until pureed. Set the mixture aside.

2. In a nonstick skillet cook tomato and remaining onion for 3 minutes. Stir in chicken and 1 cup of the tomatillo mixture; heat through. Spray a 3-quart rectangular baking dish with nonstick coating. Set aside.

3. To assemble enchiladas, pour the tomato juice into a shallow dish. Dip a tortilla in tomato juice, coating both sides. Place tortilla on a work surface. Spoon about 3 tablespoons of the chicken mixture down center of tortilla; roll up. Place, seam side down, in prepared baking dish. Repeat with remaining juice, tortillas, and chicken mixture. Spoon the remaining tomatillo mixture over the enchiladas.

4. Bake, covered, in a 350° oven about 30 minutes or until heated through. Sprinkle with cheese; bake about 5 minutes more or until the cheese melts. Makes 6 servings.

NUTRITION FACTS PER SERVING:

375 calories
13 g total fat
4 g saturated fat
67 mg cholesterol
313 mg sodium
35 g carbohydrate
2 g fiber
30 g protein

fruit & chicken kabobs

Bring the fresh style and bold flavors of the Caribbean to your backyard grill with these easy fruit-and-chicken kabobs, steeped in a sweet-and-fiery marinade.

INGREDIENTS

1 pound skinless, boneless chicken breast halves

3 tablespoons reduced-sodium soy sauce

4 teaspoons honey

4 teaspoons red wine vinegar

½ teaspoon curry powder

½ teaspoon ground allspice

¼ teaspoon bottled hot pepper sauce

1 medium red onion, cut into 1-inch wedges

1 nectarine, pitted and cut into 1-inch pieces, or 1 papaya, peeled, seeded, and cut into 1-inch pieces

2 cups hot cooked rice
 Snipped fresh parsley

Prep time: 30 minutes
Marinating time: 4 hours
Grilling time: 12 minutes

DIRECTIONS

1. Rinse chicken; pat dry with paper towels. Cut into 1-inch pieces. Place chicken in a plastic bag set in a shallow dish.

2. For marinade, in a small bowl stir together soy sauce, honey, vinegar, curry powder, allspice, and hot pepper sauce. Pour over chicken. Close bag. Marinate in the refrigerator for 4 hours, turning bag occasionally. Drain chicken, reserving the marinade.

3. In a saucepan cook the onion in a small amount of boiling water for 3 minutes; drain. On eight 6-inch metal skewers, alternately thread the chicken, nectarine or papaya pieces, and partially cooked onion.

4. Grill kabobs on the rack of an uncovered grill directly over medium coals for 12 to 14 minutes or until chicken is tender and no longer pink, turning skewers occasionally. Place marinade in a small saucepan. Bring to boiling. Boil gently, uncovered, for 1 minute. Pour marinade through a strainer, reserving the liquid.

5. Before serving, brush kabobs with the strained marinade. Serve kabobs with hot cooked rice tossed with parsley. Pass any remaining marinade. Makes 4 servings.

NUTRITION FACTS PER SERVING:

374 calories
4 g total fat
1 g saturated fat
59 mg cholesterol
462 mg sodium
54 g carbohydrate
9 g fiber
30 g protein

INGREDIENTS

- 12 ounces skinless, boneless chicken breast halves
- ¼ cup orange juice
- 2 tablespoons reduced-sodium soy sauce
- 2 teaspoons rice vinegar
- 1 teaspoon ground ginger
- 1 teaspoon toasted sesame oil
- ⅛ teaspoon crushed red pepper
- 2 teaspoons cornstarch
- 6 8-inch flour tortillas
- Nonstick spray coating
- 2 small carrots, cut into bite-size strips
- 1 cup sliced fresh mushrooms
- ½ cup thinly sliced green onions
- ½ cup sliced bamboo shoots
- 1 to 2 teaspoons cooking oil
- 2 cups shredded leaf lettuce
- ¼ cup sweet-and-sour duck sauce

moo shu chicken

Flour tortillas make an easy substitute for the pancake wrappers traditionally used in this Chinese-style burrito. If you like, use hoisin sauce in place of the duck sauce.

Prep time: 15 minutes
Marinating time: 1 hour
Cooking time: 7 minutes

DIRECTIONS

1. Rinse chicken; pat dry with paper towels. Cut into bite-size strips. Place chicken in a plastic bag set in a deep bowl. For marinade, in a small bowl combine orange juice, soy sauce, vinegar, ginger, sesame oil, and red pepper. Pour over chicken. Close bag. Marinate in refrigerator for 1 to 2 hours, turning bag frequently. Drain chicken, reserving marinade. Stir the cornstarch into reserved marinade. Set aside.

2. Wrap tortillas in foil. Heat in a 350° oven for 10 minutes. Meanwhile, spray an unheated large nonstick skillet with nonstick coating. Preheat over medium-high heat. Add carrots, mushrooms, green onions, and bamboo shoots; stir-fry for 2 minutes. Remove from skillet. Add oil to hot skillet. Add chicken; stir-fry for 2 to 3 minutes or until no longer pink. Push the chicken from center of skillet. Stir sauce; add to center of skillet. Cook and stir until bubbly. Return vegetables to skillet. Add lettuce. Stir ingredients to coat; heat through.

3. To serve, spread tortillas with duck sauce. Divide chicken mixture among tortillas; fold tortillas over filling. Makes 6 servings.

NUTRITION FACTS PER SERVING:

- 208 calories
- 6 g total fat
- 1 g saturated fat
- 30 mg cholesterol
- 371 mg sodium
- 25 g carbohydrate
- 2 g fiber
- 14 g protein

chicken burgers with pesto sauce

Ground chicken coupled with easy low-fat pesto sauce produces a perfectly seasoned burger.

INGREDIENTS

- 1 beaten egg white
- ½ cup shredded carrot
- ½ cup sliced green onions
- 2 tablespoons cornstarch
- 2 tablespoons fat-free mayonnaise dressing or salad dressing
- 1 tablespoon Dijon-style mustard
- ¼ teaspoon pepper
- 1 pound ground raw chicken or turkey
  Nonstick spray coating
- ⅓ cup reduced-sodium chicken broth
- 3 tablespoons reduced-calorie margarine

- 2 tablespoons snipped fresh parsley
- 2 tablespoons snipped fresh basil or 2 teaspoons dried basil, crushed
- 2 tablespoons grated Parmesan cheese
- 1 clove garlic, minced
- 5 whole wheat hamburger buns, split and toasted
  Lettuce leaves (optional)

Prep time: 20 minutes
Cooking time: 15 minutes

DIRECTIONS

1. In a medium mixing bowl combine egg white, carrot, green onions, cornstarch, mayonnaise or salad dressing, mustard, and pepper. Add ground chicken or turkey; mix well. On waxed paper, shape mixture into five ½-inch-thick patties.

2. Spray an unheated large nonstick skillet with nonstick coating. Cook chicken patties over medium heat until brown on both sides. Add chicken broth. Bring to boiling; reduce heat. Simmer, covered, for 15 to 20 minutes or until patties are no longer pink in the center.

3. For pesto sauce, in a small mixing bowl stir together the margarine, parsley, basil, Parmesan cheese, and garlic until well mixed and creamy. If desired, line bottoms of hamburger buns with lettuce leaves. Top with chicken patties. Spoon pesto sauce over burgers; add bun tops. Makes 5 servings.

NUTRITION FACTS PER SERVING:

277 calories
8 g total fat
2 g saturated fat
50 mg cholesterol
604 mg sodium
27 g carbohydrate
3 g fiber
24 g protein

INGREDIENTS

- 2 teaspoons cooking oil
- 1 teaspoon toasted sesame oil
- 3 cloves garlic, minced
- 2 tablespoons grated fresh ginger
- ⅓ cup white wine vinegar
- 2 tablespoons reduced-sodium soy sauce
- 3 tablespoons water
- 4 small skinless, boneless chicken breast halves (about 12 ounces total)
- 2 tablespoons water
- 1 fresh jalapeño pepper, seeded and chopped (see tip, page 21)

- ½ teaspoon sugar
- 1 medium carrot, cut into strips
- 1 cup thin strips peeled jicama
- 4 lettuce leaves
- 2 medium cucumbers, quartered lengthwise and sliced
- 1⅓ cups fresh enoki mushrooms
- 2 green onions, sliced
- 2 tablespoons chopped unsalted cocktail peanuts

szechwan chicken salad

Jicama, a crisp root vegetable, stars in this grilled chicken salad with carrot, cucumbers, and enoki mushrooms (to julienne the vegetables, see tip, page 78). A light sprinkling of peanuts adds crunch and flavor.

Prep time: 25 minutes
Marinating time: 4 hours
Grilling time: 12 minutes

DIRECTIONS

1. In a small saucepan heat cooking oil and sesame oil over medium-high heat for 1 minute. Cook and stir garlic and ginger in hot oil for 15 seconds. Remove from heat. Stir in the vinegar, soy sauce, and water. Cool completely.

2. Rinse chicken; pat dry with paper towels. Place chicken in a plastic bag set in a shallow dish. Pour half of the vinegar mixture over the chicken; reserve remaining vinegar mixture. Close bag. Marinate in the refrigerator for 4 to 24 hours, turning the bag occasionally.

3. Meanwhile, for dressing, in a bowl stir together reserved vinegar mixture, 2 tablespoons water, the jalapeño pepper, and sugar. Cover; chill for 4 to 24 hours.

4. Combine the carrot and jicama; set aside. Drain chicken, discarding marinade. Grill chicken on the lightly greased rack of an uncovered grill directly over medium coals for 12 to 15 minutes or until chicken is tender and no longer pink, turning once. Cut chicken into bite-size strips.

5. To serve, line 4 plates with lettuce. Top with carrot mixture, cucumbers, chicken, mushrooms, green onions, and peanuts. Stir dressing; drizzle over salads. Makes 4 servings.

NUTRITION FACTS PER SERVING:

200 calories
7 g total fat
1 g saturated fat
45 mg cholesterol
231 mg sodium
15 g carbohydrate
3 g fiber
20 g protein

fruit & chicken salad

Frozen juice concentrate is an ideal ingredient for making low-fat dressings. Because concentrate delivers a lot of punch in a small amount, you don't need to use much. Here, concentrate also lends body to the dressing.

½ cup fat-free dairy sour cream
½ cup fat-free mayonnaise dressing or salad dressing
1 tablespoon frozen orange juice concentrate, thawed
⅛ teaspoon ground ginger
Dash ground red pepper
3 green onions, sliced
2 cups thinly sliced celery
1½ cups seedless red or green grapes, halved
1½ cups chopped cooked chicken
½ cup dried apricots, cut into slivers

4 lettuce leaves
2 plum tomatoes, thinly sliced
1 cucumber, thinly sliced

Cut dried apricots easily

by using kitchen scissors or a sharp knife that has been sprayed with nonstick spray coating. This keeps the fruit from sticking.

Prep time: 25 minutes
Chilling time: 2 hours

DIRECTIONS

1. For dressing, stir together the sour cream, mayonnaise dressing or salad dressing, orange juice concentrate, ginger, and red pepper. Stir in green onions.

2. In a large bowl toss together the celery, grapes, chicken, and apricots. Stir in the dressing. Cover and chill for 2 to 4 hours.

3. To serve, line 4 plates with lettuce leaves. Arrange the tomatoes and cucumber on top of lettuce. Top with the chicken mixture. Makes 4 servings.

NUTRITION FACTS PER SERVING:

264 calories
3 g total fat
1 g saturated fat
44 mg cholesterol
511 mg sodium
40 g carbohydrate
5 g fiber
21 g protein

broiled pineapple chicken salad

Fresh pineapple stars in this salad. Pineapple or orange juice sweetens the tangy yogurt and curry dressing.

INGREDIENTS

4   medium skinless, boneless chicken breast halves or turkey breast tenderloin steaks (about 1 pound total)
    Nonstick spray coating
¼   of a medium pineapple, cored and cut into wedges
6   cups shredded lettuce
1   cup peeled jicama cut into bite-size pieces
1   cup coarsely shredded carrots
1   6-ounce carton tropical- or pineapple-flavored fat-free yogurt

2   tablespoons pineapple or orange juice
½   teaspoon curry powder
    Dash pepper

Prep time: 20 minutes
Broiling time: 12 minutes

DIRECTIONS

1. Rinse chicken or turkey; pat dry with paper towels. Spray the unheated rack of a broiler pan with nonstick coating. Arrange the chicken on rack. Broil 4 to 5 inches from the heat for 6 minutes. Turn the chicken. Add pineapple wedges to broiler pan. Broil 6 to 9 minutes more or until the chicken is tender and no longer pink, turning pineapple once during broiling.

2. Line 4 plates with lettuce. Cut the chicken into bite-size strips. Arrange the chicken and pineapple on each plate. Sprinkle with the jicama and carrots.

3. For dressing, stir together yogurt, pineapple or orange juice, curry powder, and pepper. Drizzle over salads. Makes 4 servings.

NUTRITION FACTS PER SERVING:

221 calories
4 g total fat
1 g saturated fat
61 mg cholesterol
95 mg sodium
21 g carbohydrate
2 g fiber
25 g protein

three-citrus chicken salad

Using a strong-flavored oil, such as olive oil, in the dressing allows you to boost the flavor without using very much. Also try orange or lemon juice instead of lime and add a fresh herb, such as basil, for variety.

INGREDIENTS

9	cups torn mixed salad greens (such as romaine, Boston or bibb lettuce, arugula, curly leaf lettuce, or red leaf lettuce)
2	cups cooked chicken cut into strips
1½	cups grapefruit sections (about 2 grapefruit)
1½	cups orange sections (about 3 oranges)
1	cup thinly sliced red onion
2	tablespoons olive oil or salad oil
2	tablespoons lime juice
2	tablespoons water
1	teaspoon Dijon-style mustard
⅛	teaspoon salt
⅛	teaspoon pepper

Section citrus fruits by cutting off the peel and white membrane. Next, remove the sections by cutting into the center of the fruit between one section and the membrane. Then turn the knife and slide it down the other side of the section next to the membrane. Remove any seeds.

Prep time: 35 minutes

DIRECTIONS

1. Divide the greens among 6 plates. Arrange the chicken, grapefruit sections, orange sections, and red onion slices on top of greens.

2. For the dressing, in a screw-top jar combine the oil, lime juice, water, mustard, salt, and pepper. Cover and shake well. Drizzle the dressing over salads. Makes 6 servings.

NUTRITION FACTS PER SERVING:

203 calories
9 g total fat
2 g saturated fat
45 mg cholesterol
116 mg sodium
16 g carbohydrate
3 g fiber
17 g protein

INGREDIENTS

- 1 **pound whole tiny new potatoes, quartered**
- 12 **ounces skinless, boneless chicken breast halves**
- 1 **tablespoon olive oil or cooking oil**
- 1 **cup sliced celery**
- 1 **cup chopped green sweet pepper**
- ½ **cup fat-free Italian salad dressing**
- 2 **tablespoons snipped fresh dill**
- 1 **tablespoon Dijon-style mustard**
- 2 **large tomatoes, halved lengthwise and sliced**
- 1 **medium cucumber, thinly sliced**
  Fresh dill (optional)

dilled chicken and potato salad

No time to cook the chicken? Use chopped roasted chicken from the deli instead.

Start to finish: 30 minutes

DIRECTIONS

1. In a covered saucepan cook potatoes in boiling lightly salted water for 6 to 8 minutes or until tender; drain.

2. Meanwhile, rinse chicken; pat dry with paper towels. Cut into bite-size strips. In a large skillet cook the chicken in hot oil over medium-high heat for 2 to 3 minutes or until tender and no longer pink. Remove from skillet.

3. In a large bowl combine the potatoes, chicken, celery, and sweet pepper. Toss gently. In a small bowl stir together the salad dressing, snipped dill, and mustard. Drizzle over chicken mixture, tossing gently to coat.

4. Arrange sliced tomatoes and cucumber on 4 plates. Spoon the chicken mixture over tomatoes and cucumber. If desired, garnish with additional fresh dill. Makes 4 servings.

NUTRITION FACTS PER SERVING:

283 calories
7 g total fat
1 g saturated fat
45 mg cholesterol
597 mg sodium
36 g carbohydrate
4 g fiber
20 g protein

asparagus-stuffed turkey rolls

If you're preparing this dish for guests, you can roll the turkey bundles ahead, cover, and refrigerate.

INGREDIENTS

4 turkey breast tenderloin steaks (about 1 pound total)

16 asparagus spears
   Nonstick spray coating

⅔ cup reduced-sodium chicken broth

2 tablespoons lemon juice

2 tablespoons orange juice

¼ teaspoon salt-free seasoning blend

⅛ teaspoon pepper

1 tablespoon water

2 teaspoons cornstarch

Slivered orange or lemon peel (optional)

Hot cooked pasta or rice (optional)

Prep time: 25 minutes
Cooking time: 6 minutes

DIRECTIONS

1. Rinse turkey; pat dry with paper towels. Place each turkey steak between 2 pieces of plastic wrap. Pound lightly with the flat side of a meat mallet to ¼-inch thickness. Remove plastic wrap. Trim asparagus spears, breaking off woody ends. Arrange 4 asparagus spears across the short end of each turkey piece. Roll up turkey; secure with wooden toothpicks, if necessary.

2. Spray an unheated large nonstick skillet with nonstick coating. Cook turkey rolls over medium heat until browned on all sides. Add chicken broth, lemon juice, orange juice, seasoning blend, and pepper. Bring to boiling; reduce heat. Simmer, covered, for 6 to 8 minutes or until turkey is tender and no longer pink.

3. Transfer the turkey to a serving platter; discard toothpicks. Keep warm. In a small bowl stir together the water and cornstarch; add to liquid in skillet. Cook and stir until thickened and bubbly. Cook and stir for 2 minutes more. Spoon over turkey. If desired, sprinkle with slivered orange or lemon peel and serve with hot cooked pasta or rice. Makes 4 servings.

NUTRITION FACTS PER SERVING:

137 calories
3 g total fat
1 g saturated fat
50 mg cholesterol
154 mg sodium
4 g carbohydrate
1 g fiber
23 g protein

INGREDIENTS

- 1 2- to 3-pound fresh or frozen turkey breast portion
- 2 teaspoons ground coriander
- ½ teaspoon onion powder
- ¼ teaspoon chili powder
  Dash ground red pepper
- 1 tablespoon margarine or butter
- 1 tablespoon lemon juice
- 1 recipe Tomatillo Guacamole
  Tomato wedges (optional)
  Lime peel strips (optional)

turkey with tomatillo guacamole

A tomatillo, often called the Mexican green tomato, resembles a small tomato with a parchment-like skin. It's available canned and fresh. In this guacamole, tomatillo replaces part of the avocado—which is high in fat.

Prep time: 20 minutes
Grilling time: 1¼ hours

DIRECTIONS

1. Thaw turkey, if frozen. Rinse turkey; pat dry with paper towels. Remove skin and excess fat from turkey. In a small saucepan cook the coriander, onion powder, chili powder, and red pepper in margarine or butter for 1 minute. Remove from heat; stir in lemon juice. Spread spice mixture on all sides of turkey. Insert a meat thermometer into the thickest portion of the breast, not touching bone (if present).

2. In a covered grill arrange medium-hot coals around a drip pan. Test for medium heat above drip pan. Place turkey on the grill rack over drip pan, but not over coals. Lower the grill hood. Grill for 1¼ to 1¾ hours or until thermometer registers 170°. Add more coals as needed. Serve turkey with Tomatillo Guacamole. If desired, garnish with tomatoes and lime strips. Makes 8 servings.

Tomatillo Guacamole: In a small mixing bowl stir together ½ of a small avocado, seeded, peeled, and chopped (about ½ cup); 2 canned tomatillos, rinsed, drained, and finely chopped (¼ cup); 1 plum tomato, chopped; 1 tablespoon canned diced green chili peppers; 2 teaspoons lemon juice; and ⅛ teaspoon garlic salt.

To test your grill for medium heat, hold your hand, palm side down, in the same location you plan to place the food. Count each second, "one thousand one, one thousand two," etc. for as long as you can hold your hand there. Four seconds means the heat is medium.

NUTRITION FACTS PER SERVING:

156 calories
6 g total fat
1 g saturated fat
50 mg cholesterol
157 mg sodium
3 g carbohydrate
0 g fiber
22 g protein

151

spinach-stuffed turkey breast

A turkey breast allows you to enjoy the flavor of roast turkey without days of leftovers. This elegant recipe features a spinach and cheese stuffing.

INGREDIENTS

- 1 2½- to 3½-pound fresh or frozen turkey breast half with bone
- 1 10-ounce package frozen chopped spinach, thawed
- ½ of an 8-ounce package reduced-fat cream cheese (Neufchâtel), softened
- 3 tablespoons grated Parmesan cheese
- 2 tablespoons water
- 1 teaspoon dried basil, crushed
- ¼ teaspoon ground nutmeg
- ¼ teaspoon pepper

To carve the turkey, start at the outside of the breast half. Slice downward, keeping the slices thin. Continue slicing slightly higher up on the breast.

Prep time: 15 minutes
Roasting time: 2½ hours

DIRECTIONS

1. Thaw turkey, if frozen. Rinse turkey; pat dry with paper towels. Drain spinach thoroughly and squeeze out excess liquid. Place spinach in food processor bowl with cream cheese, Parmesan cheese, water, basil, nutmeg, and pepper. Cover and process until well combined.

2. With a small sharp knife, loosen the breast skin from turkey and pull skin back, leaving skin attached along 1 side. Spread the spinach mixture over exposed portion of meat; pull skin back over filling. Secure skin with wooden toothpicks along sides of breast. Place turkey, skin side up, on a rack in a shallow roasting pan. Insert a meat thermometer into center of breast, below stuffing and not touching bone. Cover turkey loosely with foil.

3. Roast in a 325° oven for 2½ to 3 hours or until the thermometer registers 170°. Remove foil for the last 30 minutes of roasting. Makes 8 servings.

NUTRITION FACTS PER SERVING:

170 calories
6 g total fat
3 g saturated fat
62 mg cholesterol
176 mg sodium
3 g carbohydrate
1 g fiber
25 g protein

INGREDIENTS

- 1 2½- to 3-pound fresh or frozen turkey breast half with bone
- 1½ cups cranberries
- ½ cup coarsely shredded carrot
- ½ teaspoon finely shredded orange peel
- ½ cup orange juice
- 2 tablespoons raisins
- 2 tablespoons sugar
- Dash ground cloves
- 1 tablespoon cold water
- 2 teaspoons cornstarch
- Fresh parsley (optional)

turkey with cranberry sauce

Want to enjoy this classic combination any day of the week? Use turkey tenderloin steaks instead of the turkey breast half. Broil steaks 4 to 5 inches from the heat for 8 to 10 minutes, turning once.

Prep time: 10 minutes
Roasting time: 2½ hours

DIRECTIONS

1. Thaw turkey, if frozen. Rinse turkey; pat dry with paper towels. Remove skin and excess fat from turkey. Place turkey, bone side down, on a rack in a shallow roasting pan. Insert a meat thermometer into the thickest portion of the breast, not touching bone. Cover turkey loosely with foil.

2. Roast in a 325° oven for 2½ to 3 hours or until the thermometer registers 170°. Remove foil for the last 30 minutes of roasting.

3. Meanwhile, for sauce, in a small saucepan combine the cranberries, carrot, orange peel, orange juice, raisins, sugar, and cloves. Bring to boiling; reduce heat. Simmer, uncovered, for 3 to 4 minutes or until cranberry skins pop.

4. In a small bowl combine cold water and cornstarch. Stir into cranberry mixture in saucepan. Cook and stir until thickened and bubbly. Cook and stir for 2 minutes more.

5. Serve turkey with cranberry sauce. If desired, garnish with parsley. Makes 8 servings.

NUTRITION FACTS PER SERVING:

154 calories
2 g total fat
1 g saturated fat
50 mg cholesterol
49 mg sodium
11 g carbohydrate
1 g fiber
22 g protein

153

turkey with mixed dried fruit

A mixture of dried fruits, such as apricots, pears, and apples, lends a slightly sweet flavor to this dish. The dried fruit also makes this dish easy—the fruit is already cut up for you.

INGREDIENTS

12 ounces turkey breast tenderloin steaks
  Nonstick spray coating
1 cup apple juice or apple cider
1 cup mixed dried fruit bits
½ cup chopped onion
1½ teaspoons snipped fresh thyme or ½ teaspoon dried thyme, crushed
2 cloves garlic, minced
½ cup apple juice or apple cider

1 tablespoon cornstarch
  Hot cooked orzo or rice (optional)
  Apple slices (optional)
  Fresh thyme (optional)

Start to finish: 25 minutes

DIRECTIONS

1. Rinse turkey; pat dry with paper towels. Spray an unheated large skillet with nonstick coating. Preheat over medium-high heat. Add turkey; cook for 8 to 10 minutes or until tender and no longer pink, turning once. Remove from skillet.

2. For sauce, in the same skillet combine the 1 cup apple juice or cider, the dried fruit bits, onion, thyme, and garlic. Bring to boiling; reduce heat. Simmer, covered, for 2 to 4 minutes or just until fruit bits are tender.

3. Stir together the ½ cup apple juice or cider and the cornstarch. Add to mixture in skillet. Cook and stir until thickened and bubbly. Cook and stir for 2 minutes more. Return turkey to skillet; heat through. If desired, serve turkey and sauce with orzo or rice and garnish with apple slices and additional fresh thyme. Makes 4 servings.

NUTRITION FACTS PER SERVING:

234 calories
2 g total fat
1 g saturated fat
37 mg cholesterol
60 mg sodium
39 g carbohydrate
0 g fiber
18 g protein

INGREDIENTS

4 turkey breast tenderloin steaks
    (about 1 pound total)
   Nonstick spray coating
2 cloves garlic, minced
½ cup reduced-sodium
    chicken broth
¼ cup dry Marsala or dry sherry
1 tablespoon lemon juice
½ teaspoon salt-free
    seasoning blend
⅛ teaspoon pepper

2 tablespoons snipped
    fresh parsley
   Steamed thinly sliced carrots
    and zucchini (optional)

turkey marsala

For an alternative idea, try this dish with thinly sliced pork tenderloin or pounded boneless chicken breasts.

Start to finish: 20 minutes

DIRECTIONS

1. Rinse turkey; pat dry with paper towels. Spray an unheated large skillet with nonstick coating. Preheat over medium-high heat. Add turkey steaks and garlic; cook for 8 to 10 minutes or until turkey is tender and no longer pink, turning once. Transfer to a serving platter; cover and keep warm.

2. For sauce, in the same skillet stir together chicken broth, Marsala or sherry, lemon juice, seasoning blend, and pepper. Bring to boiling. Boil gently, uncovered, about 4 minutes or until reduced to ¼ cup liquid. Stir in parsley. Spoon sauce over turkey. If desired, serve over steamed carrots and zucchini. Makes 4 servings.

NUTRITION FACTS PER SERVING:

139 calories
3 g total fat
1 g saturated fat
50 mg cholesterol
56 mg sodium
2 g carbohydrate
0 g fiber
22 g protein

To accompany the turkey with thin ribbons of carrots and zucchini, use a vegetable peeler to make lengthwise slices down the vegetables. Steam the slices briefly just until crisp-tender.

155

turkey piccata with artichokes

Serve this dish with a cooked wild rice blend and a salad of sliced oranges, ripe olives, and mushrooms.

INGREDIENTS

Nonstick spray coating
1 pound turkey breast tenderloin steaks
¼ cup fat-free milk
1½ cups soft whole wheat bread crumbs
1 teaspoon dried Italian seasoning, crushed
1 9-ounce package frozen artichoke hearts, thawed
1¼ cups reduced-sodium chicken broth
2 shallots, sliced, or 2 tablespoons finely chopped onion
2 tablespoons lemon juice
1 tablespoon cornstarch
1 tablespoon Dijon-style mustard
½ teaspoon dried Italian seasoning, crushed
⅛ teaspoon pepper
Lemon slice twists (optional)

Shallots, one of the smaller members of the onion family, have a mild, delicate flavor and tender texture. Look for firm, well-shaped shallots that are not sprouting. Peel shallots before chopping or slicing.

Prep time: 20 minutes
Baking time: 12 minutes

DIRECTIONS

1. Spray a 15×10×1-inch baking pan with nonstick coating. Set aside. Rinse turkey; pat dry with paper towels. Cut turkey steaks into 6 serving-size pieces. Pour milk into a shallow bowl. In another shallow bowl stir together the bread crumbs and the 1 teaspoon Italian seasoning. Dip the turkey pieces in milk, then into the bread crumb mixture to coat.

2. Arrange turkey in a single layer in the prepared pan. Bake, uncovered, in a 450° oven about 12 minutes or until turkey is tender and no longer pink and crumb coating is crisp.

3. Meanwhile, for sauce, cut any large artichoke hearts in half. In a medium saucepan combine artichoke hearts, chicken broth, and shallots or onion. Bring to boiling; reduce heat. Simmer, covered, for 5 minutes. In a small bowl combine lemon juice, cornstarch, mustard, the ½ teaspoon Italian seasoning, and the pepper; add to saucepan. Cook and stir until thickened and bubbly. Cook and stir for 2 minutes more. Serve the sauce over turkey. If desired, garnish with lemon slice twists. Makes 6 servings.

NUTRITION FACTS PER SERVING:

142 calories
3 g total fat
1 g saturated fat
33 mg cholesterol
333 mg sodium
12 g carbohydrate
3 g fiber
18 g protein

INGREDIENTS

- 12 ounces turkey breast tenderloin steaks or boneless turkey breast
- ⅓ cup unsweetened pineapple juice
- 3 tablespoons rum or unsweetened pineapple juice
- 1 tablespoon brown sugar
- 1 tablespoon finely chopped lemongrass or 2 teaspoons finely shredded lemon peel
- 1 tablespoon olive oil
- 1 medium red onion, cut into thin wedges
- 2 nectarines or 3 plums, pitted and cut into thick wedges
- 1½ cups fresh or canned pineapple chunks
  Hot cooked rice (optional)
  Finely shredded lemon peel (optional)

Prep time: 15 minutes
Marinating time: 4 hours
Grilling time: 12 minutes

DIRECTIONS

1. Rinse turkey; pat dry with paper towels. Cut into 1-inch cubes. Place turkey in a plastic bag set in a shallow dish. For marinade, in a small bowl combine the ⅓ cup pineapple juice, the rum or 3 tablespoons pineapple juice, brown sugar, lemongrass or the lemon peel, and the oil. Pour over turkey. Close bag. Marinate in the refrigerator for 4 to 24 hours, turning bag occasionally.

2. Drain turkey, reserving marinade. In a small saucepan bring the marinade to boiling. Boil gently, uncovered, for 1 minute. Remove from heat. On four 12-inch skewers alternately thread turkey and onion.

3. Grill kabobs on the rack of an uncovered grill directly over medium coals for 12 to 14 minutes or until turkey is tender and no longer pink, turning once and brushing occasionally with marinade.

4. Meanwhile, on four 12-inch skewers, alternately thread nectarines or plums and pineapple. Place on grill rack next to turkey kabobs for the last 5 minutes of grilling, turning and brushing once with marinade. If desired, serve the turkey and fruit kabobs with hot cooked rice tossed with lemon peel. Makes 4 servings.

pineapple-rum turkey kabobs

Lemongrass—an essential ingredient in Indonesian and Thai cooking—imparts a woodsy, lemony flavor to the marinade for these kabobs. If you can't find fresh lemongrass at your grocery store, look for it at almost any Asian market.

NUTRITION FACTS PER SERVING:

229 calories
6 g total fat
1 g saturated fat
37 mg cholesterol
36 mg sodium
23 g carbohydrate
2 g fiber
17 g protein

157

turkey and apple stir-fry

You can use regular button mushrooms (about 2 cups sliced) instead of dried mushrooms in this dish. The dried wild mushrooms give the dish a more earthy flavor.

INGREDIENTS

- 6 dried wild mushrooms (1 cup), such as shiitake or wood ear mushrooms
- 12 ounces turkey breast tenderloin steaks
- ¾ cup cold water
- 3 tablespoons frozen orange, apple, or pineapple juice concentrate, thawed
- 2 tablespoons soy sauce
- 2 teaspoons cornstarch
- ¼ teaspoon ground ginger
- ¼ teaspoon ground cinnamon
- ⅛ to ¼ teaspoon ground red pepper

- ¼ cup sliced or slivered almonds
- 1 tablespoon cooking oil
- 2 medium green, red, orange, and/or yellow sweet peppers, cut into thin 2-inch strips (2 cups)
- 2 medium apples, cored and thinly sliced (2 cups)
- 2 cups hot cooked brown rice

Soaking time: 30 minutes
Prep time: 15 minutes
Cooking time: 9 minutes

DIRECTIONS

1. In a small bowl cover mushrooms with warm water. Soak for 30 minutes. Rinse and squeeze mushrooms to drain. Discard stems. Thinly slice caps. Set aside.

2. Rinse turkey; pat dry with paper towels. Cut turkey into 1-inch pieces. Set aside.

3. For sauce, in a small bowl stir together cold water, juice concentrate, soy sauce, cornstarch, ginger, cinnamon, and red pepper. Set aside.

4. Preheat a wok or large skillet over medium-high heat. Add almonds; stir-fry for 2 to 3 minutes or until golden. Remove almonds from wok. Let wok cool. Pour oil into wok. (Add more oil as necessary during cooking.) Add drained mushrooms, sweet peppers, and apples; stir-fry for 1 to 2 minutes or until peppers and apples are crisp-tender. Remove from wok.

5. Add turkey to hot wok; stir-fry for 3 to 4 minutes or until no longer pink. Push turkey from center of wok. Stir sauce; add to center of wok. Cook and stir until thickened and bubbly. Return apple mixture to wok. Cook and stir for 1 to 2 minutes more or until heated through. Stir in the almonds. Serve immediately over hot brown rice. Makes 4 servings.

NUTRITION FACTS PER SERVING:

363 calories
10 g total fat
2 g saturated fat
38 mg cholesterol
557 mg sodium
48 g carbohydrate
4 g fiber
22 g protein

turkey meatballs in wine sauce

If you like, make the meatballs up to 24 hours before you plan to serve them. Prepare the recipe through Step 2; cover and refrigerate the meatballs. Just before serving, continue with Step 3.

INGREDIENTS

Nonstick spray coating
1 egg white
1 cup soft bread crumbs
½ cup finely chopped onion
2 tablespoons fat-free milk
¾ teaspoon snipped fresh thyme or
   ¼ teaspoon dried thyme,
   crushed
¼ teaspoon salt
   Dash pepper
1 pound ground raw turkey
2 cups sliced fresh mushrooms
1 cup cold water
2 tablespoons cornstarch

1 teaspoon instant chicken
   bouillon granules
⅓ cup dry white wine
2 tablespoons snipped
   fresh parsley
3¾ cups hot cooked noodles
   Carrot curls (optional)

Prep time: 30 minutes
Baking time: 30 minutes

DIRECTIONS

1. Spray a 13×9×2-inch baking pan with nonstick coating. Set aside. In a medium mixing bowl stir together the egg white, bread crumbs, half of the onion, the milk, thyme, salt, and pepper. Add turkey; mix well. Shape the mixture into 1-inch meatballs. Place meatballs in the prepared pan.

2. Bake, uncovered, in a 350° oven for 30 to 35 minutes or until meatballs are no longer pink. Drain off any juices; cool slightly.

3. Spray an unheated large skillet with nonstick coating. Add mushrooms and remaining onion. Cook until onion is tender. In a bowl stir together cold water, cornstarch, and bouillon granules. Stir cornstarch mixture into mushroom mixture. Cook and stir until thickened and bubbly. Stir in meatballs and wine; heat through. Stir in parsley. Serve over hot noodles. If desired, garnish with carrot curls. Makes 5 servings.

NUTRITION FACTS PER SERVING:

333 calories
9 g total fat
2 g saturated fat
72 mg cholesterol
389 mg sodium
39 g carbohydrate
3 g fiber
20 g protein

southwestern stuffed squash

For a more exciting way to serve chili, spoon it into a squash "bowl." If you can't find butternut squash at the supermarket, use baked potatoes, omitting steps for squash.

INGREDIENTS

3   1½- to 2-pound butternut squash

8   ounces ground raw turkey
    or chicken

2   green onions, sliced

1   to 2 teaspoons chili powder

½   teaspoon dried oregano, crushed

1   15-ounce can black beans
    or pinto beans, rinsed
    and drained

1   8-ounce can tomato sauce

¼   cup sliced pitted ripe olives
    (optional)

1   fresh jalapeño pepper, seeded
    and chopped (see tip,
    page 21)

Light dairy sour cream (optional)

Green onion tops (optional)

Prep time: 20 minutes
Baking time: 55 minutes

DIRECTIONS

1. Cut off the blossom end of each squash. From 1 side of each squash, cut off a shallow lengthwise slice. Finely chop enough of the slices to equal ½ cup; set aside. Remove and discard seeds from cavities of squash.

Hollow out squash, leaving ½-inch-thick shells. Invert squash in a shallow baking pan. Bake, uncovered, in a 350° oven about 40 minutes or until squash are tender.

2. Meanwhile, in a large skillet cook turkey or chicken and chopped squash until meat is brown. Stir in the 2 green onions, the chili powder, and oregano. Cook and stir for 2 minutes more. Stir in beans, tomato sauce, olives (if desired), and jalapeño pepper. Bring to boiling. Spoon bean mixture into hollows of baked squash.

3. Bake, uncovered, in a 350° oven about 15 minutes or until heated through. If desired, serve with sour cream; garnish with green onion tops. Makes 6 servings.

NUTRITION FACTS PER SERVING:

156 calories
3 g total fat
1 g saturated fat
14 mg cholesterol
430 mg sodium
26 g carbohydrate
7 g fiber
11 g protein

INGREDIENTS

- 4 turkey breast tenderloin steaks (about 1 pound total)
- 1 teaspoon olive oil
-    Salt and pepper
- 2 peaches, pitted and cut up
- 2 plums, pitted and sliced
- 2 tablespoons lemon juice
- ½ cup lemon low-fat yogurt
- 2 tablespoons thinly sliced green onion
- ¼ teaspoon poppy seed
-    Mixed salad greens

Start to finish: 30 minutes

DIRECTIONS

1. Rinse turkey; pat dry with paper towels. Rub both sides of turkey with oil. Sprinkle with salt and pepper. Grill turkey on the rack of an uncovered grill directly over medium coals for 12 to 15 minutes or until turkey is tender and no longer pink, turning once. Cut turkey into bite-size strips.

2. In a medium bowl combine the peaches and plums. Add lemon juice; toss gently to coat. For dressing, in a small bowl combine the yogurt, green onion, and poppy seed. If necessary, stir 1 to 2 teaspoons additional lemon juice into dressing to reach drizzling consistency.

3. Divide the greens among 4 plates. (For peach bowls, see tip.) Arrange turkey and fruit on top of salad greens. Drizzle with dressing. Makes 4 servings

turkey-peach salad

Combine fresh fruit and poultry for a pleasing pair with a natural lightness. Here, grilled turkey breast, juicy peaches, and purple plums are artfully served in a hollowed-out peach "bowl" and drizzled with a light-as-air lemon-poppy seed dressing made with yogurt.

To serve salad in peach bowls, cut

2 large peaches in half crosswise; remove pits. Using a spoon, scoop out some pulp to create shallow bowls. Place on top of greens and spoon turkey and fruit into peach halves. Drizzle with dressing.

NUTRITION FACTS PER SERVING:

209 calories
4 g total fat
1 g saturated fat
51 mg cholesterol
96 mg sodium
20 g carbohydrate
2 g fiber
24 g protein

161

curry turkey and fruit salad

This light, bright salad makes a perfect entrée for a luncheon or summer supper. Select low-fat turkey or roast beef from the deli.

INGREDIENTS

2 cups strawberry halves

1 11-ounce can pineapple tidbits and mandarin orange sections, drained (juice pack), or one 11-ounce can mandarin oranges sections, drained (water pack)

¼ cup fat-free mayonnaise dressing or salad dressing

¼ cup fat-free dairy sour cream

2 tablespoons frozen orange juice concentrate

¾ to 1 teaspoon curry powder

4 to 5 tablespoons fat-free milk

6 cups torn mixed salad greens

8 ounces cooked turkey, cubed, or cooked roast beef, thinly sliced and rolled up

Toasted coconut (optional)

Toast coconut by spreading it in a single layer in a shallow baking pan. Bake in a 350° oven for 5 to 10 minutes or until light golden brown. Stir the coconut once or twice during toasting so it doesn't burn.

Prep time: 20 minutes

DIRECTIONS

1. In a medium mixing bowl toss together the strawberries and drained canned fruit. Set aside.

2. For dressing, in a bowl stir together the mayonnaise or salad dressing, sour cream, orange juice concentrate, and curry powder. Stir in enough milk to make a dressing of drizzling consistency.

3. Divide mixed greens among 4 serving plates. Top with fruit mixture and turkey or beef. Drizzle each serving with dressing. If desired, garnish with coconut. Makes 4 servings.

NUTRITION FACTS PER SERVING:

229 calories
5 g total fat
1 g saturated fat
46 mg cholesterol
284 mg sodium
28 g carbohydrate
3 g fiber
20 g protein

herbed turkey and bean salad

You lower the sodium in this recipe by using cooked dried beans instead of canned ones. If you use the canned variety for convenience, be sure to rinse the beans well before adding them to the salad.

INGREDIENTS

- ⅔ cup herb vinegar, such as tarragon, basil, or dill
- 2 tablespoons sugar
- 2 cups cooked red kidney beans, cannellini beans, and/or other white beans*
- 1 cup chopped cooked turkey or chicken
- ½ cup thinly sliced celery
- ½ cup chopped red sweet pepper
- 2 tablespoons snipped fresh parsley

  Kale leaves (optional)

Prep time: 20 minutes
Chilling time: 4 hours

DIRECTIONS

1. In a small saucepan combine vinegar and sugar. Cook and stir over medium heat until sugar dissolves.

2. In a mixing bowl combine beans, turkey or chicken, celery, sweet pepper, and parsley. Add vinegar mixture; toss to coat.

3. Cover and chill for 4 to 24 hours. If desired, serve in kale leaf-lined salad bowls. Makes 4 servings.

Note: To cook dried beans, first soak about ¾ cup of well-rinsed beans in cold water overnight. Drain and rinse. In a large saucepan cook the beans in boiling water for 1 to 1½ hours or until tender, stirring occasionally. (To keep cooked beans on hand, prepare double or triple the amount you need. Place cooked beans in an airtight, freezer-safe container. Freeze for up to 6 months.)

NUTRITION FACTS PER SERVING:

216 calories
3 g total fat
1 g saturated fat
31 mg cholesterol
48 mg sodium
31 g carbohydrate
5 g fiber
19 g protein

Crab and Fennel Risotto
Recipe, page 190

fish & seafood

grilled tuna with rosemary

Firm-fleshed fish, such as tuna, swordfish, halibut, shark, or salmon, grills nicely without falling apart.

INGREDIENTS

- 1 pound fresh or frozen tuna, swordfish, halibut, shark, or salmon steaks, cut 1 inch thick
- 2 teaspoons olive oil
- 2 teaspoons lemon juice
- 1/8 teaspoon salt
- 1/8 teaspoon pepper
- 2 cloves garlic, minced
- 2 teaspoons snipped fresh rosemary or tarragon or 1 teaspoon dried rosemary or tarragon, crushed
- 1 tablespoon capers, drained and slightly crushed
- Fresh rosemary (optional)

Prep time: 15 minutes
Grilling time: 8 minutes

DIRECTIONS

1. Thaw fish, if frozen. Rinse fish; pat dry with paper towels. Cut into 4 serving-size pieces. Brush both sides of fish with oil and lemon juice; sprinkle with salt and pepper. Rub garlic and snipped or dried rosemary or tarragon onto fish.

2. Grill fish on the rack of an uncovered grill directly over medium coals for 8 to 12 minutes or just until fish begins to flake easily with a fork, gently turning halfway through grilling. (Or, broil fish on the unheated rack of a broiler pan 4 inches from the heat for 8 to 12 minutes, gently turning halfway through broiling.)

3. To serve, top the fish with capers. If desired, garnish with additional fresh rosemary. Makes 4 servings.

NUTRITION FACTS PER SERVING:

164 calories
3 g total fat
0 g saturated fat
19 mg cholesterol
484 mg sodium
1 g carbohydrate
0 g fiber
32 g protein

lake trout with corn salsa

Ask your butcher to skin the lake trout before you bring it home. If you opt to cook it with the skin on, then place the fish, skin side down, in the baking dish.

INGREDIENTS

- 1 pound fresh or frozen lake trout or walleye fillets, ½ inch thick
- 1 cup frozen whole kernel corn
- ¼ cup water
- ½ cup small cherry tomatoes, quartered
- ½ cup finely chopped, peeled jicama
- ¼ cup snipped fresh cilantro or parsley
- 2 tablespoons lime juice
- 1 small fresh jalapeño pepper, seeded and finely chopped (see tip, page 21)
- Dash salt
- Nonstick spray coating
- 3 tablespoons fat-free Italian salad dressing
- 1 teaspoon chili powder

Prep time: 20 minutes
Baking time: 8 minutes

DIRECTIONS

1. Thaw fish, if frozen. Rinse fish; pat dry with paper towels. Cut into 4 serving-size pieces. In a small saucepan combine the corn and the water. Bring to boiling; reduce heat. Simmer, covered, for 5 minutes. Drain well.

2. For corn salsa, in a medium serving bowl combine the cooked corn, tomatoes, jicama, cilantro or parsley, lime juice, jalapeño pepper, and salt. Toss to combine. Set aside.

3. Spray a 2-quart rectangular baking dish with nonstick coating. Stir together the Italian salad dressing and chili powder; brush over fish. Place fish in the prepared baking dish. Tuck under any thin edges.

4. Bake fish, uncovered, in a 450° oven for 8 to 12 minutes or just until fish begins to flake easily with a fork. Serve fish with corn salsa. Makes 4 servings.

NUTRITION FACTS PER SERVING:

157 calories
1 g total fat
0 g saturated fat
45 mg cholesterol
196 mg sodium
13 g carbohydrate
1 g fiber
24 g protein

salmon with wilted greens

This fish dinner packs in all the vitamin C and almost half of the vitamin A you need for an entire day—all for under 300 calories.

INGREDIENTS

1 pound fresh or frozen salmon steaks, cut ¾ inch thick

3 tablespoons orange juice concentrate

3 tablespoons water

2 tablespoons reduced-sodium soy sauce

1 tablespoon honey

2 teaspoons cooking oil

1 teaspoon toasted sesame oil

½ teaspoon grated ginger or ¼ teaspoon ground ginger

6 cups torn mixed salad greens, such as spinach, Swiss chard, radicchio, or mustard, beet, or collard greens

1 medium orange, peeled and sectioned

1 small red sweet pepper, cut into thin strips (½ cup)

Prep time: 15 minutes
Broiling time: 6 minutes

DIRECTIONS

1. Thaw fish, if frozen. Rinse fish; pat dry with paper towels. Cut into 4 serving-size pieces. Set aside. For dressing, in a small bowl combine the orange juice concentrate, water, soy sauce, honey, cooking oil, sesame oil, and ginger.

2. Broil fish on the greased unheated rack of a broiler pan 4 inches from the heat for 6 to 9 minutes or just until fish begins to flake easily with a fork, brushing with 1 tablespoon of the dressing halfway through broiling. (Or, grill fish on the greased rack of an uncovered grill directly over medium coals for 6 to 9 minutes, gently turning and brushing with 1 tablespoon of the dressing halfway through grilling.)

Cover and keep fish warm while preparing the greens.

3. In a large salad bowl combine greens and orange sections. In a large skillet bring the remaining dressing to boiling. Boil gently, uncovered, for 1 minute. Add red pepper strips. Remove from heat. Pour over greens mixture, tossing to coat.

4. To serve, divide the greens mixture among 4 serving plates. Top with the fish. Serve immediately.

NUTRITION FACTS PER SERVING:

255 calories
9 g total fat
2 g saturated fat
31 mg cholesterol
406 mg sodium
15 g carbohydrate
2 g fiber
27 g protein

INGREDIENTS

- 1 **pound fresh or frozen orange roughy or other fish fillets, ½ to ¾ inch thick**
- **Nonstick spray coating**
- ¼ **cup cornmeal**
- ½ **teaspoon dried thyme, crushed**
- ¼ **teaspoon lemon-pepper seasoning**
- 1 **egg white**
- 2 **tablespoons water**
- ¼ **cup fine dry bread crumbs**

- 2 **tablespoons toasted wheat germ**
- 1 **tablespoon snipped fresh parsley**
- ½ **teaspoon paprika**
- 1 **8-ounce carton plain fat-free yogurt**
- ¼ **cup lemon fat-free yogurt**
- 1 **teaspoon dried dillweed**
- **Few dashes bottled hot pepper sauce**
- **Lemon wedges (optional)**

crispy orange roughy with dilled yogurt sauce

If you're fond of crispy fried fish, this flavorful alternative will convert you to light eating.

Prep time: 15 minutes
Baking time: 4 minutes

DIRECTIONS

1. Thaw fish, if frozen. Rinse fish; pat dry with paper towels. Cut into 4 serving-size pieces. Spray a shallow baking pan with nonstick coating. Set aside.

2. In a shallow dish combine cornmeal, thyme, and lemon-pepper seasoning. In another shallow bowl beat egg white and water until frothy. In a third shallow bowl combine bread crumbs, wheat germ, parsley, and paprika. Dip fish fillets into cornmeal mixture, shaking off any excess. Dip into egg white mixture, then coat with bread crumb mixture. Place the fish in the prepared baking pan, tucking under any thin edges.

3. Bake in a 450° oven just until fish begins to flake easily with a fork (allow 4 to 6 minutes per ½-inch thickness of fish).

4. Meanwhile, for sauce, in a small bowl stir together plain yogurt, lemon yogurt, dillweed, and hot pepper sauce. Serve sauce with fish. If desired, garnish with lemon. Makes 4 servings.

To thaw fish,

remove it from the freezer the night before you serve it. Place it, unopened, in a container in the refrigerator—it should be thawed by the next evening. If necessary, you can place the wrapped package of fish under cold running water to hasten the process. Never thaw fish at room temperature.

NUTRITION FACTS PER SERVING:

221 calories
3 g total fat
0 g saturated fat
62 mg cholesterol
271 mg sodium
20 g carbohydrate
1 g fiber
29 g protein

169

fennel and fish au gratin

Bulb shaped with feathery, dill-like leaves, fennel emits a mild anise flavor. Try this tasty dish—and become a fennel fan.

INGREDIENTS

- 1 pound fresh or frozen orange roughy, salmon, or other fish fillets, ½ to ¾ inch thick
- 2 fennel bulbs with leaves
- 3 carrots, julienned (1½ cups) (see tip, page 78)
- 1¼ cups fat-free milk
- 3 tablespoons all-purpose flour
- 2 tablespoons dry white wine (optional)
- ⅛ teaspoon salt
- ⅛ teaspoon pepper
- 2 tablespoons grated Parmesan cheese
- 1 tablespoon fine dry bread crumbs
- 2 teaspoons margarine or butter, melted

Prep time: 30 minutes
Baking time: 10 minutes

DIRECTIONS

1. Thaw fish, if frozen. Rinse fish; pat dry with paper towels. Cut into 4 serving-size pieces. Set aside.

2. Remove upper stalks from fennel, including feathery leaves; reserve leaves and discard stalks. Discard any wilted outer layers on fennel bulbs; cut off a thin slice from each base. Wash fennel and pat dry. Quarter each fennel bulb lengthwise and remove core; julienne each quarter lengthwise (see tip, page 78). Chop enough of the reserved fennel leaves to make ¼ cup.

3. In a large covered saucepan cook julienned fennel and the carrots in a small amount of boiling water for 8 to 10 minutes or until tender; drain. Transfer vegetables to a 2-quart square or rectangular baking dish. Rinse saucepan.

4. Meanwhile, in a large skillet cook the fish in a small amount of simmering water just until fish begins to flake easily with a fork (allow 4 to 6 minutes per ½-inch thickness of fish); drain. Arrange fish on top of vegetables in baking dish.

5. For sauce, in the large saucepan combine the milk and flour. Cook and stir over medium heat until thickened and bubbly. Stir in the ¼ cup chopped fennel leaves, the wine (if desired), salt, and pepper. Pour sauce over fish and vegetables. Combine Parmesan cheese, bread crumbs, and margarine or butter; sprinkle over the sauce. Bake, uncovered, in a 350° oven about 10 minutes or until heated through. Makes 4 servings.

NUTRITION FACTS PER SERVING:

199 calories
4 g total fat
1 g saturated fat
49 mg cholesterol
308 mg sodium
16 g carbohydrate
1 g fiber
24 g protein

sole with feta and tomatoes

A well-seasoned tomato sauce and sharp, salty feta cheese jazz up the delicate flavor of sole.

INGREDIENTS

- 1¼ pounds fresh or frozen sole or other fish fillets, ½ to ¾ inch thick
- 1 14½-ounce can low-sodium tomatoes, undrained and cut up
- 8 green onions, thinly sliced
- 2 tablespoons lemon juice
- 1 teaspoon dried Italian seasoning, crushed
- ¼ teaspoon pepper
  Nonstick spray coating

- 3 cups hot cooked spinach fettuccine
- 2 tablespoons crumbled feta cheese or 2 tablespoons sliced pitted ripe olives

Prep time: 25 minutes
Baking time: 20 minutes

DIRECTIONS

1. Thaw fish, if frozen. Rinse fish; pat dry with paper towels. Cut into 4 serving-size pieces. Set aside.

2. For sauce, in a large skillet combine undrained tomatoes, green onions, lemon juice, Italian seasoning, and pepper. Bring to boiling; reduce heat. Simmer, uncovered, for 8 to 10 minutes or until nearly all the liquid has evaporated.

3. Spray a 2-quart square or rectangular baking dish with nonstick coating. Arrange fish in prepared dish. Tuck under any thin edges. Spoon the sauce over fish.

4. Bake fish, covered, in a 350° oven for 20 to 25 minutes or just until fish begins to flake easily with a fork. Serve fish and sauce on top of fettuccine. Sprinkle with feta cheese or olives. Makes 4 servings.

When baking or broiling fish fillets, fold under the thin ends so the fish is an even thickness. This prevents the ends from cooking too quickly and drying out before the rest of the fish is done.

NUTRITION FACTS PER SERVING:

299 calories
4 g total fat
2 g saturated fat
74 mg cholesterol
220 mg sodium
34 g carbohydrate
2 g fiber
31 g protein

grilled rosemary trout with lemon butter

INGREDIENTS

- 4 teaspoons butter, softened
- 1 tablespoon finely chopped shallot or onion
- 1 teaspoon finely shredded lemon peel
- 2 fresh rainbow trout, pan dressed and boned (8 to 10 ounces each)
- 1 tablespoon snipped fresh rosemary
- 1 tablespoon lemon juice
- 2 teaspoons olive oil
- 2 medium tomatoes, halved crosswise
- 1 tablespoon snipped fresh parsley

Taste the delicious reason lemon and butter remain the timeless, classic accompaniments to fish! This recipe is so simple you'll want to tote it along on your next fishing trip.

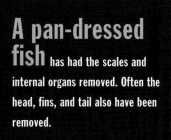

A pan-dressed fish has had the scales and internal organs removed. Often the head, fins, and tail also have been removed.

Prep time: 15 minutes
Grilling time: 6 minutes

DIRECTIONS

1. In a small bowl stir together the butter, half of the shallot or onion, and the lemon peel; sprinkle with salt and coarsely ground pepper. Set aside.

2. Rinse fish; pat dry with paper towels. Spread each fish open and place skin sides down. Rub the remaining shallot or onion and the rosemary onto fish. Sprinkle with additional salt and pepper and drizzle with lemon juice and olive oil.

3. Grill fish, skin sides down, on the greased rack of an uncovered grill directly over medium coals for 6 to 8 minutes or just until fish begins to flake easily.

4. Meanwhile, place tomatoes, cut sides up, on grill rack; dot each with ¼ teaspoon of the butter mixture. Grill tomatoes about 5 minutes or until heated through. Remove fish and tomatoes from grill. Cut each fish in half lengthwise. In a small saucepan melt the remaining butter mixture; serve with fish and tomatoes. Sprinkle fish with parsley. Makes 4 servings.

NUTRITION FACTS PER SERVING:

206 calories
10 g total fat
3 g saturated fat
75 mg cholesterol
109 mg sodium
4 g carbohydrate
1 g fiber
24 g protein

cod with lemon cream sauce

Generally low in fat and calories, fish is great for dieters. Here, spinach noodles make both a colorful backdrop and filling accompaniment (a ¾-cup serving has 158 calories).

INGREDIENTS

- 1 pound fresh or frozen cod or other fish fillets, ½ to ¾ inch thick
- 1½ cups water
- 1 tablespoon lemon juice
- ½ cup finely chopped carrot
- ½ cup finely chopped onion
- ½ cup fat-free milk
- 1 teaspoon cornstarch
- 1 teaspoon snipped fresh dill or ¼ teaspoon dried dillweed
- ½ teaspoon instant chicken bouillon granules
- Hot cooked spinach noodles or other desired hot cooked noodles (optional)

Start to finish: 20 minutes

DIRECTIONS

1. Thaw fish fillets, if frozen. Rinse fish; pat dry with paper towels.

2. In a 12-inch skillet combine water and lemon juice. Bring to boiling. Add fish. Reduce heat. Simmer, covered, just until fish begins to flake easily with a fork (allow 4 to 6 minutes per ½-inch thickness of fish). Remove fish from skillet and keep warm.

3. In a small covered saucepan cook the carrot and onion in a small amount of boiling water about 3 minutes or until crisp-tender. Drain well. In a small bowl stir together milk, cornstarch, dill, and bouillon granules. Stir into vegetables in saucepan. Cook and stir until thickened and bubbly. Cook and stir for 2 minutes more.

4. Serve the vegetable sauce over fish. If desired, serve with hot cooked noodles. Makes 4 servings.

When selecting fresh fish, choose only fillets or steaks that have a sweet, mild smell, not a strong odor. Look for fish that appears moist and recently cut.

NUTRITION FACTS PER SERVING:

114 calories
1 g total fat
0 g saturated fat
45 mg chalesteral
199 mg sodium
5 g carbohydrate
1 g fiber
20 g protein

red snapper with ginger sauce

Fresh ginger imparts a tantalizing zing to this distinctive Oriental-style sauce.

INGREDIENTS

- 1 pound fresh or frozen red snapper or other firm fish fillets, ¾ inch thick
- ¼ cup light soy sauce
- 3 tablespoons dry white or red wine or water
- 2 tablespoons sliced green onion
- 1 tablespoon grated ginger
- 1 clove garlic, quartered
  Nonstick spray coating
- 2 cups red or green sweet pepper strips and/or sliced zucchini
  Thin, long green onion strips (optional)

It's best to cook fresh fish the same day you buy it. If that's not possible, store it in the coldest part of the refrigerator for up to 2 days, or freeze it.

Prep time: 20 minutes
Broiling time: 6 minutes

DIRECTIONS

1. Thaw fish, if frozen. Rinse fish; pat dry with paper towels. Cut into 4 serving-size pieces. Set aside.

2. For sauce, in a blender container or food processor bowl combine the soy sauce, wine or water, sliced green onion, ginger, and garlic. Cover and blend or process until pureed. Set aside.

3. Spray the unheated rack of a broiler pan with nonstick coating. Place fish and sweet pepper strips or zucchini slices on rack. Tuck under any thin edges of fish. Broil 4 inches from heat for 6 to 9 minutes or just until fish begins to flake easily with a fork and vegetables are tender, brushing fish and vegetables with sauce halfway through broiling.

4. Place the remaining sauce in a small saucepan and bring to boiling. Boil gently, uncovered, for 1 minute. Transfer the fish and vegetables to a serving platter. Spoon the remaining sauce over fish. If desired, garnish with green onion strips. Makes 4 servings.

NUTRITION FACTS PER SERVING:

148 calories
2 g total fat
0 g saturated fat
42 mg cholesterol
607 mg sodium
4 g carbohydrate
0 g fiber
25 g protein

sweet-pepper-stuffed sole

Fines herbes transforms a simple wine sauce from ordinary to delicious. This herb mix usually contains chervil, parsley, chives, and tarragon. Look for it with the other dried herbs in your grocery store.

INGREDIENTS

- 4 4-ounce fresh or frozen sole or flounder fillets, ¼ to ½ inch thick
- 2 small red, yellow, and/or green sweet peppers, cut into thin bite-size strips
- 4 green onions, halved lengthwise and cut into 3-inch-long pieces
- 2 teaspoons margarine or butter
- ⅓ cup dry white wine or chicken broth
- ¼ teaspoon dried fines herbes, crushed
- ⅛ teaspoon salt (optional)
- ⅛ teaspoon black pepper
- 1 tablespoon cold water
- 2 teaspoons cornstarch
   Hot cooked wild rice and/or brown rice (optional)

Prep time: 30 minutes
Baking time: 25 minutes

DIRECTIONS

1. Thaw fish, if frozen. Rinse fish; pat dry with paper towels. Set aside. In a medium covered saucepan cook the sweet peppers and green onions in a small amount of boiling water for 3 minutes. Drain well.

2. Dot each fish fillet with ½ teaspoon of the margarine or butter. Place one-fourth of the pepper mixture across the center of each fillet. Starting from a short side, roll up the fish fillets. Secure with wooden toothpicks. Place fish, seam sides down, in a shallow baking dish. Stir together the wine or broth, fines herbes, salt (omit if using broth), and black pepper; drizzle over fish.

3. Bake, covered, in a 350° oven for 25 to 30 minutes or just until fish begins to flake easily with a fork. Transfer the fish to a serving platter. Keep warm.

4. For sauce, measure pan juices; add enough water to measure ¾ cup. In a small saucepan combine the 1 tablespoon cold water and the cornstarch; stir in pan juices. Cook and stir over medium heat until thickened and bubbly. Cook and stir for 2 minutes more. If desired, serve the fish on top of rice. Spoon the sauce over fish. Makes 4 servings.

NUTRITION FACTS PER SERVING:

148 calories
3 g total fat
1 g saturated fat
60 mg cholesterol
184 mg sodium
4 g carbohydrate
0 g fiber
22 g protein

fish and sweet peppers

This simple recipe clamors for glistening fresh fish, for these ingredients won't mask its delicate flavor.

INGREDIENTS

1 pound fresh or frozen cod or other fish fillets, ½ to ¾ inch thick

¾ cup chicken broth

1 medium onion, sliced and separated into rings

½ teaspoon finely shredded lemon peel

1 tablespoon lemon juice

2¼ teaspoons snipped fresh oregano or marjoram or ¾ teaspoon dried oregano or marjoram, crushed

1 clove garlic, minced

2 small green and/or red sweet peppers, cut into bite-size strips (1½ cups)

1 tablespoon cold water

1½ teaspoons cornstarch

1 lemon, halved and sliced (optional)

Prep time: 25 minutes
Cooking time: 7 minutes

DIRECTIONS

1. Thaw fish, if frozen. Rinse fish; pat dry with paper towels. Cut into 4 serving-size pieces. Set aside.

2. In a large skillet combine the chicken broth, onion, lemon peel, lemon juice, oregano or marjoram, and garlic. Bring to boiling; reduce heat. Simmer, covered, about 3 minutes or until onion is tender.

3. Arrange the fish on top of onion mixture in skillet. Add sweet peppers. Cook, covered, over medium heat just until fish begins to flake easily with a fork (allow 4 to 6 minutes per ½-inch thickness of fish). Using a slotted spoon, transfer fish and vegetable mixture to a serving platter. Keep warm.

4. Combine cold water and cornstarch. Add to pan juices. Cook and stir until thickened and bubbly. Cook and stir for 2 minutes more. Spoon over the fish and vegetables. If desired, garnish with lemon slices. Makes 4 servings.

NUTRITION FACTS PER SERVING:

116 calories
1 g total fat
0 g saturated fat
45 mg cholesterol
211 mg sodium
6 g carbohydrate
1 g fiber
20 g protein

INGREDIENTS

- 1 **pound fresh or frozen skinless salmon or other fish fillets, ½ to ¾ inch thick**
- ½ **teaspoon garlic-pepper seasoning or seasoned pepper**
- 1½ **cups water**
- 1 **pound asparagus spears**
- 1 **small onion, sliced**
- ½ **cup dry white wine or reduced-sodium chicken broth**
- ¼ **cup fat-free mayonnaise dressing or salad dressing**
- 2 **tablespoons fat-free milk or water**
- 1 **teaspoon finely shredded lime peel or lemon peel**
- 1 **tablespoon lime juice or lemon juice**
   Fresh watercress and/or lettuce leaves (optional)

cold poached salmon with asparagus

Prepare this make-ahead dish as a spring or summer cold entrée, or use small servings for an elegant first course.

Prep time: 20 minutes
Cooking time: 8 minutes
Chilling time: 6 hours

DIRECTIONS

1. Thaw fish, if frozen. Rinse fish; pat dry with paper towels. Cut into 4 serving-size pieces. Rub fish fillets with garlic-pepper seasoning or seasoned pepper; set aside.

2. In a large skillet bring the water to boiling. Meanwhile, wash asparagus; snap off and discard woody bases. If desired, scrape off scales. Cook the asparagus in the boiling water, covered, for 4 to 8 minutes or until crisp-tender. Remove asparagus, reserving liquid in skillet. Rinse asparagus in cold water; drain and cool.

3. Add the onion and wine or broth to skillet; return to boiling. Add fish. Reduce heat. Simmer, covered, just until fish begins to flake easily with a fork (allow 4 to 6 minutes per ½-inch thickness of fish). Using a slotted spoon, remove fish from skillet; cool. Discard the cooking liquid, including onion. Transfer fish and asparagus to separate storage containers and chill for 6 to 24 hours.

4. For dressing, in a small bowl stir together the mayonnaise dressing or salad dressing, milk or water, lime or lemon peel, and lime or lemon juice. If desired, line 4 plates with watercress and/or lettuce. Arrange the fish and asparagus on top of greens. Spoon some of the dressing over fish. Pass the remaining dressing. Makes 4 servings.

NUTRITION FACTS PER SERVING:

162 calories
4 g total fat
1 g saturated fat
20 mg cholesterol
271 mg sodium
8 g carbohydrate
2 g fiber
18 g protein

mahimahi with yellow pepper sauce

Roasting peppers enhances their naturally sweet flavor and becomes the key to this recipe. To shorten prep time, roast the peppers ahead, then cover and chill for up to 24 hours.

Prep time: 55 minutes
Broiling time: 6 minutes

INGREDIENTS

- 1 pound skinless mahimahi or other firm fish fillets, ¾ to 1 inch thick
- 2 yellow or red sweet peppers
- ½ cup plain fat-free yogurt
- 1 tablespoon fresh parsley leaves
- 1½ teaspoons snipped fresh basil or ½ teaspoon dried basil, crushed
- ½ teaspoon finely shredded lemon peel
- ⅛ teaspoon black pepper
  Nonstick spray coating
- 1 tablespoon lemon juice
  Fat-free milk
  Hot cooked rice (optional)
  Sliced tomatoes (optional)
  Lime or lemon slices (optional)

DIRECTIONS

1. Thaw fish, if frozen. Rinse fish; pat dry with paper towels. Cut fish into 4 serving-size pieces. Set aside.

2. Quarter sweet peppers; remove stems, seeds, and membranes. Place pepper pieces, cut sides down, on a foil-lined baking sheet. Bake in a 450° oven for 15 to 20 minutes or until skins are blistered and dark. Fold up foil on baking sheet around peppers to form a packet, sealing edges. Let stand about 20 minutes to loosen skins. With a small sharp knife, peel skin from peppers.

Discard skin. Cut 6 narrow strips of roasted pepper; halve the strips and reserve for garnish.

3. For sauce, place the remaining roasted sweet pepper in a blender container or food processor bowl. Cover and blend or process until nearly smooth, stopping and scraping sides of container as necessary. Add yogurt, parsley, basil, lemon peel, and black pepper. Cover and blend or process until combined. Transfer to a small saucepan. Cover; set aside.

4. Spray the unheated rack of a broiler pan with nonstick coating. Place fish on the rack; tuck under any thin edges. Brush fish with lemon juice. Broil 4 inches from the heat just until fish begins to flake easily with a fork

(allow 4 to 6 minutes per ½-inch thickness of fish). If fish is 1 inch thick, gently turn it halfway through broiling. Heat and stir the sauce over medium-low heat until warm (do not boil). Stir up to 2 tablespoons milk into sauce until it reaches the desired consistency.

5. If desired, serve fish on top of rice. Spoon the sauce over fish. Garnish with

reserved sweet pepper strips and, if desired, tomatoes and lime or lemon slices. Makes 4 servings.

NUTRITION FACTS PER SERVING:

127 calories
1 g total fat
0 g saturated fat
84 mg cholesterol
125 mg sodium
6 g carbohydrate
0 g fiber
23 g protein

wasabi-glazed whitefish with vegetable slaw

Though its presence in this recipe is subtle, fans of fiery wasabi—the bright-green Japanese horseradish condiment—will notice its head-clearing heat. Wasabi is found in powdered or paste form in Japanese markets or in larger supermarkets.

INGREDIENTS

- 4 4-ounce fresh white-fleshed skinless fish fillets, about ¾ inch thick
- 2 tablespoons light soy sauce
- 1 teaspoon toasted sesame oil
- ½ teaspoon sugar
- ¼ teaspoon wasabi powder or 1 tablespoon prepared horseradish
- 1 medium zucchini, coarsely shredded (about 1⅓ cups)
- 1 cup sliced radishes
- 1 cup fresh pea pods
- 3 tablespoons snipped fresh chives
- 3 tablespoons rice vinegar

Prep time: 15 minutes
Grilling time: 6 minutes

DIRECTIONS

1. Rinse fish; pat dry with paper towels. In a small bowl combine the soy sauce, ½ teaspoon of the sesame oil, ¼ teaspoon of the sugar, and the wasabi powder or horseradish. Brush the soy mixture over fish.

2. Place fish on a greased grill rack or in a well-greased grill basket. Grill on an uncovered grill directly over medium coals for 6 to 9 minutes or just until fish begins to flake easily with a fork, gently turning halfway through grilling.

3. Meanwhile, for vegetable slaw, in a medium bowl combine the zucchini, radishes, pea pods, and 2 tablespoons of the chives. Stir together the vinegar, remaining sesame oil, and remaining sugar. Drizzle over the zucchini mixture; toss to coat. Sprinkle the remaining chives over fish. Serve fish with vegetable slaw. Makes 4 servings.

Types of fish that work well

for this distinctive Asian recipe include whitefish, sea bass, orange roughy, or other similar fish fillets.

NUTRITION FACTS PER SERVING:

141 calories
3 g total fat
1 g saturated fat
60 mg cholesterol
363 mg sodium
6 g carbohydrate
1 g fiber
24 g protein

sweet-and-sour fish

Oriental-style sweet-and-sour dishes are usually fried, but this version uses poached lean fish. Although we trimmed the calories and fat, we kept the great flavor.

INGREDIENTS

1 pound fresh or frozen halibut, swordfish, tuna, or other fish steaks, cut 1 inch thick

2 tablespoons brown sugar

2 tablespoons vinegar

2 tablespoons reduced-sodium soy sauce

4 teaspoons cornstarch

⅔ cup reduced-sodium chicken broth

1 medium green or red sweet pepper, cut into 1-inch squares

1 medium carrot, thinly bias sliced

½ cup seedless grapes, halved

2 cups hot cooked rice

Start to finish: 30 minutes

DIRECTIONS

1. Thaw fish, if frozen. Rinse fish; pat dry with paper towels. Cut into 1-inch cubes. In a large covered saucepan cook fish in boiling water about 5 minutes or just until fish begins to flake easily with a fork. Drain well. Keep warm.

2. Meanwhile, in a small bowl combine the brown sugar, vinegar, soy sauce, and cornstarch. Set aside.

3. In a medium saucepan combine the chicken broth, sweet pepper, and carrot. Bring to boiling; reduce heat. Simmer, covered, about 3 minutes or until vegetables are crisp-tender.

4. Stir brown sugar mixture into vegetable mixture. Cook and stir until thickened and bubbly. Cook and stir for 2 minutes more. Gently stir in fish and grapes. Cook about 1 minute more or until heated through. Serve over hot cooked rice. Makes 4 servings.

NUTRITION FACTS PER SERVING:

294 calories
3 g total fat
1 g saturated fat
36 mg cholesterol
446 mg sodium
38 g carbohydrate
1 g fiber
27 g protein

INGREDIENTS

- 12 ounces fresh or frozen skinless, boneless fish
- ¼ cup dry white wine or chicken broth
- ¼ cup chicken broth
- 2 tablespoons lime juice
- 2 teaspoons cornstarch
- 1 teaspoon honey
- ¼ teaspoon ground ginger
- ¼ teaspoon ground coriander
- ⅛ teaspoon black pepper
  Nonstick spray coating
- 1 medium cucumber, seeded and cut into 2×½-inch sticks
- 1 medium zucchini, cut into 2×½-inch sticks
- 1 medium red or green sweet pepper, cut into ¾-inch squares
- 1 teaspoon cooking oil
- 3 cups hot cooked linguine
  Lime wedges (optional)

lime-sauced fish and linguine

For fish stir-fries, such as this one, select a firm fish. Swordfish, shark, sea bass, cod, or orange roughy all work well.

Start to finish: 35 minutes

DIRECTIONS

1. Thaw fish, if frozen. Rinse fish; pat dry with paper towels. Cut into ¾-inch pieces. Set aside.

2. For sauce, in a small bowl stir together the wine, chicken broth, lime juice, cornstarch, honey, ginger, coriander, and black pepper. Set aside.

3. Spray an unheated wok or large skillet with nonstick coating. Preheat over medium-high heat. Add the cucumber and zucchini; stir-fry for 1½ minutes. Add the sweet pepper; stir-fry about 1½ minutes more or until crisp-tender. Remove vegetables from wok.

4. Add the oil to hot wok. Add fish; stir-fry for 2 to 3 minutes or just until fish begins to flake easily with a fork. Push the fish from center of wok. Stir sauce; add to center of wok. Cook and stir until thickened and bubbly. Return cooked vegetables to wok. Cook and stir about 2 minutes or until heated through. Serve immediately with linguine. If desired, garnish with lime wedges. Makes 4 servings.

NUTRITION FACTS PER SERVING:

312 calories
6 g total fat
1 g saturated fat
34 mg cholesterol
130 mg sodium
39 g carbohydrate
3 g fiber
23 g protein

salmon salad

This salad will remind you of a Caesar salad—without the raw eggs, anchovies, high fat, and calories. Plain yogurt adds the creamy texture to the garlic-and-lemon dressing.

INGREDIENTS

- 2 tablespoons olive oil
- 5 cloves garlic, thinly sliced
- 2 tablespoons lemon juice
- 1 tablespoon Worcestershire sauce
- 1 tablespoon Dijon-style mustard
- 1 tablespoon water
- ½ teaspoon pepper
- ⅓ cup plain fat-free yogurt
- 12 ounces fresh or frozen skinless, boneless salmon fillets, 1 inch thick
  Nonstick spray coating
- 10 cups torn romaine
- ½ cup thinly sliced red onion
- ¼ cup freshly grated Parmesan cheese
- 1 cup cherry tomatoes, halved
- ½ cup pitted ripe olives, halved (optional)

Prep time: 20 minutes
Marinating time: 30 minutes
Broiling time: 8 minutes

DIRECTIONS

1. For dressing, in a small saucepan heat olive oil over medium-low heat. Add the garlic. Cook and stir for 1 to 2 minutes or until garlic is light golden. Transfer garlic to a blender container. Add lemon juice, Worcestershire sauce, mustard, water, and pepper. Cover and blend until combined. Remove 2 tablespoons of the garlic mixture; set aside. Add the yogurt to the remaining garlic mixture in blender. Cover and blend until smooth. Chill until serving time.

2. Thaw fish, if frozen. Rinse fish; pat dry with paper towels. Brush the reserved garlic mixture evenly over fish. Cover and marinate in refrigerator for 30 minutes.

3. Spray the unheated rack of a broiler pan with nonstick coating. Place fish on rack; tuck under any thin edges. Broil 4 to 5 inches from the heat for 8 to 12 minutes or just until fish begins to flake easily with a fork, gently turning halfway through broiling.

4. Meanwhile, in a large bowl combine the romaine, red onion, and Parmesan cheese. Add the chilled yogurt dressing; toss to coat. Divide the romaine mixture among 4 plates. Top with the fish, cherry tomatoes, and ripe olives (if desired). Makes 4 servings.

NUTRITION FACTS PER SERVING:

234 calories
13 g total fat
3 g saturated fat
21 mg cholesterol
331 mg sodium
12 g carbohydrate
4 g fiber
19 g protein

tuna-vegetable salad

For a great sandwich, spread the tuna mixture between slices of whole wheat bread and top with tomato and lettuce.

INGREDIENTS

- 1 cup chopped celery and/or chopped seeded cucumber
- ½ cup shredded carrot
- 2 tablespoons sliced green onion
- ⅓ cup fat-free mayonnaise dressing or salad dressing
- 1½ teaspoons snipped fresh dill or ½ teaspoon dried dillweed
- ½ teaspoon finely shredded lemon peel
- ⅛ teaspoon garlic powder
- ⅛ teaspoon pepper
- 1 6½-ounce can low-sodium chunk light or white tuna (water pack), drained and broken into chunks
- 4 medium tomatoes, sliced Fresh dill (optional)

Prep time: 15 minutes
Chilling time: 1 hour

DIRECTIONS

1. In a medium mixing bowl combine the celery or cucumber, carrot, and green onion. Stir in the mayonnaise dressing or salad dressing, snipped or dried dill, lemon peel, garlic powder, and pepper. Gently fold in tuna. Cover and chill mixture for 1 to 4 hours.

2. To serve, divide the sliced tomatoes among 4 plates. Spoon the tuna mixture over tomato slices.

If desired, garnish with additional fresh dill. Makes 4 servings.

NUTRITION FACTS PER SERVING:

109 calories
1 g total fat
0 g saturated fat
15 mg cholesterol
314 mg sodium
13 g carbohydrate
3 g fiber
13 g protein

183

linguine with garlic shrimp

No need to fear the amount of garlic in this delicious dish since it's roasted to a mellow, buttery paste. It also has many other uses—spread it on Italian bread, stir it into mashed potatoes, or add it to mayonnaise for sandwiches.

INGREDIENTS

- 12 ounces fresh or frozen, peeled and deveined shrimp
- 2 large bulbs garlic
- 8 ounces packaged dried plain and/or spinach linguine or fettuccine
- 2 cups sliced fresh mushrooms
- 1 medium yellow or green sweet pepper, chopped
- 1 tablespoon olive oil or cooking oil
- ½ cup water
- 1 tablespoon snipped fresh basil or 1 teaspoon dried basil, crushed
- 2 teaspoons cornstarch
- 1½ teaspoons snipped fresh oregano or ½ teaspoon dried oregano, crushed
- ½ teaspoon instant chicken bouillon granules
- ⅛ teaspoon black pepper
- 2 medium tomatoes, peeled, seeded, and chopped
- ¼ cup finely shredded Parmesan cheese

Prep time: 30 minutes
Cooking time: 45 minutes

DIRECTIONS

1. Thaw shrimp, if frozen. Rinse shrimp; pat dry with paper towels. Set aside.

2. For garlic paste, cut ½ inch off the pointed top portions of garlic bulbs. Remove the outer papery layers of the garlic. Place both bulbs on a square piece of foil. Bring edges of foil together to form a pouch. Seal. Bake garlic in a 375° oven for 35 to 40 minutes or until very soft. When cool enough to handle, use your fingers to press garlic pulp from each clove. Mash pulp with a spoon or fork to make a smooth paste (you should have about 2 to 3 tablespoons). Set aside.

3. Cook the pasta according to package directions. Drain. Cover to keep warm.

4. Meanwhile, in a large saucepan cook mushrooms and sweet pepper in hot oil until pepper is tender.

5. In a small bowl stir together the garlic paste, water, basil, cornstarch, oregano, bouillon granules, and black pepper. Add to mushroom mixture in saucepan. Cook and stir until thickened and bubbly. Add the shrimp to the mushroom mixture. Simmer, covered, about 2 minutes or until shrimp are opaque. Stir in tomatoes; heat through.

6. To serve, spoon the shrimp mixture over pasta. Sprinkle with Parmesan cheese. Toss to combine. Makes 4 servings.

NUTRITION FACTS PER SERVING:

357 calories
7 g total fat
2 g saturated fat
126 mg cholesterol
397 mg sodium
49 g carbohydrate
6 g fiber
24 g protein

poached shrimp with green chili rice

Look for the tomatillos used in this dish in the produce section of a supermarket or a Mexican grocery store.

INGREDIENTS

- 1 pound fresh or frozen shrimp in shells
- 8 fresh tomatillos, husked and cut up
- 1 medium onion, cut up
- 1 fresh jalapeño, serrano, or banana pepper, seeded and cut up (see tip, page 21)
- 1 tablespoon chopped mild green chili pepper (canned or fresh)
- 1 tablespoon fresh cilantro or parsley leaves
- 1 clove garlic, quartered
- ½ teaspoon sugar
- ½ teaspoon dried oregano, crushed
- ¼ teaspoon salt-free seasoning blend
- 2 cups hot cooked rice
- 1 cup water
- 1 cup dry white wine or reduced-sodium chicken broth
- 2 lemon or lime slices
- ¼ teaspoon peppercorns
  Fresh cilantro or parsley (optional)

Start to finish: 40 minutes

DIRECTIONS

1. Thaw shrimp, if frozen. Peel and devein shrimp. Rinse shrimp; pat dry with paper towels. Set aside.

2. For green chili rice, in a blender container or food processor bowl combine the tomatillos; onion; jalapeño, serrano, or banana pepper; mild green chili pepper; the 1 tablespoon cilantro or parsley; the garlic; sugar; oregano; and seasoning blend. Cover and blend or process until smooth, stopping and scraping sides of container as necessary. Transfer mixture to a medium saucepan; heat through. Stir in hot cooked rice; cover and keep warm.

3. In a Dutch oven or large saucepan combine the water, wine or broth, lemon or lime slices, and peppercorns. Bring to boiling; add shrimp. Reduce heat. Simmer, uncovered, for 1 to 3 minutes or until shrimp are opaque. Drain. Spoon the green chili rice onto a serving platter; top with the shrimp. If desired, garnish with additional cilantro or parsley. Makes 4 servings.

To peel shrimp,

open the shell along the underside. Starting at the head, pull back the shell and discard. Gently pull on the tail to remove. Use a sharp knife to cut along the center of the back and remove the black vein.

NUTRITION FACTS PER SERVING:

247 calories
2 g total fat
0 g saturated fat
131 mg cholesterol
177 mg sodium
31 g carbohydrate
1 g fiber
17 g protein

185

lemony shrimp and asparagus

If you purchase shrimp in shells, buy about 1 pound. By the time you remove and discard the shells, the shrimp will weigh about 12 ounces.

INGREDIENTS

- 12 ounces fresh or frozen, peeled and deveined shrimp
- 1 pound fresh asparagus, trimmed and cut into 2-inch pieces, or one 10-ounce package frozen cut asparagus
- 1 medium red or green sweet pepper, cut into thin strips
- 2 cloves garlic, minced
- ⅔ cup water
- 1 tablespoon reduced-sodium soy sauce
- 1 teaspoon finely shredded lemon peel
- 1 tablespoon lemon juice
- 2 teaspoons cornstarch
- 2 cups hot cooked rice

Start to finish: 25 minutes

DIRECTIONS

1. Thaw shrimp, if frozen. Rinse shrimp; pat dry with paper towels. In a medium covered saucepan cook the asparagus in a small amount of boiling water for 3 minutes. Add the shrimp, sweet pepper, and garlic. Return to boiling. Cook, covered, for 1 to 2 minutes more or until shrimp are opaque. Drain.

2. Meanwhile, in a large saucepan stir together the ⅔ cup water, the soy sauce, lemon peel, lemon juice, and cornstarch. Cook and stir until thickened and bubbly. Cook and stir for 2 minutes more. Stir in the vegetable-shrimp mixture; heat through. Serve with hot cooked rice. Makes 4 servings.

NUTRITION FACTS PER SERVING:

200 calories
1 g total fat
0 g saturated fat
131 mg cholesterol
287 mg sodium
29 g carbohydrate
2 g fiber
19 g protein

mixed seafood with pasta

Frozen scallops and shrimp work as well as fresh, but you'll need to use fresh clams. When buying clams, look for moist shells without cracks or chips and choose those that close when gently tapped.

INGREDIENTS

- 8 ounces fresh or frozen, peeled and deveined shrimp
- 6 ounces fresh or frozen sea scallops
- 12 small fresh clams in shells
- 1 cup water
- 1 medium yellow sweet pepper, cut into ¾-inch pieces
- ½ cup chopped onion
- 1 tablespoon *each* snipped fresh basil and oregano or 1 teaspoon *each* dried basil and oregano, crushed
- 2 cloves garlic, minced
- ½ teaspoon instant chicken bouillon granules
- ¼ teaspoon black pepper
- 2 tablespoons cornstarch
- 2 tablespoons cold water
- 2 medium tomatoes, seeded and chopped
- 3 cups hot cooked spaghetti or linguine
- ¼ cup grated Parmesan cheese
- 2 tablespoons snipped fresh parsley

Prep time: 15 minutes
Soaking time: 45 minutes
Cooking time: 10 minutes

DIRECTIONS

1. Thaw shrimp and scallops, if frozen. Halve any large scallops. Rinse shrimp and scallops; pat dry with paper towels. Set aside.

2. Scrub clams under cold running water. In a large container cover clams with salted water, using 8 cups cold water to 3 tablespoons salt. Soak for 15 minutes; drain and rinse. Discard water. Repeat 2 more times.

3. In a large skillet combine the clams, 1 cup water, sweet pepper, onion, dried herbs (if using), garlic, bouillon, and black pepper.

Cook, covered, about 5 minutes or until onion is tender and clams open. Remove clams; discard any unopened ones.

4. Stir together cornstarch and 2 tablespoons cold water; stir into onion mixture. Cook and stir until thickened and bubbly. Stir in shrimp, scallops, and fresh herbs (if using). Cook 3 to 4 minutes or until shrimp and scallops are opaque. Stir in tomatoes and clams; heat through. Serve with pasta. Sprinkle with Parmesan cheese and parsley. Makes 6 servings.

NUTRITION FACTS PER SERVING:

214 calories
3 g total fat
1 g saturated fat
76 mg cholesterol
285 mg sodium
28 g carbohydrate
1 g fiber
19 g protein

187

shrimp salad

This salad has the makings of an elegant meal and deserves consideration for a special celebration menu. The flavors of asparagus and shrimp flourish with the addition of the balsamic vinaigrette.

INGREDIENTS

- 2 tablespoons dried tomato pieces (not oil-packed)
- ¼ cup balsamic vinegar
- 2 tablespoons olive oil
- 1 tablespoon snipped fresh basil
- 2 teaspoons Dijon-style mustard
- 2 cloves garlic, minced
- ¼ teaspoon sugar
- ⅛ teaspoon pepper
- 12 ounces fresh or frozen, peeled and deveined shrimp
- 4 cups water
- 1 clove garlic
- 8 ounces asparagus, cut into 2-inch pieces
- 6 cups torn mixed salad greens
- 2 medium pears, cored and thinly sliced

Cook shrimp quickly; overcooking toughens them. Cook shrimp just until they curl, the shells (if present) turn pink, and their flesh turns opaque.

Prep time: 20 minutes
Cooking time: 5 minutes
Chilling time: 4 hours

DIRECTIONS

1. In a small bowl pour enough boiling water over tomato pieces to cover. Soak for 2 minutes. Drain.

2. For dressing, in a screw-top jar combine the tomato pieces, vinegar, olive oil, basil, mustard, the 2 cloves garlic, the sugar, and pepper. Cover and shake well. If desired, cover and chill for up to 24 hours.

3. Thaw shrimp, if frozen. Rinse shrimp; pat dry with paper towels. In a large saucepan bring the water and the 1 clove garlic to boiling; add asparagus. Return to boiling; reduce heat. Simmer, uncovered, for 4 minutes.

4. Add shrimp to saucepan. Return to boiling; reduce heat. Simmer, uncovered, for 1 to 3 minutes more or until shrimp are opaque. Drain, discarding garlic. Rinse under cold running water; drain well. Cover and chill for 4 to 24 hours.

5. To serve, divide greens and pears among 4 plates. Top with shrimp and asparagus. Shake dressing; drizzle over salads. Serves 4.

NUTRITION FACTS PER SERVING:

221 calories
8 g total fat
1 g saturated fat
131 mg cholesterol
260 mg sodium
21 g carbohydrate
4 g fiber
17 g protein

shrimp with tarragon dressing

This flavorful salad is an easy make-ahead. Arrange the potatoes and shrimp on lettuce-lined plates. Make the dressing. Cover and chill salads and dressing until you're ready to serve. Just before serving, drizzle the dressing over the salads.

INGREDIENTS

- 1 pound fresh or frozen shrimp in shells
- 3 medium potatoes, sliced ¼ inch thick
- ¼ cup light mayonnaise dressing or salad dressing
- ¼ cup buttermilk or plain low-fat yogurt
- 2 green onions, sliced
- 2 tablespoons snipped fresh parsley
- 1 teaspoon snipped fresh tarragon or ¼ teaspoon dried tarragon, crushed
- 1 clove garlic, minced
- 4 cups water
- 2 tablespoons vinegar
- ½ teaspoon salt
  Lettuce leaves
- 8 cherry tomatoes (optional)

Start to finish: 40 minutes

DIRECTIONS

1. Thaw shrimp, if frozen. Peel and devein shrimp, leaving tails on if desired. Rinse shrimp; pat dry with paper towels. Cover and chill until needed.

2. In a covered saucepan cook the potatoes in a small amount of lightly salted boiling water for 8 to 12 minutes or until tender. Drain well. Set aside.

3. Meanwhile, for dressing, in a blender container combine the mayonnaise dressing or salad dressing, buttermilk or yogurt, green onions, parsley, tarragon, and garlic. Cover and blend until smooth. Set aside.

4. In a large saucepan combine the water, vinegar, and salt. Bring to boiling. Add shrimp. Reduce heat. Simmer, uncovered, for 1 to 3 minutes or until shrimp are opaque. Drain. Rinse with cold water; drain.

5. Arrange the potato slices and shrimp on 4 lettuce-lined plates. If necessary, stir some water into the dressing to make of drizzling consistency. Drizzle dressing over potatoes and shrimp. If desired, garnish with cherry tomatoes. Makes 4 servings.

To store fresh shrimp, first rinse them under cold running water, then drain well. Cover and store in the refrigerator for up to 2 days.

NUTRITION FACTS PER SERVING:

237 calories
6 g total fat
1 g saturated fat
131 mg cholesterol
553 mg sodium
28 g carbohydrate
1 g fiber
17 g protein

crab and fennel risotto

A celerylike vegetable, fennel has a delicate licorice flavor. The seed from the fennel plant is a spice traditionally used in Italian sausage. (Recipe also pictured on pages 164–165.)

INGREDIENTS

- 2 fennel bulbs with leaves
- 1 cup sliced fresh shiitake, porcini, or button mushrooms
- ½ teaspoon fennel seed, crushed
- 1 tablespoon olive oil
- 1 cup Arborio or medium-grain rice
- 3¼ cups water
- 1 teaspoon chicken bouillon granules
- ⅛ teaspoon pepper
- 1 cup cooked crabmeat; one 6½-ounce can crabmeat, drained, flaked, and cartilage removed; or one 6-ounce package frozen cooked crabmeat, thawed and drained
- ½ cup asparagus, cut into 1-inch pieces
- ⅓ cup thinly sliced green onions
- Fennel leaves (optional)

If the asparagus spears are thick,

halve the spears lengthwise, then cut into 1-inch pieces. Cook in a small amount of boiling water until crisp-tender. Add to the risotto.

Prep time: 20 minutes
Cooking time: 20 minutes

DIRECTIONS

1. Remove upper stalks from fennel, including feathery leaves; reserve leaves and discard stalks. Discard any wilted outer layers on fennel bulbs; cut off a thin slice from each base.

Wash fennel and pat dry. Quarter each fennel bulb lengthwise and remove core. Slice the fennel; measure 1 cup sliced fennel. Chop enough of the reserved fennel leaves to make 1 tablespoon. Set aside.

2. In a large saucepan cook the 1 cup fennel, the mushrooms, and fennel seed in hot oil until tender. Stir in the uncooked rice. Cook and stir over medium heat for 2 minutes. Carefully stir in the water, bouillon granules, and pepper. Bring to boiling; reduce heat. Simmer, covered, for 20 minutes (do not lift cover). Remove saucepan from heat.

3. Stir the crabmeat, asparagus, and green onions into the rice mixture. Let stand, covered, for 5 minutes.

(The rice should be tender but slightly firm, and the mixture should be creamy. If necessary, stir in a little water to reach desired consistency.)

4. Stir in the chopped fennel leaves. If desired, garnish with additional fennel leaves. Makes 4 servings.

NUTRITION FACTS PER SERVING:

307 calories
5 g total fat
1 g saturated fat
22 mg cholesterol
401 mg sodium
54 g carbohydrate
6 g fiber
13 g protein

crab and asparagus gratin

This easy seafood casserole brings color, taste, and a change of pace to the table. Round out the meal with a tossed spinach and orange salad and a crusty baguette.

INGREDIENTS

1 pound fresh or frozen split crab legs

1 10-ounce package frozen cut asparagus

1 tablespoon margarine or butter

1 cup sliced fresh mushrooms

¼ cup finely chopped onion

1 tablespoon cornstarch

⅛ teaspoon salt

⅛ teaspoon ground nutmeg
   Dash pepper

1 cup fat-free milk

2 tablespoons chopped almonds, toasted (see tip, page 108)

2 tablespoons grated Parmesan cheese

Prep time: 35 minutes
Baking time: 10 minutes

DIRECTIONS

1. Thaw crab legs, if frozen. Remove meat from shells; cut meat into 1-inch pieces. Cook the asparagus according to package directions; drain well. Set asparagus aside.

2. In a medium saucepan melt the margarine or butter over medium heat. Add the mushrooms and onion; cook until onion is tender. Stir in cornstarch, salt, nutmeg, and pepper. Add milk all at once. Cook and stir until thickened and bubbly. Cook and stir for 2 minutes more. Stir in crabmeat and asparagus.

3. Spoon the crab mixture into 4 individual 10- to 14-ounce au gratin dishes or oval casseroles.

4. In a small bowl stir together the almonds and Parmesan cheese. Sprinkle over casseroles.

5. Bake in a 400° oven about 10 minutes or until mixture is heated through. Makes 4 servings.

Crab legs are readily available precooked and frozen. Or, you can use 6 ounces of refrigerated or thawed, frozen crab-flavored fish pieces.

NUTRITION FACTS PER SERVING:

153 calories
7 g total fat
1 g saturated fat
26 mg cholesterol
649 mg sodium
10 g carbohydrate
2 g fiber
15 g protein

191

saffron lobster with couscous

Invest in a small amount of saffron for this delectable dish of lobster in a creamy wine sauce. It is well worth it.

INGREDIENTS

- 4 4-ounce frozen lobster tails, thawed
- 6 cups water
- 2 lemon slices
- 4 peppercorns
- 1 bay leaf
- ½ cup reduced-sodium chicken broth
- 4 shallots, peeled and chopped (⅓ cup)
- 2 cloves garlic, minced
- 1½ cups chopped tomatoes
- 1½ teaspoons snipped fresh thyme or ½ teaspoon dried thyme, crushed
- ¼ teaspoon lemon-pepper seasoning
- Dash powdered saffron or ⅛ teaspoon thread saffron
- 2 tablespoons cornstarch
- 1 cup fat-free milk
- ¼ cup dry white wine or reduced-sodium chicken broth
- 2 cups hot cooked couscous or rice
- Fresh thyme (optional)

Instead of lobster tails, you can use 1½ cups cooked lobster meat. Omit the simmering directions and the 6 cups water, lemon slices, peppercorns, and bay leaf. Begin with Step 2 of the recipe directions.

Start to finish: 45 minutes

DIRECTIONS

1. Rinse lobster; pat dry with paper towels. In a large saucepan combine the water, lemon slices, peppercorns, and bay leaf; bring to boiling. Add lobster tails; return to boiling. Reduce heat. Simmer, uncovered, for 4 to 8 minutes or until shells turn bright red and meat is opaque. Drain, discarding the cooking liquid. Cool lobster; remove meat from shells. Chop meat; set aside.

2. In a large skillet heat the chicken broth. Add the shallots and garlic. Cook, uncovered, over medium heat about 3 minutes or until the shallots are tender.

3. Stir in the tomatoes, snipped or dried thyme, lemon-pepper seasoning, and saffron. Simmer, uncovered, for 5 minutes. In a small bowl stir cornstarch into milk; add to skillet. Cook and stir until thickened and bubbly. Cook and stir for 2 minutes more. Stir in the chopped lobster meat and wine or broth. Cook about 1 minute more or until heated through. Serve the lobster mixture over hot cooked couscous or rice. If desired, garnish with additional fresh thyme. Makes 4 servings.

NUTRITION FACTS PER SERVING:

237 calories
1 g total fat
0 g saturated fat
40 mg cholesterol
325 mg sodium
37 g carbohydrate
1 g fiber
17 g protein

lobster newburg

Milk replaces cream in this lightened version of an easy-to-fix classic. Serve it for a special lunch with friends or a romantic brunch for two.

INGREDIENTS

- 2 teaspoons margarine or butter
- 1 tablespoon all-purpose flour
- ¼ teaspoon salt
- 1½ cups milk
- 2 beaten egg yolks
- 8 ounces cubed fresh or frozen cooked lobster meat or refrigerated chunk-style lobster-flavored fish pieces
- 1 tablespoon dry sherry
- ⅛ teaspoon white or black pepper
  Dash ground red pepper
- 2 English muffins, split and toasted
  Snipped fresh chives (optional)

NUTRITION FACTS PER SERVING:

223 calories
6 g total fat
1 g saturated fat
149 mg cholesterol
629 mg sodium
22 g carbohydrate
1 g fiber
19 g protein

Start to finish: 20 minutes

DIRECTIONS

1. In a medium saucepan melt the margarine or butter. Stir in the flour and salt. Add the milk all at once. Cook and stir until thickened and bubbly. Cook and stir for 1 minute more.

2. Stir about half of the hot mixture into the beaten egg yolks. Return the egg mixture to saucepan. Cook and stir until thickened and bubbly.

3. Stir in the lobster meat, dry sherry, white or black pepper, and ground red pepper. Heat through.

4. Serve the lobster mixture over English muffin halves. If desired, garnish with snipped chives. Makes 4 servings.

193

chilled lobster with curry dressing

Reserve this salad for a special celebration. Most supermarkets regularly carry lobster, a true treat that is not difficult to prepare.

INGREDIENTS

- **2** fresh or frozen medium rock lobster tails (about 5 ounces each)
- **6** cups water
- **2** tablespoons light mayonnaise dressing or salad dressing
- **2** tablespoons light dairy sour cream
- **1** tablespoon snipped fresh parsley
- **1** teaspoon lime juice or lemon juice
- **¼** to **½** teaspoon curry powder
- **1** to 2 drops bottled hot pepper sauce

Leaf lettuce (optional)
Tomato wedges (optional)
Cucumber strips (optional)

Rock lobsters have no claws,

so almost all of the meat is found in the tail. When buying frozen lobster tails, look for packages that are intact with no evidence of ice or juices. The meat should be free of dry or frosty areas.

Prep time: 20 minutes
Cooking time: 6 minutes
Chilling time: 2 hours

DIRECTIONS

1. Thaw lobster, if frozen. Rinse lobster; pat dry with paper towels. In a large saucepan bring the water to boiling. Add lobster tails; return to boiling. Reduce heat. Simmer, uncovered, for 6 to 10 minutes or until shells turn bright red and meat is opaque. Drain. Cover and chill for 2 to 24 hours.

2. For dressing, in a small mixing bowl stir together the mayonnaise dressing or salad dressing, sour cream, parsley, lime or lemon juice, curry powder, and hot pepper sauce. Cover and chill until serving time.

3. To serve, if desired, line 2 plates with leaf lettuce. Arrange the tomato wedges and cucumber strips on plates. Place lobster tails on a cutting surface, shell sides down. With kitchen shears, cut along both sides of the tail and remove the membrane to expose the meat. Cut meat lengthwise. Place 1 lobster tail on each plate. Serve with chilled dressing. Makes 2 servings.

194

NUTRITION FACTS PER SERVING:

155 calories
7 g total fat
2 g saturated fat
63 mg cholesterol
453 mg sodium
4 g carbohydrate
0 g fiber
18 g protein

INGREDIENTS

1   9-ounce package refrigerated spinach or plain fettuccine

12   ounces fresh or frozen bay or sea scallops

¾   cup reduced-sodium chicken broth

½   cup dry white wine

3   cloves garlic, minced

½   teaspoon dried oregano, crushed

½   teaspoon dried rosemary, crushed

¼   teaspoon cracked black pepper

4   teaspoons cornstarch

3   tablespoons snipped fresh parsley

scallops scampi-style

Shrimp scampi, listed on restaurant menus, is shrimp cooked in garlic, butter, white wine, and herbs. Our version of the popular dish features tender, sweet scallops.

Start to finish: 20 minutes

DIRECTIONS

1. Cook pasta according to package directions, omitting oil; drain. Keep warm.

2. Meanwhile, thaw scallops, if frozen. Halve or quarter any large scallops. Rinse scallops; pat dry with paper towels. In a large saucepan combine chicken broth, ¼ cup of the wine, the garlic, oregano, rosemary, and cracked pepper. Bring to boiling. Add scallops; return to boiling. Reduce heat. Simmer, covered, for 1 to 2 minutes or until scallops are opaque. Drain, reserving the cooking liquid. Return liquid to saucepan.

3. In a small bowl combine the remaining wine and the cornstarch. Add to the cooking liquid. Cook and stir until thickened and bubbly. Cook and stir for 2 minutes more. Stir in scallops and parsley; heat through. Serve scallop mixture over cooked pasta. Makes 4 servings.

Sea scallops can be quite large.

For this recipe, halve or quarter them. The meat of either type of scallop can be creamy white, tan, or creamy pink.

NUTRITION FACTS PER SERVING:

272 calories
2 g total fat
0 g saturated fat
72 mg cholesterol
223 mg sodium
40 g carbohydrate
0 g fiber
19 g protein

scallops and artichoke stir-fry

Accent this light-and-lemony stir-fry by serving it over couscous, a quick-cooking grain commonly used in North African cuisine. Look for couscous near the rice or pasta in your grocery store.

INGREDIENTS

12 ounces fresh or frozen bay or sea scallops
¾ cup water
3 tablespoons lemon juice
1 tablespoon cornstarch
1 teaspoon sugar
1 teaspoon instant chicken bouillon granules
⅛ teaspoon black pepper
1 8- or 9-ounce package frozen artichoke hearts
    Nonstick spray coating
2 medium green and/or red sweet peppers, cut into thin bite-size strips
2 cups sliced fresh shiitake, oyster, or brown mushrooms
1 tablespoon cooking oil
2 cups hot cooked couscous

Start to finish: 30 minutes

DIRECTIONS

1. Thaw scallops, if frozen. Halve any large scallops. Rinse scallops; pat dry with paper towels. Set aside.

2. For sauce, in a small bowl combine the water, lemon juice, cornstarch, sugar, bouillon granules, and black pepper. Set aside.

3. Place the artichokes in a colander. Run cold water over them until partially thawed. Halve any large pieces. Set artichokes aside.

4. Spray an unheated nonstick wok or large skillet with nonstick coating. Preheat over medium-high heat. Add the artichokes; stir-fry for 2 minutes. Add the sweet peppers and mushrooms; stir-fry for 2 to 4 minutes or until peppers are crisp-tender. Remove the vegetables from wok.

5. Add the oil to hot wok. Add the scallops; stir-fry about 2 minutes or until opaque. Push the scallops from center of wok.

6. Stir sauce; add to center of wok. Cook and stir until thickened and bubbly. Return the cooked vegetables to wok. Cook and stir about 2 minutes or until heated through. Serve immediately over hot cooked couscous. Makes 4 servings.

NUTRITION FACTS PER SERVING:

208 calories
5 g total fat
1 g saturated fat
26 mg cholesterol
409 mg sodium
28 g carbohydrate
8 g fiber
17 g protein

INGREDIENTS

- 8 ounces fresh or frozen sea scallops
- 8 cups torn fresh spinach
- 2 cups sliced fresh mushrooms
- 1 cup shredded carrots
- 4 slices bacon, cut into ½-inch pieces
- ½ teaspoon chili powder
- ⅛ to ¼ teaspoon ground red pepper
- ¼ to ⅓ cup chutney, snipped
- ¼ cup water
- 1 to 2 teaspoons Dijon-style mustard

seared scallop and spinach salad

Give an old favorite—bacon-spinach salad—a new lease on life by adding sea scallops to the usual lineup. The scallops are dusted with chili powder and red pepper before searing—a guaranteed wake-up call for eaters.

Start to finish: 30 minutes

DIRECTIONS

1. Thaw scallops, if frozen. Rinse scallops; pat dry with paper towels. Set aside. In a large bowl toss together the spinach, mushrooms, and carrots. Set aside.

2. In a large nonstick skillet cook bacon over medium heat until crisp. Drain bacon, reserving 1 tablespoon drippings in skillet.

3. In a bowl combine chili powder and red pepper. Add scallops; toss lightly to coat.

4. Cook the scallops in the reserved bacon drippings over medium heat for 2 to 3 minutes or until scallops are opaque. Remove scallops from skillet; set aside. Add the chutney, water, and mustard to skillet. Cook and stir over medium-high heat until bubbly. Spoon over the spinach mixture, tossing lightly to coat.

5. Divide spinach mixture among 4 plates. Top with the scallops. Sprinkle with the bacon. Makes 4 servings.

Select fresh shucked scallops

that are firm and free of excess cloudy liquid. Make sure they are sweet smelling. You may refrigerate them in their own liquid in a closed container for up to 2 days.

NUTRITION FACTS PER SERVING:

160 calories
4 g total fat
1 g saturated fat
22 mg cholesterol
324 mg sodium
19 g carbohydrate
5 g fiber
14 g protein

197

Succotash Soup & Dumplings
Recipe, page 222

soups

mexican beef stew

This savory country stew is a harmonious blend of robust beef and assorted vegetables—mild ancho peppers, squash, potatoes, tomatoes, and corn.

INGREDIENTS

- 12 ounces beef stew meat, cut into ¾-inch cubes
- 1 tablespoon cooking oil
- 2 cups water
- ½ teaspoon salt
- ¼ teaspoon black pepper
- 1 to 2 dried ancho peppers
- 2 cups chopped, peeled tomatoes (2 large) or one 14½-ounce can tomatoes, undrained and cut up
- 1 medium onion, cut up
- 2 cloves garlic, minced
- ¼ teaspoon ground cumin
- 2 medium potatoes, cut into 1-inch cubes
- 1 large fresh ear of corn, cut into 1-inch pieces, or 1 cup frozen whole kernel corn
- 1 medium zucchini or yellow summer squash, halved lengthwise and sliced 1 inch thick

---

Beef round steak or chuck roast are good cuts to use for stew meat. Remove and discard excess fat from the meat before cutting it into cubes.

Prep time: 20 minutes
Cooking time: 1⅔ hours

DIRECTIONS

1. In a large saucepan cook the meat in hot oil until browned. Drain off fat. Add the water, salt, and black pepper to saucepan. Bring to boiling; reduce heat. Simmer, covered, for 1 hour.

2. Meanwhile, cut dried peppers open; discard stems and seeds. Cut peppers into small pieces. Place in a small bowl; add enough boiling water to cover. Soak for 45 to 60 minutes or until softened. Drain well.

3. In a blender container or food processor bowl combine drained pepper pieces, the fresh or canned tomatoes, onion, garlic, and cumin. Cover and blend or process until nearly smooth. Stir into meat mixture in saucepan.

4. Stir in the potatoes and corn. Bring to boiling; reduce heat. Simmer, covered, for 30 minutes.

5. Stir in the zucchini or yellow squash. Cook about 10 minutes more or until meat and vegetables are tender. Makes 4 servings.

NUTRITION FACTS PER SERVING:

336 calories
14 g total fat
4 g saturated fat
63 mg cholesterol
340 mg sodium
33 g carbohydrate
5 g fiber
23 g protein

teriyaki beef soup

Cut up the beef and vegetables the evening before to get this soup on the table even faster. The next day, you'll be able to toss the whole meal together in the time it takes to cook the rice.

INGREDIENTS

- 8 ounces boneless beef sirloin steak
- 2 teaspoons olive oil
- 1 large shallot, sliced
- 4 cups water
- 1 cup unsweetened apple juice
- 2 carrots, julienned (see tip, page 78)
- ⅓ cup long grain rice
- 1 tablespoon grated fresh ginger
- 3 cloves garlic, minced
- 1 teaspoon instant beef bouillon granules
- 2 cups coarsely chopped broccoli
- 1 to 2 tablespoons reduced-sodium teriyaki sauce
- 1 tablespoon dry sherry (optional)

Start to finish: 40 minutes

DIRECTIONS

1. Trim fat from meat. Cut meat into bite-size strips. In a large saucepan heat olive oil over medium-high heat. Add the meat and shallot. Cook and stir for 2 to 3 minutes or until the meat is tender. Remove meat mixture with a slotted spoon. Set aside.

2. In the same saucepan combine the water, apple juice, carrots, uncooked rice, ginger, garlic, and bouillon granules. Bring to boiling; reduce heat. Simmer, covered, about 15 minutes or until the carrots are tender.

3. Stir in the broccoli and meat mixture. Simmer, covered, for 3 minutes. Stir in the teriyaki sauce and dry sherry (if desired). Makes 5 servings.

NUTRITION FACTS PER SERVING:

197 calories
6 g total fat
2 g saturated fat
30 mg cholesterol
382 mg sodium
22 g carbohydrate
2 g fiber
13 g protein

meatball soup

This meal in a bowl features mini-meatballs made with lean ground beef. It resembles a recipe called "wedding soup," which is found in some Italian restaurants in America.

INGREDIENTS

Nonstick spray coating
1 beaten egg
½ cup soft bread crumbs
2 tablespoons grated Parmesan or Romano cheese
1 tablespoon snipped fresh parsley
1 tablespoon finely chopped onion
¼ teaspoon garlic powder
⅛ teaspoon ground red pepper
8 ounces lean ground beef
2 cups water
1 15-ounce can garbanzo beans, rinsed and drained
1 14½-ounce can beef broth
1 14½-ounce can low-sodium stewed tomatoes
1 9-ounce package frozen Italian green beans
1 cup sliced fresh mushrooms
1½ teaspoons dried Italian seasoning, crushed
½ teaspoon fennel seed, crushed (optional)

There are so many types of mushrooms available, experiment with different varieties. It's usually easy to find the mild-flavored common white or brown mushrooms. For a richer, earthier flavor, try shiitakes, morels, or portobellos.

Start to finish: 45 minutes

DIRECTIONS

1. Spray a 2-quart square baking dish with nonstick coating. Set aside. In a medium bowl combine the egg, bread crumbs, Parmesan or Romano cheese, parsley, onion, garlic powder, and red pepper. Add the ground beef; mix well. Shape the mixture into 36 meatballs. Place the meatballs in prepared the baking dish.

2. Bake, uncovered, in a 375° oven for 15 to 20 minutes or until juices run clear. Drain well. Set the meatballs aside.

3. Meanwhile, in a large saucepan stir together water, garbanzo beans, beef broth, undrained tomatoes, Italian green beans, mushrooms, Italian seasoning, and fennel seed (if desired). Bring to boiling; reduce heat. Simmer, covered, for 10 minutes. Stir in meatballs. Heat through. Makes 6 servings.

NUTRITION FACTS PER SERVING:

211 calories
7 g total fat
3 g saturated fat
64 mg cholesterol
438 mg sodium
22 g carbohydrate
5 g fiber
16 g protein

INGREDIENTS

- 1 15-ounce can black beans, rinsed and drained
- 1 14½-ounce can beef broth
- 1¾ cups water
- 12 ounces cooked lean boneless pork, cut into bite-size strips
- 3 plantains, peeled and cubed
- 1 cup chopped tomatoes
- ½ of a 16-ounce package (2 cups) frozen pepper stir-fry vegetables (yellow, green, and red sweet peppers and onion)
- 1 tablespoon grated fresh ginger
- 1 teaspoon ground cumin
- ¼ teaspoon salt
- ¼ teaspoon crushed red pepper
- 3 cups hot cooked rice

Crushed red pepper (optional)

Fresh pineapple slices (optional)

caribbean-style pork stew

The flavor of a plantain depends on the ripeness. A ripe, black-skinned plantain tastes like a banana. The taste of an almost-ripe, yellow plantain resembles that of sweet potatoes. Unripe, green plantains taste starchy until cooked.

Start to finish: 30 minutes

DIRECTIONS

1. In a Dutch oven combine the beans, beef broth, and water. Bring to boiling.

2. Add the meat, plantains, and tomatoes to the bean mixture. Stir in the frozen vegetables, ginger, cumin, salt, and the ¼ teaspoon red pepper.

3. Return to boiling; reduce heat. Simmer, covered, about 10 minutes or until plantains are tender. Serve with hot cooked rice. If desired, sprinkle with additional crushed red pepper and garnish with pineapple slices. Makes 6 servings.

When you have the time (and to save time later) cook extra rice and save it. Place cooked rice in an airtight container and store it in the refrigerator for up to 1 week or in the freezer for up to 6 months.

NUTRITION FACTS PER SERVING:

425 calories
9 g total fat
3 g saturated fat
52 mg cholesterol
547 mg sodium
66 g carbohydrate
6 g fiber
26 g protein

lentil, barley, and ham soup

If you're watching your sodium intake, look for lower-sodium ham at your supermarket. It will reduce the sodium in each serving of this hearty soup by about 130 mg.

INGREDIENTS

- ½ cup dry lentils
- ¾ cup chopped onion
- ½ cup chopped celery
- 1 clove garlic, minced
- 2 tablespoons margarine or butter
- 5 cups water
- 1½ teaspoons snipped fresh oregano or ½ teaspoon dried oregano, crushed
- 1½ teaspoons snipped fresh basil or ½ teaspoon dried basil, crushed
- ¾ teaspoon snipped fresh rosemary or ¼ teaspoon dried rosemary, crushed
- ¼ teaspoon pepper
- 1½ cups diced reduced-fat and reduced-sodium cooked ham
- 1 cup thinly sliced carrots
- ½ cup quick-cooking barley
- 1 14½-ounce can tomatoes, undrained and cut up

Freeze or chill soup leftovers

and you'll have a quick meal for another day. (Don't freeze soups made with milk products.) To reheat soup, cook in a covered saucepan over medium heat, stirring often. Break up frozen soup during reheating.

Prep time: 25 minutes
Cooking time: 50 minutes

DIRECTIONS

1. Rinse and drain lentils; set aside. In a large saucepan cook the onion, celery, and garlic in hot margarine or butter until tender. Stir in the lentils, water, oregano, basil, rosemary, and pepper.

2. Bring to boiling; reduce heat. Simmer, covered, for 30 minutes. Stir in the ham, carrots, and uncooked barley.

Return to boiling; reduce heat. Simmer, covered, about 20 minutes more or just until carrots are tender. Stir in the tomatoes. Heat through. Makes 6 servings.

NUTRITION FACTS PER SERVING:

211 calories
6 g total fat
1 g saturated fat
16 mg cholesterol
602 mg sodium
28 g carbohydrate
3 g fiber
13 g protein

lamb and orzo soup with spinach

Orzo, also called rosamarina, is a tiny pasta shaped like long grains of rice. It's ideal for soups!

INGREDIENTS

- 2½ pounds lamb shanks
- 4 cups water
- 4 cups reduced-sodium chicken broth or vegetable broth
- 2 bay leaves
- 1 tablespoon snipped fresh oregano or 1 teaspoon dried oregano, crushed
- 1½ teaspoons snipped fresh marjoram or ½ teaspoon dried marjoram, crushed
- ½ teaspoon salt
- ¼ teaspoon pepper
- 2 carrots, julienned (see tip, page 78)
- 1 cup sliced celery
- ¾ cup orzo (rosamarina)
- 3 cups torn spinach or ½ of a 10-ounce package frozen chopped spinach, thawed and well drained

  Finely shredded Parmesan cheese (optional)

  Sliced pitted ripe olives (optional)

Prep time: 30 minutes
Cooking time: 1½ hours

DIRECTIONS

1. In a large Dutch oven combine the lamb shanks, water, chicken or vegetable broth, bay leaves, oregano, marjoram, salt, and pepper. Bring to boiling; reduce heat. Simmer, covered, for 1¼ to 1½ hours or until the meat is tender.

2. Remove the meat from broth; set aside to cool. Strain the broth through a large sieve or colander lined with 2 layers of 100% cotton cheesecloth; discard herbs. Skim fat from broth; return broth to Dutch oven. Cut the meat off bones and coarsely chop meat; discard bones.

3. Stir the chopped meat, carrots, celery, and orzo into the broth. Return to boiling; reduce heat. Simmer, covered, about 15 minutes or until vegetables and orzo are tender. Stir in the spinach. Cook for 1 to 2 minutes more or just until spinach wilts. If desired, serve with Parmesan cheese and ripe olives. Makes 6 servings.

Serve soups and stews at just the right temperature by heating the individual bowls or mugs. Just before serving, run the containers under hot tap water, then dry with a towel. The warm containers help the soup stay hot.

NUTRITION FACTS PER SERVING:

226 calories
5 g total fat
2 g saturated fat
59 mg cholesterol
544 mg sodium
20 g carbohydrate
1 g fiber
25 g protein

205

chicken stew with tortellini

This one-dish, healthful stew boasts an Italian flair. Just add a tossed green salad and Italian bread to complete the meal.

INGREDIENTS

- 1 14½-ounce can reduced-sodium chicken broth
- 2 cups water
- 6 cups torn beet or turnip greens or torn spinach
- 1½ cups sliced carrots
- 1 medium zucchini or yellow summer squash, halved lengthwise and cut into ½-inch slices
- 1 cup packaged dried cheese-filled tortellini
- 1 red or green sweet pepper, coarsely chopped
- 1 medium onion, cut into bite-size wedges
- 1 teaspoon dried basil, crushed
- ½ teaspoon salt-free seasoning blend
- ½ teaspoon dried oregano, crushed
- ¼ teaspoon black pepper
- 2 cups chopped cooked chicken
   Coarsely ground black pepper (optional)

When a recipe calls for cooked chicken, you can use a package of frozen chopped cooked chicken. Or, purchase a deli-roasted chicken. A cooked whole chicken will yield 1½ to 2 cups chopped meat. If you have more time, you can poach chicken. For 2 cups chopped cooked chicken, poach 12 ounces skinless, boneless chicken breasts for 12 to 14 minutes.

Start to finish: 45 minutes

DIRECTIONS

1. In a large kettle or Dutch oven combine the chicken broth and water. Bring to boiling. Stir in the greens or spinach, carrots, zucchini or yellow squash, tortellini, sweet pepper, onion, basil, seasoning blend, oregano, and the ¼ teaspoon black pepper. Reduce heat. Simmer, covered, about 15 minutes or until tortellini and vegetables are nearly tender.

2. Stir in cooked chicken. Cook, covered, about 5 minutes more or until tortellini and vegetables are tender. If desired, sprinkle with coarsely ground black pepper. Makes 6 servings.

NUTRITION FACTS PER SERVING:

234 calories
6 g total fat
1 g saturated fat
45 mg cholesterol
530 mg sodium
22 g carbohydrate
3 g fiber
22 g protein

INGREDIENTS

- 1 pound skinless, boneless chicken breast halves
- 6 cups chicken broth
- ½ cup chopped onion
- ½ cup chopped green sweet pepper
- 1 clove garlic, minced
- 1 tablespoon cooking oil
- 1 cup chopped tomato (1 large) or one 7½-ounce can tomatoes, undrained and cut up
- ¾ teaspoon dried oregano, crushed
- 1 teaspoon finely shredded lime peel
- 3 tablespoons lime juice
- 6 6-inch corn tortillas or 7-inch flour tortillas
- Nonstick spray coating
- Fresh habanero or jalapeño peppers, rinsed, seeded, and chopped (optional) (see tip, page 21)
- Thin lime slices (optional)

chicken and lime soup

This tangy, out-of-the-ordinary soup contains a generous amount of tender chicken, which contrasts well with the crisp tortilla strips.

Start to finish: 1¼ hours

DIRECTIONS

1. Rinse chicken; pat dry with paper towels. In a large Dutch oven bring chicken broth to boiling. Add the chicken; reduce heat.

Simmer, covered, about 15 minutes or until chicken is tender and no longer pink. Remove chicken from broth; set aside to cool. Shred the chicken. Set aside. Strain the broth through a large sieve or colander lined with 2 layers of 100% cotton cheesecloth. Set aside.

2. In the same Dutch oven cook the onion, sweet pepper, and garlic in hot oil until tender. Stir in the strained broth, tomatoes, and oregano. Bring to boiling. Stir in the lime peel and lime juice. Reduce heat. Simmer, covered, for 20 minutes. Stir in the shredded chicken. Heat through.

3. Meanwhile, cut the tortillas in half. Cut crosswise into ½-inch-wide strips. Spray the strips lightly with cooking spray. Arrange the strips in a single layer on a baking sheet. Bake in a 350° oven about 10 minutes or until lightly browned and crisp.

4. To serve, ladle soup into bowls. Top each serving with tortilla strips. If desired, garnish with habanero or jalapeño peppers and lime slices. Makes 6 servings.

NUTRITION FACTS PER SERVING:

220 calories
7 g total fat
1 g saturated fat
41 mg cholesterol
856 mg sodium
18 g carbohydrate
1 g fiber
22 g protein

chicken chili with rice

Tomatillos, sometimes referred to as Mexican green tomatoes, resemble small green tomatoes and often are used in Mexican cooking. They add a unique taste to salads, salsas, and this chunky soup.

INGREDIENTS

3 cloves garlic, minced

1 fresh jalapeño pepper, seeded and finely chopped (see tip, page 21)

1 tablespoon cooking oil

2 cups frozen small whole onions

1 cup reduced-sodium chicken broth or chicken broth

2 teaspoons chili powder

1 teaspoon ground cumin

1 teaspoon dried oregano, crushed

¼ teaspoon salt

⅛ teaspoon ground white pepper

⅛ teaspoon ground red pepper

1 19-ounce can white kidney (cannellini) beans, rinsed and drained

1 cup chopped cooked chicken

1 cup chopped fresh tomatillos

2 cups hot cooked rice or couscous

Start to finish: 35 minutes

DIRECTIONS

1. In a large saucepan cook the garlic and jalapeño pepper in hot oil for 30 seconds. Carefully stir in the onions, chicken broth, chili powder, cumin, oregano, salt, white pepper, and red pepper.

2. Bring to boiling; reduce heat. Simmer, covered, for 20 minutes. Add the beans, chicken, and tomatillos. Cook and stir until heated through. Serve the chicken mixture over rice. Makes 4 servings.

NUTRITION FACTS PER SERVING:

335 calories
8 g total fat
1 g saturated fat
34 mg cholesterol
417 mg sodium
51 g carbohydrate
8 g fiber
23 g protein

INGREDIENTS

- 2½ cups reduced-sodium chicken broth
- 2 small apples, chopped
- 2 medium carrots, chopped
- 1 cup water
- 1 7½-ounce can tomatoes, undrained and cut up
- 1 stalk celery, chopped
- ⅓ cup long grain rice
- ¼ cup chopped onion
- ¼ cup raisins

- 1 tablespoon snipped fresh parsley
- 1 to 1½ teaspoons curry powder
- 1 teaspoon lemon juice
- ¼ teaspoon coarsely ground pepper
- ⅛ teaspoon ground mace or nutmeg
- 1½ cups chopped cooked chicken or turkey

easy mulligatawny soup

Serve your guests a simplified version of the classic, curry-flavored Indian soup.

Prep time: 25 minutes
Cooking time: 20 minutes

DIRECTIONS

1. In a large saucepan combine the chicken broth, apples, carrots, water, tomatoes, celery, uncooked rice, onion, raisins, parsley, curry powder, lemon juice, pepper, and mace or nutmeg.

2. Bring to boiling; reduce heat. Simmer, covered, about 20 minutes or until rice is tender. Stir in the chicken or turkey; heat through. Makes 4 servings.

NUTRITION FACTS PER SERVING:

275 calories
6 g total fat
2 g saturated fat
51 mg cholesterol
439 mg sodium
34 g carbohydrate
4 g fiber
22 g protein

Keep soup garnishes simple. A

sprinkling of snipped fresh herbs or sliced green onions adds color to any soup, while croutons offer a little crunch. A slice of lemon, a little grated cheese, a few chopped nuts, sieved cooked egg white or yolk, or shredded radishes add complementary color to many soups.

chicken and dumplings

You won't have to forego Mom's chicken and dumplings again. Skinning the chicken before you cook it keeps the calories and fat in check, making it kinder to your waistline.

INGREDIENTS

- 4 **chicken thighs (about 1½ pounds total), skinned**
- 2½ **cups water**
- 1 **cup sliced carrots**
- 1 **cup sliced celery**
- ½ **cup chopped onion**
- 2 **teaspoons instant chicken bouillon granules**
- ¾ **teaspoon snipped fresh sage or ¼ teaspoon dried sage, crushed**
- 2 **tablespoons cold water**
- 4 **teaspoons cornstarch**
- 1 **recipe Dumplings**

Prep time: 30 minutes
Cooking time: 45 minutes

DIRECTIONS

1. Rinse chicken; pat dry with paper towels. In a large saucepan combine chicken, the 2½ cups water, the carrots, celery, onion, bouillon granules, and sage. Bring to boiling; reduce heat. Simmer, covered, for 35 minutes.

2. Remove chicken from saucepan; set aside. Skim fat from broth.

3. Stir together the 2 tablespoons cold water and the cornstarch. Stir into broth in saucepan. Cook and stir until thickened and bubbly. Return chicken to saucepan.

4. Meanwhile, prepare the Dumplings. Drop the dumpling mixture from a tablespoon into 8 mounds directly on top of the bubbling chicken mixture. Cover tightly and simmer about 10 minutes (do not lift cover) or until a wooden toothpick inserted in a dumpling comes out clean. To serve, ladle the chicken mixture and dumplings into bowls. Makes 4 servings.

Dumplings: In a medium mixing bowl stir together 1 cup all-purpose flour, 1 tablespoon snipped fresh parsley, 2 teaspoons baking powder, and ⅛ teaspoon salt. In a small bowl combine 1 beaten egg, ¼ cup fat-free milk, and 2 tablespoons cooking oil. Stir egg mixture into the flour mixture with a fork just until moistened.

NUTRITION FACTS PER SERVING:

341 calories
14 g total fat
3 g saturated fat
103 mg cholesterol
808 mg sodium
33 g carbohydrate
3 g fiber
20 g protein

chipotle chile pepper soup

If you've never tried chipotle (chih-POHT-lay) peppers, here's your chance. As well as adding the heat, these peppers add a pleasant smoked flavor to this cilantro-seasoned chicken soup.

INGREDIENTS

1 large onion, finely chopped
4 cloves garlic, minced
1 tablespoon olive oil or cooking oil
12 ounces skinless, boneless chicken breast halves, cut into bite-size pieces
1 14½-ounce can chicken broth
2 teaspoons chopped canned chipotle peppers in adobo sauce
½ teaspoon sugar
¼ teaspoon salt
2 cups chopped tomatoes or one 14½-ounce can low-sodium diced tomatoes
¼ cup snipped fresh cilantro

The sugar cuts
the sharpness of the tomatoes, giving a mellow, rich flavor to the soup without adding noticeable sweetness.

Start to finish: 35 minutes

DIRECTIONS

1. In a Dutch oven cook the onion and garlic in hot oil over medium-high heat about 4 minutes or until onion is tender. Add the chicken. Cook and stir for 2 minutes. Stir in chicken broth, chipotle peppers, sugar, and salt.

2. Bring to boiling; reduce heat. Simmer, uncovered, for 15 minutes. Remove from heat. Stir in tomatoes and cilantro. Makes 3 servings.

NUTRITION FACTS PER SERVING:

246 calories
9 g total fat
2 g saturated fat
60 mg cholesterol
735 mg sodium
14 g carbohydrate
3 g fiber
26 g protein

211

italian fish soup

In Italy, there are as many versions of *zuppa di pesce*, or fish soup, as there are coastal towns. Serve fish soup as the Italians do—with a slice of toasted Italian bread.

INGREDIENTS

- 8 ounces fresh or frozen haddock, bass, sole, or other fish fillets
- 6 ounces fresh or frozen, peeled and deveined shrimp
- 3 cups water
- 2 medium tomatoes, peeled and cut up
- 1 cup thinly sliced carrots (2 medium)
- ½ cup dry white wine or water
- ½ cup chopped celery (2 stalks)
- ⅓ cup chopped onion
- 2 teaspoons instant chicken bouillon granules
- 2 cloves garlic, minced
- 2 bay leaves
- ½ teaspoon dried marjoram, crushed
- ½ teaspoon finely shredded orange peel
  Dash bottled hot pepper sauce
- ¼ cup tomato paste
- 4 slices Italian bread, toasted

Adding wine to soup

often enhances its flavor. A dry white table wine adds zest to fish soup, crab or lobster bisque, or creamy chowder. A strongly flavored soup with beef benefits from a tablespoon of dry red table wine. And sherry or Madeira blends well with veal or chicken soup.

Prep time: 25 minutes
Cooking time: 18 minutes

DIRECTIONS

1. Thaw the fish fillets and shrimp, if frozen. Cut the fish into 1-inch pieces; halve the shrimp lengthwise. Rinse the fish and shrimp; pat dry with paper towels. Chill until needed.

2. In a large saucepan combine the 3 cups water, the tomatoes, carrots, wine or water, celery, onion, bouillon granules, garlic, bay leaves, marjoram, orange peel, and hot pepper sauce. Bring to boiling; reduce heat. Simmer, covered, for 15 to 20 minutes or until vegetables are nearly tender. Stir in tomato paste.

3. Stir the fish and shrimp into the tomato mixture. Bring mixture just to boiling; reduce heat. Simmer, covered, for 3 to 5 minutes more or just until fish begins to flake easily with a fork and shrimp are opaque. Discard bay leaves.

4. To serve, place a slice of bread in each of 4 soup bowls. Ladle soup into bowls. Makes 4 servings.

NUTRITION FACTS PER SERVING:

252 calories
3 g total fat
0 g saturated fat
96 mg cholesterol
780 mg sodium
30 g carbohydrate
5 g fiber
24 g protein

INGREDIENTS

8	ounces fresh or frozen fish fillets
2	cups water
2	cups frozen mixed vegetables
1	14½-ounce can tomatoes, undrained and cut up
1	cup thinly sliced celery
¾	cup chopped onion
4	teaspoons snipped fresh oregano or 1 teaspoon dried oregano, crushed
1½	teaspoons instant chicken bouillon granules
1	clove garlic, minced
	Several dashes bottled hot pepper sauce

vegetable-fish soup

Serve this flavorful vegetable-filled soup in just 30 minutes. Watch the soup carefully once you add the fish. Cook it just until it begins to flake easily when tested with a fork. Overcooked fish will be tough and chewy.

Start to finish: 30 minutes

DIRECTIONS

1. Thaw fish, if frozen. Rinse fish; pat dry with paper towels. Cut the fish into 1-inch pieces. Set aside.

2. In a large saucepan combine the water, frozen vegetables, tomatoes, celery, onion, dried oregano (if using), bouillon granules, garlic, and hot pepper sauce. Bring to boiling; reduce heat. Simmer, covered, about 10 minutes or until vegetables are tender.

3. Stir in the fish and fresh oregano (if using). Return just to boiling; reduce heat. Simmer gently, covered, for 3 to 5 minutes or just until the fish begins to flake easily with a fork. Makes 4 servings.

Check out your grocer's freezer case for vegetable combos. You'll find a huge selection of frozen mixtures in all types and colors. In addition, frozen vegetables are quick, easy to prepare, and packed with as much or more nutrition than fresh vegetables.

NUTRITION FACTS PER SERVING:

166 calories
2 g total fat
0 g saturated fat
27 mg cholesterol
623 mg sodium
23 g carbohydrate
4 g fiber
15 g protein

213

gingered shrimp soup

Rice wine, ginger, and tofu mark the Asian influence on this soup. Follow it up with a scoop of lemon sherbet for a light, yet satisfying meal.

INGREDIENTS

- 8 ounces fresh or frozen, peeled and deveined shrimp
- 3 cups reduced-sodium chicken broth
- 1½ cups water
- ¼ cup rice wine or dry sherry
- 1 tablespoon reduced-sodium soy sauce
- 2 cloves garlic, minced
- 1 teaspoon grated fresh ginger
- ½ teaspoon toasted sesame oil
- ¼ teaspoon pepper
- 4 ounces firm tofu (fresh bean curd), cubed
- 1 cup fresh pea pods, halved crosswise, or ½ of a 6-ounce package frozen pea pods, halved crosswise
- ¾ cup thinly bias-sliced carrots
- ¼ cup thinly sliced green onions

Shrimp are sold by the pound.

The price per pound usually is determined by the size of the shrimp—the bigger the shrimp, the higher the price and the fewer per pound.

Start to finish: 35 minutes

DIRECTIONS

1. Thaw shrimp, if frozen. Halve shrimp lengthwise. Rinse shrimp; pat dry with paper towels. Set aside.

2. In a large saucepan combine the broth, water, rice wine or sherry, soy sauce, garlic, ginger, sesame oil, and pepper. Bring to boiling.

3. Stir in the shrimp, tofu, fresh pea pods (if using), carrots, and green onions. Return to boiling; reduce heat. Simmer, covered, for 1 to 3 minutes or until shrimp turn opaque. Stir in frozen pea pods (if using); heat through. Makes 4 servings.

NUTRITION FACTS PER SERVING:

155 calories
4 g total fat
1 g saturated fat
87 mg cholesterol
736 mg sodium
9 g carbohydrate
2 g fiber
17 g protein

INGREDIENTS

- 8 medium ripe tomatoes, peeled, if desired, and chopped (about 2½ pounds total)
- 1 medium cucumber, chopped
- 1 medium green or red sweet pepper, seeded and chopped
- ¾ cup low-sodium vegetable juice or low-sodium tomato juice
- ½ cup clam juice
- ¼ cup chopped onion
- 3 tablespoons red wine vinegar
- 2 tablespoons snipped fresh cilantro
- 2 tablespoons olive oil
- 1 clove garlic, minced
- ¼ teaspoon ground cumin
- 1 8-ounce package frozen, peeled, cooked small shrimp, thawed
- Fat-free dairy sour cream (optional)

shrimp gazpacho

Gazpacho—a Spanish soup with tomatoes and onions—traditionally is served cold. We've made this gazpacho into a complete meal by adding succulent shrimp for a zingy thrill of a chill.

Prep time: 35 minutes
Chilling time: 4 hours

DIRECTIONS

1. In a large bowl combine the tomatoes, cucumber, sweet pepper, vegetable or tomato juice, clam juice, onion, vinegar, cilantro, olive oil, garlic, and cumin. Gently fold the shrimp into the tomato mixture.

2. Cover and chill for 4 to 24 hours to allow flavors to blend. To serve, ladle soup into bowls. If desired, top each with a spoonful of sour cream. Makes 6 servings.

Cholesterol is something shrimp have a lot of; but they have some great attributes—they're low in fat, saturated fat, and calories. So go ahead and satisfy your craving—just watch your total cholesterol intake from all foods.

NUTRITION FACTS PER SERVING:

141 calories
6 g total fat
1 g saturated fat
74 mg cholesterol
154 mg sodium
15 g carbohydrate
4 g fiber
11 g protein

clam chowder

This lightened version of clam chowder saves you about 220 calories and 18 grams of fat per serving over a traditional recipe made with cream.

INGREDIENTS

2	6½-ounce cans minced clams
1½	cups cubed potatoes
½	cup chopped onion
½	cup chopped celery
1	tablespoon snipped fresh thyme or ½ teaspoon dried thyme, crushed
2½	cups fat-free milk
4	teaspoons cornstarch
⅓	cup shredded carrot
1	teaspoon instant chicken bouillon granules
2	slices turkey bacon, cooked and chopped (optional)
	Fresh thyme (optional)

To make a dish more nutritious,

omit peeling many vegetables and fruits, such as potatoes, carrots, apples, and nectarines. Not only will the dish be faster and easier to prepare, but you'll also increase its fiber content.

Start to finish: 35 minutes

DIRECTIONS

1. Drain clams, reserving liquid. Set clams aside. Add enough water to clam liquid to equal 1 cup liquid. In a 2-quart saucepan combine the clam liquid, potatoes, onion, celery, and snipped or dried thyme. Bring to boiling; reduce heat. Simmer, covered, about 10 minutes or until potatoes are just tender.

2. Meanwhile, gradually stir about ¼ cup of the milk into cornstarch. Add to mixture in saucepan along with the remaining milk, the carrot, and bouillon granules.

3. Cook and stir over medium heat until slightly thickened and bubbly. Reduce heat. Cook and stir for 2 minutes more. Stir in the drained clams. Heat through. To serve, ladle soup into bowls. If desired, garnish with cooked turkey bacon and additional fresh thyme. Makes 4 servings.

NUTRITION FACTS PER SERVING:

169 calories
2 g total fat
0 g saturated fat
60 mg cholesterol
364 mg sodium
27 g carbohydrate
2 g fiber
14 g protein

make-ahead minestrone

You can serve this meatless soup immediately, but chilling the soup allows the flavors to blend. If you like, serve it country-style over thick slices of toasted Italian bread.

INGREDIENTS

- 3   14½-ounce cans beef broth
- 1   15½-ounce can red kidney beans, rinsed and drained
- 1   15-ounce can garbanzo beans, rinsed and drained
- 1   14½-ounce can low-sodium stewed tomatoes
- 1   11½-ounce can vegetable juice
- 1   6-ounce can low-sodium tomato paste
- 2   teaspoons sugar
- 1   teaspoon dried Italian seasoning, crushed
- 1½ cups loose-pack frozen mixed vegetables (such as an Italian blend)
- 2   cups fresh spinach leaves, cut into strips
- 2   cups cooked pasta (1 cup uncooked), such as small shells or mostaccioli
     Finely shredded Parmesan cheese (optional)

Prep time: 15 minutes
Cooking time: 10 minutes
Chilling time: 6 hours

DIRECTIONS

1. In a large kettle combine the beef broth, beans, stewed tomatoes, vegetable juice, tomato paste, sugar, and Italian seasoning. Bring to boiling. Stir in the mixed vegetables. Reduce heat. Simmer, covered, about 10 minutes or until vegetables are tender. Remove from heat; cool. Cover and refrigerate for 6 to 24 hours. (Or, to serve immediately, stir in the spinach and cooked pasta. Heat through.)

2. To serve, reheat the soup over medium heat. Stir in the spinach and cooked pasta. Heat through. To serve, ladle soup into bowls. If desired, sprinkle with Parmesan cheese. Makes 8 servings.

NUTRITION FACTS PER SERVING:

214 calories
2 g total fat
0 g saturated fat
0 mg cholesterol
975 mg sodium
41 g carbohydrate
9 g fiber
12 g protein

If you're concerned about your sodium intake, use two 15½-ounce cans reduced-sodium dark red kidney beans in place of the regular kidney beans and garbanzo beans, and 1½ cups of no salt added vegetable juice in place of the 11½-ounce can of vegetable juice.

cheesy vegetable chowder

Gruyère cheese is known for its rich, sweet, nutty flavor. We recommend aged Gruyère, which usually is produced in France. Processed Gruyère just can't compare in flavor with the aged variety.

INGREDIENTS

- 2 cups vegetable broth
- 2 cups cubed potatoes
- ¾ cup chopped onion
- ½ cup chopped celery
- 1 tablespoon snipped fresh thyme or ½ teaspoon dried thyme, crushed
- ⅛ teaspoon black pepper
- 2 cups cut fresh corn or frozen whole kernel corn
- 2 cups chopped cabbage
- ¼ cup chopped green sweet pepper
- 2 cups fat-free milk
- 2 tablespoons all-purpose flour
- 1 cup shredded Gruyère or Swiss cheese (4 ounces)
- Fresh thyme (optional)

When a recipe calls for vegetable broth, you can use canned broth, bouillon granules, or prepare a homemade stock. An easy way to make your own stock is to keep saving the water in which vegetables are boiled. Freeze the liquid in a covered container, and in time you'll have a basic stock that's ready to use.

218

Start to finish: 40 minutes

DIRECTIONS

1. In a large saucepan combine the vegetable broth, potatoes, onion, celery, snipped or dried thyme, and black pepper. Bring to boiling; reduce heat. Simmer, covered, for 10 minutes. Stir in the corn, cabbage, and sweet pepper. Cook, covered, about 5 minutes more or until the potatoes and corn are just tender, stirring occasionally.

2. Meanwhile, in a screw-top jar combine ½ cup of the milk and the flour. Shake well. Add to the potato mixture in the saucepan along with the remaining milk. Cook and stir until thickened and bubbly. Cook and stir for 1 minute more. Remove from heat.

3. Add the Gruyère or Swiss cheese to the potato mixture, stirring until melted. To serve, ladle soup into bowls. If desired, garnish with additional fresh thyme. Makes 5 servings.

NUTRITION FACTS PER SERVING:

288 calories
9 g total fat
5 g saturated fat
26 mg cholesterol
512 mg sodium
41 g carbohydrate
6 g fiber
15 g protein

INGREDIENTS

- ½ cup dry baby lima beans or garbanzo beans
- ½ cup dry pinto beans or kidney beans
- ½ cup dry navy beans or great northern beans
- 4 cups cold water
- 1 cup chopped celery
- 1 cup chopped onion
- 1 cup chopped carrot
- 3 cloves garlic, minced
- 1 tablespoon olive oil or cooking oil
- 3 cups water
- 1 14½-ounce can vegetable broth
- 1 teaspoon dried thyme, crushed
- ½ teaspoon dried marjoram, crushed
- ¼ teaspoon pepper
- 1 14½-ounce can diced tomatoes
- 1½ cups low-sodium vegetable juice
- Fresh marjoram (optional)

mixed bean soup

If you don't want to store extra beans, buy a package of mixed dried beans instead of the three different kinds. Prepare the recipe as directed using 1½ cups of the bean mix.

Prep time: 40 minutes
Standing time: 1 hour
Cooking time: 1¼ hours

DIRECTIONS

1. Rinse beans; transfer to a 4-quart Dutch oven. Add the 4 cups water. Bring to boiling; reduce heat. Simmer, uncovered, for 2 minutes; remove from heat. Cover and let stand for 1 hour. (Or, omit simmering; in a covered Dutch oven soak beans in cold water overnight.) Drain and rinse beans in a colander.

2. In the same Dutch oven cook the celery, onion, carrot, and garlic in the hot oil until tender, stirring once or twice. Add the beans. Stir in the 3 cups water, the vegetable broth, thyme, dried marjoram, and pepper.

3. Bring to boiling; reduce heat. Simmer, covered, for 1¼ to 1½ hours or until beans are tender. Stir in the undrained tomatoes and the vegetable juice. Heat through. To serve, ladle the soup into bowls. If desired, garnish with fresh marjoram. Makes 5 servings.

Fat-smart cooks

know to look for recipes that are full of beans. Unlike other high-protein sources, such as meat and cheese, beans contain almost no saturated fat and no cholesterol. In addition, they're high in fiber.

NUTRITION FACTS PER SERVING:

267 calories
4 g total fat
1 g saturated fat
0 mg cholesterol
594 mg sodium
49 g carbohydrate
5 g fiber
14 g protein

spring vegetable soup

This Italian-style soup plays up asparagus, fava beans, peas, and young artichokes, with a hint of flavor from fresh fennel and pancetta.

INGREDIENTS

- 12 baby artichokes
- 6 cups chicken broth or reduced-sodium chicken broth
- 1 cup small boiling onions, peeled and halved, or pearl onions
- 4 ounces pancetta (Italian bacon) or 5 slices bacon, crisp-cooked, drained, and cut into small pieces
- 1 teaspoon fennel seed, crushed
- ¼ teaspoon pepper
- 2 cups cooked or canned fava or lima beans, rinsed and drained
- 12 ounces asparagus spears, trimmed and cut into 1-inch pieces
- 1 medium fennel bulb, chopped
  Fresh fennel leaves

To cook fresh or frozen fava or lima beans,

simmer, covered, in a small amount of boiling water for 15 to 25 minutes or until tender. Drain and cool slightly. When cool, remove skins from fava beans. For 2 cups of cooked fava beans, purchase 2 pounds of fava beans in the pod.

Prep time: 30 minutes
Cooking time: 20 minutes

DIRECTIONS

1. Remove the tough outer green leaves from artichokes (inside leaves will be more tender and greenish yellow). Snip off about 1 inch from the leaf tops, cutting where the green meets the yellow. Trim the stems. Quarter artichokes lengthwise; set aside.

2. In a 4-quart Dutch oven combine the chicken broth, onions, pancetta or bacon, fennel seed, and pepper. Bring to boiling; reduce heat. Simmer, covered, for 10 minutes. Stir in the artichokes and beans. Cook for 5 minutes. Stir in the asparagus and chopped fennel. Cook about 5 minutes more or until the vegetables are tender.

3. To serve, ladle the soup into bowls. Garnish each serving with fennel leaves. Makes 4 servings.

NUTRITION FACTS PER SERVING:

152 calories
3 g total fat
1 g saturated fat
4 mg cholesterol
695 mg sodium
21 g carbohydrate
6 g fiber
11 g protein

INGREDIENTS

1   15½-ounce can red kidney beans,
    rinsed and drained
1   15-ounce can great northern
    beans, rinsed and drained
1   14½-ounce can low-sodium
    tomatoes, undrained and
    cut up
1   8-ounce can low-sodium
    tomato sauce
1   cup water
¾   cup chopped green sweet pepper
½   cup chopped onion
1   tablespoon chili powder
2   cloves garlic, minced

1   teaspoon sugar
1   teaspoon snipped fresh basil or
    ½ teaspoon dried basil,
    crushed
½   teaspoon ground cumin
¼   teaspoon salt
    Dash ground red pepper
2   cups hot cooked rice

vegetarian chili with rice

Brighten a rainy day with cumin-scented bowls of chili. Mix up a batch of corn bread to serve with this colorful chili.

Prep time: 20 minutes
Cooking time: 15 minutes

NUTRITION FACTS PER SERVING:

377 calories
2 g total fat
0 g saturated fat
0 mg cholesterol
365 mg sodium
77 g carbohydrate
9 g fiber
20 g protein

DIRECTIONS

1. In a large saucepan combine beans, tomatoes, tomato sauce, water, sweet pepper, onion, chili powder, garlic, sugar, basil, cumin, salt, and red pepper. Bring to boiling; reduce heat. Simmer, covered, for 15 minutes, stirring occasionally.

2. Ladle chili into bowls. Top with cooked rice. Makes 4 servings.

succotash soup and dumplings

To cut fresh corn from the cob, hold each ear of corn so an end rests on a cutting board. Then, with a sharp knife, cut down the ear from top to bottom, cutting through the base of each kernel. (Recipe also pictured on pages 198–199)

INGREDIENTS

- **3** **cups water**
- **2** **cups cut fresh corn or one 10-ounce package frozen whole kernel corn**
- **1** **cup frozen lima beans**
- **½** **cup chopped celery**
- **½** **cup sliced carrot**
- **½** **cup chopped onion**
- **1** **tablespoon snipped fresh dill or ½ teaspoon dried dillweed**
- **2** **teaspoons instant vegetable bouillon granules**
- **1** **recipe Cornmeal Dumplings**
- **⅓** **cup packaged instant mashed potato flakes**

Start to finish: 45 minutes

DIRECTIONS

1. In a large saucepan combine the 3 cups water, the corn, lima beans, celery, carrot, onion, dill, and bouillon granules. Bring to boiling; reduce heat. Simmer, covered, for 8 to 10 minutes or until the vegetables are almost tender.

2. Meanwhile, prepare Cornmeal Dumplings. Set aside. Stir potato flakes into the soup. Cook and stir until slightly thickened and bubbly.

3. Drop the dumpling mixture from a tablespoon into 8 mounds directly on top of the bubbling soup. Cover tightly and simmer for 10 to 12 minutes (do not lift cover) or until a wooden toothpick inserted in a dumpling comes out clean. To serve, ladle soup and dumplings into bowls. Makes 4 servings.

Cornmeal Dumplings: In a medium saucepan combine 1 cup water, ⅓ cup yellow cornmeal, ¼ teaspoon salt, and dash pepper. Cook and stir until thickened and bubbly. Remove from heat; cool slightly. Add 1 beaten egg, beating until smooth. In a small bowl stir together ⅔ cup all-purpose flour, 1 tablespoon grated Parmesan cheese, 1 tablespoon snipped fresh parsley, and 1 teaspoon baking powder. Stir into the cornmeal mixture with a fork just until moistened.

NUTRITION FACTS PER SERVING:

279 calories
3 g total fat
1 g saturated fat
55 mg cholesterol
765 mg sodium
55 g carbohydrate
4 g fiber
11 g protein

INGREDIENTS

- 1 cup dry lentils
- ½ cup chopped onion
- 1½ to 2 teaspoons curry powder
- 2 teaspoons cooking oil
- 2½ cups water
- 2 cups cubed peeled rutabagas or turnips
- 1 cup sliced carrots
- ¼ teaspoon salt
- ⅛ teaspoon pepper
- 1 9-ounce package frozen cut green beans
- 3 cups vegetable juice

curried lentil stew

High in protein and fiber, lentils give an enticing earthy vegetable flavor to all types of soups and stews. Look for lentils near the dried beans in your supermarket.

Start to finish: 45 minutes

DIRECTIONS

1. Rinse and drain lentils; set aside. In a large saucepan cook onion and curry powder in hot oil for 3 minutes, stirring occasionally. Add the lentils, water, rutabagas or turnips, carrots, salt, and pepper. Bring to boiling; reduce heat. Simmer, covered, for 15 to 20 minutes or until vegetables and lentils are almost tender.

2. Stir the frozen green beans into the lentil mixture. Return to boiling; reduce heat. Simmer, covered, for 6 to 8 minutes more or until the vegetables and lentils are tender. Stir in the vegetable juice. Heat through. Makes 6 servings.

NUTRITION FACTS PER SERVING:

- 106 calories
- 2 g total fat
- 0 g saturated fat
- 0 mg cholesterol
- 566 mg sodium
- 24 g carbohydrate
- 4 g fiber
- 5 g protein

223

Roasted Sweet Pepper Salad
Recipe, page 240

sides

zucchini alla romana

For best results, select zucchini that are small, firm, and free of cuts and soft spots. Pass over large zucchini. They tend to have tough skins and lots of seeds. If you're lucky enough to find baby squash, use them instead.

INGREDIENTS

- 2 cloves garlic
- 2 teaspoons olive oil
- 4 cups sliced zucchini (4 to 5 small)
- 1 teaspoon dried mint or basil, crushed, or 1 tablespoon snipped fresh mint or basil
- ¼ teaspoon salt
  Dash pepper
- 2 tablespoons finely shredded Parmesan or Romano cheese

When storing herbs by the bunch, place them in a loose-fitting bag in the crisper drawer of your refrigerator. Or trim the stem ends and place themv in a tall container of water, immersing the stems about 2 inches. Cover the leaves loosely with a plastic bag and refrigerate.

Prep time: 8 minutes
Cooking time: 5 minutes

DIRECTIONS

1. In a large skillet cook the whole garlic cloves in hot oil until lightly browned; discard garlic. Add the zucchini, dried mint or basil (if using), salt, and pepper to the oil in the skillet.

2. Cook, uncovered, over medium heat about 5 minutes or until the zucchini is crisp-tender, stirring occasionally. To serve, sprinkle with the Parmesan cheese and fresh mint or basil (if using). Makes 6 servings.

NUTRITION FACTS PER SERVING:

35 calories
2 g total fat
1 g saturated fat
2 mg cholesterol
130 mg sodium
3 g carbohydrate
1 g fiber
2 g protein

INGREDIENTS

- 1 pound broccoli, cut into flowerets
- 1 red or yellow sweet pepper, cut into 1-inch pieces
- 2 tablespoons reduced-calorie margarine
- 1 teaspoon finely shredded lemon peel
- 1 tablespoon lemon juice
- ⅛ teaspoon black pepper

broccoli and peppers

If you don't have a steamer basket, improvise with a metal colander to prepare this dish.

Prep time: 10 minutes
Cooking time: 8 minutes

DIRECTIONS

1. Place broccoli and sweet pepper in a steamer basket over simmering water. Steam, covered, for 8 to 12 minutes or until vegetables are crisp-tender. Arrange vegetables on a serving platter.

2. Meanwhile, in a small saucepan melt the margarine. Stir in the lemon peel, lemon juice, and black pepper. Drizzle over the vegetables. Makes 6 servings.

NUTRITION FACTS PER SERVING:

42 calories
2 g total fat
0 g saturated fat
0 mg cholesterol
63 mg sodium
5 g carbohydrate
3 g fiber
2 g protein

lemony asparagus and new potatoes

With spring comes fresh asparagus and new potatoes. This recipe showcases both in a healthful side dish with a snippet of lemon and thyme.

INGREDIENTS

- 12 ounces asparagus spears
- 8 whole tiny new potatoes, cut into quarters (about 10 ounces)
- 2 teaspoons olive oil or cooking oil
- ½ teaspoon finely shredded lemon peel
- ¼ teaspoon salt
- ¼ teaspoon dried thyme, crushed
  Fresh thyme (optional)

Prep time: 10 minutes
Cooking time: 18 minutes

DIRECTIONS

1. Snap off and discard the woody bases from asparagus. If desired, scrape off the scales. Cut into 2-inch pieces. Set aside.

2. In a 2-quart covered saucepan cook the potatoes in a small amount of boiling water for 10 minutes. Add the asparagus. Cook, covered, about 8 minutes more or until the asparagus is crisp-tender and the potatoes are tender. Drain. Transfer the vegetables to a serving bowl.

3. Meanwhile, in a small bowl combine the oil, lemon peel, salt, and dried thyme. Pour over the vegetables, tossing gently to coat. If desired, garnish with fresh thyme. Makes 4 servings.

NUTRITION FACTS PER SERVING:

105 calories
3 g total fat
0 g saturated fat
0 mg cholesterol
141 mg sodium
19 g carbohydrate
2 g fiber
3 g protein

INGREDIENTS

- 2 **fennel bulbs with leaves**
- ½ **cup apple juice or apple cider**
- ¼ **cup cider vinegar**
- 1 **teaspoon instant chicken bouillon granules**
- 3 **cloves garlic, minced**
- 1 **tablespoon cooking oil**
- 1 **10-ounce package shredded red cabbage (about 4 cups)**
- 2 **tablespoons brown sugar**
- ¼ **teaspoon fennel seed, crushed**

red cabbage with fennel

Fennel's feathery green leaves look like fresh dill but have a delicate anise flavor.

Start to finish: 30 minutes

DIRECTIONS

1. Remove upper stalks from fennel, including feathery leaves; reserve leaves and discard stalks. Discard any wilted outer layers on fennel bulbs; cut off a thin slice from each base. Wash fennel and pat dry. Quarter each fennel bulb lengthwise. Chop enough of the reserved fennel leaves to make 2 teaspoons; set aside along with a few sprigs of the feathery leaves.

2. In a small bowl combine the apple juice or cider and vinegar. In a medium saucepan combine the fennel wedges, ½ cup of the apple juice mixture, the bouillon granules, and garlic. Bring to boiling; reduce heat. Simmer, covered, for 14 to 16 minutes or until the fennel is tender.

3. Meanwhile, pour oil into a large skillet or wok. Preheat over medium-high heat. Add the cabbage; stir-fry for 3 to 5 minutes or until cabbage is crisp-tender. Combine the remaining apple juice mixture and the brown sugar; stir into cabbage along with the fennel seed. Cook and stir about 1 minute more or until heated through.

4. Transfer the cabbage to a serving platter. Remove the fennel wedges from the liquid with a slotted spoon. Place on top of cabbage. Garnish with the reserved chopped fennel leaves and the reserved sprigs. Makes 4 to 6 servings.

NUTRITION FACTS PER SERVING:

107 calories
4 g total fat
1 g saturated fat
0 mg cholesterol
258 mg sodium
19 g carbohydrate
13 g fiber
2 g protein

229

roasted veggies with balsamic vinegar

Roasting brings out the natural sweetness of vegetables. These earthy and elegant roasted green beans and summer squash balance just about any entrée—steaks, chicken, pork chops, or salmon.

INGREDIENTS

8 ounces green beans, ends trimmed
1 small onion, cut into thin wedges
1 clove garlic, minced
1 tablespoon olive oil
Dash salt
Dash pepper
2 medium yellow summer squash, halved lengthwise and sliced ¼ inch thick
⅓ cup balsamic vinegar

Start to finish: 25 minutes

DIRECTIONS

1. In a shallow roasting pan combine the green beans, onion, and garlic. Drizzle with the olive oil; sprinkle with salt and pepper. Toss the mixture until the vegetables are evenly coated. Spread into a single layer.

2. Roast in a 450° oven for 8 minutes. Stir in the squash. Roast for 5 to 7 minutes more or until vegetables are tender and slightly browned.

3. Meanwhile, in a small saucepan bring the balsamic vinegar to boiling over medium-high heat; reduce heat. Boil gently about 5 minutes or until the vinegar is reduced by half (the vinegar will thicken slightly).

4. Drizzle the vinegar over roasted vegetables; toss until vegetables are evenly coated. Makes 4 to 6 servings.

NUTRITION FACTS PER SERVING:

81 calories
4 g total fat
1 g saturated fat
0 mg cholesterol
45 mg sodium
12 g carbohydrate
1 g fiber
1 g protein

sweet-and-sour onions

These onions, in a piquant sauce of vinegar and brown sugar, provide a perfect accompaniment for roasted beef, pork, or chicken.

INGREDIENTS

- 3 cups pearl white and/or red onions or one 16-ounce package frozen small whole onions
- 2 teaspoons margarine or butter
- ¼ cup white wine vinegar or balsamic vinegar
- 2 tablespoons brown sugar
- ⅛ teaspoon pepper
- 1 ounce prosciutto or thinly sliced cooked ham, cut into short thin strips

Start to finish: 35 minutes

DIRECTIONS

1. In a medium covered saucepan cook the unpeeled pearl onions (if using) in a small amount of boiling water about 10 minutes or until onions are just tender. Drain. Cool onions slightly; trim ends and remove skins. (Or, cook the frozen onions in a medium saucepan according to package directions; drain.)

2. In the same saucepan melt the margarine or butter over medium heat. Stir in the vinegar, brown sugar, and pepper. Cook and stir about 30 seconds or until combined. Stir in the onions and the prosciutto or ham.

3. Cook, uncovered, for 7 to 8 minutes more or until the onions are golden brown and slightly glazed, stirring occasionally. Makes 4 servings.

NUTRITION FACTS PER SERVING:

94 calories
2 g total fat
0 g saturated fat
3 mg cholesterol
372 mg sodium
16 g carbohydrate
2 g fiber
3 g protein

Everyone knows vegetables are good for them, but do they know why? Vegetables provide our bodies with vitamins A and C, folic acid, iron, magnesium, and other important nutrients. In addition, they're low in fat and high in fiber. Vegetables are so important to our diets, that health experts recommend 3 to 5 servings a day.

grilled herbed vegetables

For easy cleanup and fuss-free cooking, grill or bake mixed veggies of your choice in a foil packet.

INGREDIENTS

- 1 tablespoon olive oil
- 2 teaspoons snipped fresh rosemary or ½ teaspoon dried rosemary, crushed; or 2 tablespoons snipped fresh basil or 1 teaspoon dried basil, crushed
- 1 clove garlic, minced
- ¼ teaspoon salt
- 4 cups mixed vegetables, such as eggplant chunks; halved small yellow summer squash, zucchini, or pattypan squash; green beans; red onion wedges; and/or sliced yellow, red, or green sweet pepper
- Black pepper

Prep time: 5 minutes
Standing time: 2 hours
Grilling time: 20 minutes

DIRECTIONS

1. In a medium mixing bowl combine the olive oil, rosemary or basil, garlic, and salt. Let the mixture stand for 2 hours.

2. Add the vegetables to the oil mixture, tossing to coat. Spoon the vegetable mixture onto a 24×12-inch piece of heavy foil. Bring the opposite edges of foil together; seal tightly with a double fold. Fold in the remaining ends to completely enclose the vegetables, leaving a little space for steam to build.

3. Grill the vegetable packet on the rack of an uncovered grill directly over medium-hot coals about 20 minutes or until vegetables are tender, turning the packet over halfway through grilling. (Or, bake the vegetable packet in a 350° oven about 25 minutes or until tender.) Season the vegetables to taste with black pepper. Makes 4 servings.

NUTRITION FACTS PER SERVING:

63 calories
4 g total fat
0 g saturated fat
0 mg cholesterol
136 mg sodium
8 g carbohydrate
3 g fiber
1 g protein

risotto primavera

Risotto usually takes an inordinate amount of patience to prepare, due to all the stirring, stirring, stirring at the stove. Our Test Kitchen modified this recipe so it's easier to make. For cooks who want a more classic risotto, we've included the traditional method of adding a little broth at a time while stirring constantly.

INGREDIENTS

- ¼ cup thinly sliced celery
- ¼ cup thinly sliced shallots or green onions
- 2 cloves garlic, minced
- ⅛ teaspoon pepper
- 1 tablespoon margarine or butter
- 1 cup Arborio or long grain rice
- 1 14½-ounce can reduced-sodium chicken broth
- 1¾ cups water
- ½ cup fresh or frozen peas, thawed
- ½ cup coarsely chopped yellow summer squash and/or zucchini
- ½ teaspoon finely shredded lemon peel
- Fresh herbs (optional)

Prep time: 15 minutes
Cooking time: 25 minutes
Standing time: 5 minutes

DIRECTIONS

1. In a 3-quart saucepan cook the celery, shallots or green onions, garlic, and pepper in hot margarine or butter until tender. Add the uncooked rice. Cook and stir for 2 minutes.

2. Carefully stir in the chicken broth and water. Bring to boiling; reduce heat. Simmer, covered, for 25 minutes. (Do not lift cover.) Remove from heat.

3. Stir in the peas, yellow squash or zucchini, and lemon peel. Let stand, covered, for 5 minutes. Serve immediately. If desired, garnish with fresh herbs. Makes 6 servings.

Traditional Method: Cook celery mixture as directed; add the uncooked rice. Cook and stir for 2 minutes. In another saucepan bring the broth and water to boiling; reduce heat and simmer. Slowly add ¾ cup of the broth to rice mixture, stirring constantly. Cook and stir over medium heat until the liquid is absorbed. Continue to add broth, ¾ cup at a time, and continue to cook and stir until the rice is slightly creamy and just tender. (This should take about 20 minutes.)

During cooking, adjust the heat as necessary to keep the broth at a gentle simmer. Stir in the peas, yellow squash or zucchini, and lemon peel. Let stand, covered, for 5 minutes. Serve immediately.

NUTRITION FACTS PER SERVING:

156 calories
3 g total fat
0 g saturated fat
0 mg cholesterol
227 mg sodium
29 g carbohydrate
1 g fiber
4 g protein

233

brown rice pilaf

Shredded carrot adds a slight sweetness and a splash of color to this pilaf. Use wild mushrooms, such as shiitake, chanterelle, or porcini, for a more exotic dish.

INGREDIENTS

- 1 cup water
- 1 teaspoon instant chicken bouillon granules
- 1 cup sliced fresh mushrooms
- ¾ cup quick-cooking brown rice
- ½ cup shredded carrot
- ¾ teaspoon snipped fresh marjoram or ¼ teaspoon dried marjoram, crushed
- Dash pepper
- ¼ cup thinly sliced green onions
- 1 tablespoon snipped fresh parsley
- Fresh marjoram (optional)

Choose mushrooms by their caps. Look for caps that are closed around the stem; wide-open caps are a sign of age. Color should be uniform but depends upon the variety; white, off-white, and tan are most common.

Prep time: 10 minutes
Cooking time: 12 minutes
Standing time: 5 minutes

DIRECTIONS

1. In a medium saucepan stir together the water and bouillon granules. Bring to boiling. Stir in the mushrooms, uncooked rice, carrot, snipped or dried marjoram, and pepper. Return to boiling; reduce heat. Simmer, covered, for 12 minutes.

2. Remove from heat. Let stand, covered, for 5 minutes. Add the green onions and parsley; toss lightly with a fork. If desired, garnish with additional fresh marjoram. Makes 4 servings.

NUTRITION FACTS PER SERVING:

60 calories
1 g total fat
0 g saturated fat
0 mg cholesterol
230 mg sodium
13 g carbohydrate
2 g fiber
2 g protein

pasta and fresh tomato sauce

INGREDIENTS

- 4 ounces packaged dried rotini (corkscrew) or fusilli pasta
- 2 cups coarsely chopped plum tomatoes
- 2 teaspoons olive oil
- ¼ teaspoon salt
- 3 tablespoons shredded fresh basil
- ¼ cup shaved or grated Parmesan or Romano cheese
- ¼ teaspoon pepper

This pasta sauce, the essence of simplicity, contains chopped plum tomatoes lightly sautéed in a little olive oil and seasoned with basil. Served on the side, it's the ideal accompaniment to beef, chicken, or seafood.

Start to finish: 20 minutes

DIRECTIONS

1. Cook the pasta according to package directions; drain well.

2. Meanwhile, in a medium saucepan combine the tomatoes, olive oil, and salt. Cook over medium-low heat until heated through and tomatoes start to juice out slightly. Stir in the basil.

3. Divide the pasta among 4 plates. Top with the tomato mixture. Sprinkle with the Parmesan or Romano cheese and the pepper. Makes 4 servings.

Here's a slick trick
for shredding fresh basil. Layer the basil leaves on top of each other, then roll up the leaves into a tight spiral. Using a sharp knife, cut the basil into fine strips.

NUTRITION FACTS PER SERVING:

184 calories
5 g total fat
2 g saturated fat
5 mg cholesterol
260 mg sodium
28 g carbohydrate
2 g fiber
7 g protein

235

garlic asparagus & pasta with lemon cream

Delicate asparagus requires tender, loving care to show off its simple perfection. Providing just the coddling it needs are succulent baby squash, curly pasta ribbons, and a low-fuss, lemon-infused cream sauce. (Recipe also pictured on the cover.)

INGREDIENTS

6 ounces dried mafalda or rotini
1 tablespoon margarine or butter
2 cups asparagus cut into
     2-inch pieces
8 baby sunburst squash and/or
     pattypan squash, halved
     (4 ounces)*
2 cloves garlic, minced
1 12-ounce can (1⅓ cups)
     evaporated fat-free milk
1 tablespoon all-purpose flour
¼ cup Parmesan cheese
2 teaspoons finely shredded
     lemon peel

Keep cooked pasta hot
by draining it quickly. Don't let it stand in the colander longer than necessary. Then return the pasta to the hot cooking pan immediately. The heat of the pan will help keep the pasta warm.

Start to finish: 25 minutes

DIRECTIONS

1. Cook pasta according to package directions; drain and keep warm.

2. Meanwhile, in a large skillet melt margarine or butter; add asparagus, squash, and garlic. Cook, stirring frequently, for 2 to 3 minutes or until vegetables are crisp-tender. Remove with a slotted spoon and add to pasta.

3. In a medium saucepan stir the evaporated milk into the flour. Cook and stir over medium heat until mixture is thickened and bubbly. Cook and stir for 1 minute more. Add the ¼ cup Parmesan cheese and lemon peel. Heat through.

4. To serve, pour sauce over pasta and vegetables. Toss to coat. If desired, serve with additional Parmesan cheese. Makes 6 side-dish or 4 main-dish servings.

*Note: One medium yellow squash or zucchini cut into 16 pieces can be substituted for the baby sunburst squash and/or pattypan squash.

NUTRITION FACTS PER SERVING:

213 calories
4 g total fat
1 g saturated fat
5 mg cholesterol
144 mg sodium
33 g carbohydrate
2 g fiber
11 g protein

INGREDIENTS

Nonstick spray coating

1½ cups fat-free milk

½ cup cornmeal

½ cup cold water

¼ teaspoon salt

¼ cup plain low-fat yogurt

¼ cup grated Parmesan cheese

Dash ground red pepper

Spaghetti or pizza sauce, heated (optional)

cheesy polenta squares

Polenta, an Italian favorite, is made from cornmeal. For a zesty flavor, top it with warm spaghetti or pizza sauce.

Prep time: 20 minutes
Standing time: 30 minutes
Baking time: 10 minutes

DIRECTIONS

1. Spray an 8×8×2-inch baking pan with nonstick coating. Set aside. In a medium saucepan bring the milk to simmering.

2. Meanwhile, in a bowl combine cornmeal, cold water, and salt. Slowly add the cornmeal mixture to simmering milk, stirring constantly. Cook and stir until mixture returns to simmering. Reduce heat to low. Cook, uncovered, about 10 minutes or until thick, stirring frequently. Spread in prepared pan. Let stand for 30 to 40 minutes or until firm.

3. Meanwhile, in a small bowl combine the yogurt, Parmesan cheese, and ground red pepper. Set aside.

4. Spray an oval baking dish or 15×10×1-inch baking pan with nonstick coating. Cut the cornmeal mixture into 12 squares; place in the prepared dish or pan. Spoon the yogurt mixture over the polenta squares.

5. Bake, uncovered, in a 425° oven for 10 to 12 minutes or until top is golden brown and polenta is heated through. If desired, serve with warm spaghetti or pizza sauce. Makes 6 servings.

NUTRITION FACTS PER SERVING:

89 calories
2 g total fat
1 g saturated fat
5 mg cholesterol
206 mg sodium
13 g carbohydrate
1 g fiber
5 g protein

237

marinated tomato platter

When "keep it simple" is your mealtime motto, reach for this easy, fresh salad recipe. Ripe tomatoes and garden zucchini star, with a drizzle of an oil-and-vinegar dressing.

INGREDIENTS

- 3 tablespoons olive oil
- 3 tablespoons white wine vinegar
- 1 tablespoon thinly sliced green onion or snipped chives
- 2 teaspoons honey mustard
- ⅛ teaspoon pepper
- 2 medium zucchini or cucumbers
   Leaf lettuce (optional)
- 3 large red and/or yellow tomatoes, sliced
- ¼ cup crumbled feta cheese with tomato and basil or plain feta cheese (1 ounce)

Cheeses once considered exotic are now widely available, and because they are so flavorful, a little goes a long way. Consider flavored fetas, any of the blue cheeses (such as Gorgonzola, Maytag blue, or Roquefort), goat cheese (chèvre), Parmesan or Pecorino Romano.

Prep time: 15 minutes
Chilling time: 30 minutes

DIRECTIONS

1. For dressing, in a screw-top jar combine the olive oil, vinegar, green onion or chives, mustard, and pepper. Cover and shake well. Chill until needed.

2. Cut the zucchini or cucumbers in half lengthwise. Seed cucumbers, if using. Using a vegetable peeler, cut zucchini or cucumber halves into thin, lengthwise strips (½ to 1 inch wide).

3. Line a serving platter with leaf lettuce (if desired) and top with the sliced tomatoes. Arrange the zucchini or cucumber strips among the tomatoes, tucking and folding the strips as desired.

4. Shake dressing; drizzle over vegetables. Cover and chill for at least 30 minutes. Before serving, sprinkle the vegetables with feta cheese. Makes 6 servings.

NUTRITION FACTS PER SERVING:

117 calories
9 g total fat
3 g saturated fat
9 mg cholesterol
138 mg sodium
7 g carbohydrate
2 g fiber
3 g protein

INGREDIENTS

- ¾ cup packaged dried rotini (corkscrew) pasta or elbow macaroni
- 1 cup broccoli flowerets
- 1 cup cauliflower flowerets
- 1 9-ounce package frozen artichoke hearts
- ½ cup thinly sliced carrot
- ¼ cup sliced green onions
- ½ cup reduced-calorie Italian salad dressing
- Leaf lettuce (optional)

vegetable and pasta toss

Double all of the ingredients and tote this simple pasta salad to your next potluck. No one will guess it's low in calories. Use any flavor of fat-free or reduced-calorie dressing you like.

Prep time: 25 minutes
Chilling time: 2 hours

DIRECTIONS

1. Cook the pasta according to package directions, except omit any oil; add the broccoli and cauliflower to boiling pasta for the last 1 minute of cooking. Drain. Rinse with cold water; drain well.

2. Meanwhile, cook the artichoke hearts according to package directions. Drain. Rinse with cold water; drain well. Halve any large pieces.

3. In a large mixing bowl combine the pasta mixture, artichoke hearts, carrot, and green onions. Add the Italian dressing; toss to coat.

4. Cover and chill for 2 to 24 hours. If desired, serve on lettuce-lined salad plates. Makes 6 servings.

NUTRITION FACTS PER SERVING:

91 calories
2 g total fat
0 g saturated fat
1 mg cholesterol
208 mg sodium
16 g carbohydrate
4 g fiber
4 g protein

roasted sweet pepper salad

Use any leftovers of this flavorful salad for an extra-special sandwich topping. It's especially tasty on a grilled chicken sandwich. (Also pictured on pages 224–225.)

(Also pictured on pages 224–225.)

INGREDIENTS

6 medium red, yellow, and/or green sweet peppers

3 tablespoons balsamic vinegar

2 tablespoons capers, drained

2 tablespoons snipped fresh basil or 1 teaspoon dried basil, crushed

1 tablespoon snipped fresh oregano or 1 teaspoon dried oregano, crushed

1 tablespoon olive oil

2 cloves garlic, minced

¼ teaspoon black pepper

Lettuce leaves

What are capers?
They're the unopened flower buds on a bush that's grown primarily in Europe. The buds are packed in a vinegar brine and usually are drained, and sometimes rinsed, before using. Tangy and pungent, they have a flavor that can't easily be substituted.

Start to finish: 55 minutes

DIRECTIONS

1. Halve sweet peppers; remove stems, seeds, and membranes. Place pepper halves, cut sides down, on a foil-lined baking sheet. Bake in a 450° oven for 15 to 20 minutes or until skins are blistered and dark. Fold up foil on baking sheet around peppers to form a packet, sealing edges. Let stand about 20 minutes to loosen skins. With a small sharp knife, peel skin from peppers. Discard skin. Cut the peppers into strips.

2. In a medium bowl combine the sweet pepper strips, the vinegar, capers, basil, oregano, oil, garlic, and black pepper; toss to coat. Serve immediately or cover and chill for up to 24 hours. Serve on lettuce-lined salad plates. Makes 6 to 8 servings.

NUTRITION FACTS PER SERVING:

58 calories
3 g total fat
0 g saturated fat
0 mg cholesterol
55 mg sodium
9 g carbohydrate
3 g fiber
1 g protein

INGREDIENTS

1 16-ounce package frozen white whole kernel corn (shoe peg), thawed
1 16-ounce package frozen baby peas, thawed
1 cup chopped, peeled jicama
⅔ cup chopped celery
½ cup thinly sliced green onions
¼ cup chopped red and/or orange sweet pepper
½ cup seasoned rice vinegar
2 tablespoons brown sugar

1 tablespoon snipped fresh parsley
½ teaspoon salt
¼ teaspoon ground white pepper
1 tablespoon snipped fresh mint

white corn and baby pea salad

A tangy vinaigrette-style dressing perks up a crunchy combo of white shoe peg corn, baby peas, jicama, and fresh mint.

Prep time: 15 minutes
Chilling time: 1 hour

DIRECTIONS

1. In a large mixing bowl combine the corn, peas, jicama, celery, green onions, and sweet pepper.

2. For dressing, in a screw-top jar combine the vinegar, brown sugar, parsley, salt, and white pepper. Cover and shake well. Pour over the corn mixture; toss gently to coat. Stir in mint. Cover and chill for 1 to 2 hours. Makes 10 to 12 servings.

NUTRITION FACTS PER SERVING:

90 calories
0 g total fat
0 g saturated fat
0 mg cholesterol
151 mg sodium
21 g carbohydrate
2 g fiber
4 g protein

241

new potato-green bean salad

This salad offers a wonderful choice for potlucks and summertime picnics and parties.

INGREDIENTS

2 pounds whole tiny new potatoes, halved or quartered, or 6 medium red potatoes, cubed

1 9-ounce package frozen French-style green beans or cut green beans, cooked and drained

Shredded lettuce

4 plum tomatoes, cut into wedges

1 recipe Yogurt-French Dressing

Prep time: 30 minutes
Cooling time: 20 minutes
Chilling time: 2 hours

DIRECTIONS

1. In a large covered saucepan cook the potatoes in boiling water for 15 to 20 minutes or just until tender. Drain; cool for 20 minutes. Cover and chill potatoes and beans for 2 to 24 hours.

2. To serve, line a serving platter with lettuce. Arrange the potatoes, green beans, and tomato wedges on lettuce. Drizzle the Yogurt-French Dressing over the vegetables. Serve immediately. Makes 6 servings.

Yogurt-French Dressing: In a small bowl stir together ¼ cup bottled fat-free French salad dressing; 3 tablespoons plain fat-free yogurt; 1 tablespoon fat-free mayonnaise dressing or salad dressing; and 1 green onion, sliced.

NUTRITION FACTS PER SERVING:

110 calories
1 g total fat
0 g saturated fat
1 mg cholesterol
134 mg sodium
24 g carbohydrate
2 g fiber
3 g protein

INGREDIENTS

- 2 cups shredded cabbage
- 1 cup julienned, peeled jicama (see tip, page 78)
- 1 medium apple, chopped, or 1 medium peach or nectarine, peeled, pitted, and chopped
- ½ of a small red onion, chopped (about ¼ cup)
- 3 tablespoons light mayonnaise dressing or salad dressing
- 2 tablespoons snipped fresh cilantro or parsley
- 1 tablespoon cider vinegar
- 1½ teaspoons sugar
- Dash to ⅛ teaspoon ground red pepper
- Purple kale (optional)

jicama coleslaw

Jicama actually resembles a large brown turnip. The thin, pale brown skin peels off easily to reveal a pure white potato-like meat that has a clean, crisp bite and a mildly sweet flavor. It's best when peeled just before using, and you can eat it raw or cooked.

Prep time: 20 minutes
Chilling time: 2 hours

DIRECTIONS

1. In a large mixing bowl combine the cabbage; jicama; apple, peach, or nectarine; and red onion.

2. In a small bowl stir together the mayonnaise dressing or salad dressing, cilantro or parsley, vinegar, sugar, and ground red pepper. Pour the dressing over cabbage mixture, tossing to coat. Cover and chill for 2 to 4 hours. Transfer to a salad bowl. If desired, garnish with kale. Makes 4 servings.

Store whole jicamas in the refrigerator for up to 3 weeks. If you cut them up, wrap in plastic wrap and refrigerate up to 1 week.

NUTRITION FACTS PER SERVING:

- 91 calories
- 4 g total fat
- 1 g saturated fat
- 0 mg cholesterol
- 91 mg sodium
- 14 g carbohydrate
- 2 g fiber
- 1 g protein

243

roasted pepper and onion salad

For a burst of color, use a combination of green, red, and yellow sweet peppers.

INGREDIENTS

- **5** medium sweet peppers
- **1** red onion, cut into thin wedges
- **2** tablespoons white wine vinegar
- **2** tablespoons water
- **1** tablespoon snipped fresh basil or 1 teaspoon dried basil, crushed
- **1** tablespoon olive oil or salad oil
- **¼** teaspoon salt-free seasoning blend
  Lettuce leaves
- **1** tablespoon snipped fresh chives or 1 teaspoon dried chives

With its mild flavor, the familiar green bell pepper is still a favorite, but more and more cooks are turning to sweet peppers in other hues to brighten their dishes. Orange, purple, yellow, red, and chocolate varieties are available at various times in most grocery stores.

Start to finish: 55 minutes

DIRECTIONS

1. Halve sweet peppers; remove stems, seeds, and membranes. Place pepper halves, cut sides down, along with the onion wedges on a foil-lined baking sheet. Bake in a 450° oven for 15 to 20 minutes or until pepper skins are blistered and dark. (Cover onion loosely with foil after 10 to 15 minutes to prevent overbrowning.) Remove onion wedges; set aside. Fold up foil on baking sheet around peppers to form a packet, sealing edges. Let stand 20 minutes to loosen skins. With a small sharp knife, peel skin from peppers. Discard skin. Cut peppers into ½-inch-wide strips.

2. For dressing, in a blender container or food processor bowl combine ⅓ cup of 1 color of pepper strips, the vinegar, water, basil, oil, and seasoning blend. Cover and blend or process until smooth.

3. Line 4 salad plates with lettuce leaves. Arrange the remaining pepper strips and onion wedges on lettuce. Sprinkle with chives. Drizzle dressing over each serving. Makes 4 servings.

NUTRITION FACTS PER SERVING:

81 calories
4 g total fat
1 g saturated fat
0 mg cholesterol
5 mg sodium
12 g carbohydrate
3 g fiber
2 g protein

244

mixed greens and fruit salad

Enjoy this tossed salad with fresh berries in the summer or with canned mandarin orange sections during winter.

INGREDIENTS

4   cups torn mixed salad greens
1   cup sliced fresh mushrooms
1   cup fresh blueberries, raspberries, quartered strawberries, and/or canned mandarin orange sections, drained
⅓   cup orange juice
4   teaspoons salad oil
4   teaspoons brown mustard
1½ teaspoons sugar
1½ teaspoons snipped fresh mint or
¼   teaspoon dried mint, crushed
¼   teaspoon salt
⅛   teaspoon pepper

Prep time: 15 minutes

DIRECTIONS

1. In a large bowl gently toss together the salad greens, mushrooms, and fruit.

2. For dressing, in a screw-top jar combine the orange juice, oil, brown mustard, sugar, mint, salt, and pepper. Cover and shake well. Drizzle the dressing over the greens mixture; toss gently to coat. Makes 4 servings

With the rich array of lettuces and greens

on the market these days, you can select varieties for color and for sharp and sweet tastes. Consider smooth-textured Bibb, light-green Boston, crunchy romaine, and red and green leaf lettuce. They mix nicely with specialty greens such as tangy arugula, bitter radicchio, and peppery watercress.

NUTRITION FACTS PER SERVING:

97 calories
5 g total fat
1 g saturated fat
0 mg cholesterol
248 mg sodium
12 g carbohydrate
3 g fiber
3 g protein

245

Fresh Pear Custard Tart
Recipe, page 252

desserts

berry-lemon trifle

This heavenly dessert starts with angel food cake—
either a homemade or a bakery cake will do.

INGREDIENTS

- 2 cups cubed angel food cake
- 1 8-ounce carton lemon fat-free yogurt
- ¼ of an 8-ounce container frozen light whipped dessert topping, thawed
- 1 cup mixed fresh berries, such as raspberries, blueberries, or sliced strawberries
- Fresh mint (optional)

How did angel food cake earn such a heavenly name? Maybe it's because a slice (¹⁄₁₂ of a cake) has about 130 calories and less than 1 gram of fat. A similar serving of homemade chocolate cake has over 300 calories and 13 grams of fat. When you want to splurge, angel food cake is definitely more saintly.

Prep time: 12 minutes

DIRECTIONS

1. Divide angel food cake cubes among 4 individual dessert dishes. In a small mixing bowl fold together the yogurt and whipped topping.

2. Spoon the yogurt mixture on top of the cake cubes. Sprinkle with berries. If desired, garnish with fresh mint. Makes 4 servings.

NUTRITION FACTS PER SERVING:

104 calories
2 g total fat
0 g saturated fat
1 mg cholesterol
152 mg sodium
19 g carbohydrate
1 g fiber
3 g protein

INGREDIENTS

- ⅓ cup granulated sugar
- 3 tablespoons all-purpose flour
- ⅔ cup milk
- 1 egg
- 1 egg yolk
- ¼ cup ground toasted almonds (see tip, page 108)
- 1 tablespoon butter or margarine
- 1 teaspoon vanilla
- ¼ teaspoon almond extract
- 3 egg yolks

- ¼ teaspoon vanilla
- ½ cup milk
- 3 tablespoons butter or margarine, melted
- ½ cup all-purpose flour
- ¼ cup granulated sugar
- 3 egg whites
- Cooking oil
- Sliced almonds, toasted
- Sifted powdered sugar
- Mixed fresh berries (optional)

almond cream crepes

In France, it's customary to touch the handle of the pan during cooking and make a wish while the crepe is turned.

Prep time: 1 hour
Baking time: 10 minutes

DIRECTIONS

1. For filling, in a small saucepan combine the ⅓ cup granulated sugar and the 3 tablespoons flour. Add the ⅔ cup milk; cook and stir until thickened and bubbly. Cook and stir for 1 minute more. Beat the whole egg and the 1 egg yolk together slightly. Gradually stir half of the hot mixture into the beaten eggs. Return all of the mixture to the saucepan. Cook and stir over low heat for 2 minutes (do not boil). Remove from heat. Stir in the ground almonds, the 1 tablespoon butter or margarine, the 1 teaspoon vanilla, and the almond extract. Cover and set aside.

2. Meanwhile, for crepes, in a small mixing bowl stir together the 3 egg yolks and the ¼ teaspoon vanilla; stir in the ½ cup milk and the 3 tablespoons melted butter or margarine. Stir in the ½ cup flour and the ¼ cup granulated sugar until smooth. In a medium mixing bowl beat the egg whites with an electric mixer until stiff peaks form (tips stand straight). Gently fold the batter into beaten egg whites.

3. Brush a 6-inch skillet with cooking oil; heat over medium heat. Spoon a generous tablespoon of batter into the skillet; spread with back of spoon into a 4- to 5-inch circle. Cook over medium heat for 30 to 45 seconds or until the underside is brown. Turn and cook just until the other side is light brown. Invert onto paper towels. Cover; keep warm. Repeat with remaining batter to make 24 crepes.

4. To assemble, spread about 2 teaspoons of the filling onto each crepe; fold in half, then fold in half again to form a triangle. Place the crepes in an ungreased 3-quart rectangular baking dish. Bake, uncovered, in a 350° oven about 10 minutes or until heated through. Sprinkle with sliced almonds and powdered sugar. If desired, serve with fresh berries. Makes 12 servings.

NUTRITION FACTS PER SERVING:

152 calories
8 g total fat
2 g saturated fat
90 mg cholesterol
78 mg sodium
17 g carbohydrate
0 g fiber
4 g protein

249

apple crumble

Sliced, peeled pears make an equally delicious stand-in for the cooking apples.

Nonstick spray coating

8 cups sliced, peeled
cooking apples

1 tablespoon lemon juice

½ cup rolled oats

¼ cup all-purpose flour

¼ cup packed brown sugar

1 teaspoon ground cinnamon

¼ teaspoon ground nutmeg

3 tablespoons butter, chilled

Vanilla low-fat yogurt (optional)

Honey (optional)

There's no better low-fat

choice for dessert than fresh fruit. Choose the best quality you can find for the most after-dinner satisfaction. Fruits should be plump, brightly colored, and heavy for their size (this indicates moistness). Avoid fruits with mold, mildew, bruises, cuts, or other blemishes.

Prep time: 20 minutes
Baking time: 40 minutes

DIRECTIONS

1. Spray a 2-quart square baking dish with nonstick coating. Place the apples in the prepared dish. Sprinkle with the lemon juice.

2. In a medium bowl stir together the rolled oats, flour, brown sugar, cinnamon, and nutmeg. Using a pastry blender, cut in the butter until the mixture resembles coarse crumbs. Sprinkle oat mixture evenly over apples.

3. Bake in a 350° oven for 40 to 45 minutes or until the apples are tender. Serve warm. If desired, top with yogurt sweetened with a little honey. Makes 6 servings.

NUTRITION FACTS PER SERVING:

211 calories
7 g total fat
3 g saturated fat
15 mg cholesterol
70 mg sodium
38 g carbohydrate
4 g fiber
2 g protein

cherry-peach cobbler

We cut the calories and fat by using fat-free yogurt to tenderize the biscuit-like topping on this traditional homespun cobbler.

INGREDIENTS

- 1 cup all-purpose flour
- 2 tablespoons sugar
- 1½ teaspoons baking powder
- ¼ teaspoon ground nutmeg
- 2 tablespoons margarine or butter
- ½ cup sugar
- 4 teaspoons cornstarch
- ⅓ cup water
- 3 cups fresh or frozen unsweetened sliced, peeled peaches
- 2 cups fresh or frozen unsweetened pitted tart red cherries
- ⅓ cup plain fat-free yogurt
- ¼ cup refrigerated or frozen egg product, thawed
- Ground nutmeg (optional)

Prep time: 15 minutes
Baking time: 20 minutes

DIRECTIONS

1. For topping, in a mixing bowl stir together the flour, the 2 tablespoons sugar, the baking powder, and the ¼ teaspoon nutmeg. Using a pastry blender, cut in the margarine or butter until the mixture resembles coarse crumbs. Set aside.

2. For filling, in a large saucepan stir together the ½ cup sugar and the cornstarch. Stir in water. Add the peach slices and cherries. Cook and stir until thickened and bubbly. Keep the filling hot while finishing topping.

3. To finish topping, stir together the yogurt and egg product. Add the yogurt mixture to flour mixture, stirring just until moistened.

4. Transfer the filling to a 2-quart square baking dish. Drop the topping from a spoon into 8 mounds directly on top of the hot filling.

5. Bake cobbler in a 400° oven about 20 minutes or until a wooden toothpick inserted into topping comes out clean. Serve warm. If desired, sprinkle with additional ground nutmeg. Makes 8 servings.

NUTRITION FACTS PER SERVING:

- 202 calories
- 3 g total fat
- 1 g saturated fat
- 0 mg cholesterol
- 120 mg sodium
- 41 g carbohydrate
- 2 g fiber
- 4 g protein

fresh pear custard tart

Be sure to use ripe pears for this tart. Pears that are too firm or unripe will make it difficult to eat. If you're really in a pinch, substitute sliced, well-drained canned pears. (Recipe also pictured on pages 246 and 247.)

INGREDIENTS

1 recipe Single-Crust Pastry
½ cup granulated sugar
2 tablespoons cornstarch
2 cups fat-free milk
2 beaten eggs
4 teaspoons finely chopped crystallized ginger
1 teaspoon vanilla
⅔ cup pear nectar

1½ teaspoons cornstarch
3 small ripe pears
½ cup fresh berries (such as raspberries, blackberries, and/or blueberries)
Sifted powdered sugar (optional)
Fresh mint (optional)
Edible flowers (optional)

Prep time: 1 hour
Chilling time: 1 hour

DIRECTIONS

1. Prepare the Single-Crust Pastry. For filling, in a medium heavy saucepan combine the granulated sugar and the 2 tablespoons cornstarch. Stir in milk. Cook and stir over medium heat until thickened and bubbly. Cook and stir for 2 minutes more. Remove from heat.

2. Gradually stir about 1 cup of the hot mixture into beaten eggs. Return all of the mixture to the saucepan. Stir in the ginger. Cook and stir until thickened and bubbly. Reduce heat. Cook and stir for 2 minutes more. Remove

from heat. Stir in the vanilla. Pour into the baked tart shell. Cover and chill until ready to assemble.

3. Meanwhile, for glaze, in a small saucepan combine the pear nectar and the 1½ teaspoons cornstarch. Cook and stir until thickened and bubbly. Cook and stir for 2 minutes more. Remove from heat. Cover and cool to room temperature.

4. To assemble the tart, peel, core, and thinly slice the pears. Arrange in a concentric pattern over the filling. Pour the cooled glaze over pears, spreading evenly. Cover and chill for 1 to 4 hours. To serve, top with berries. If desired, dust with powdered sugar and garnish with fresh mint and edible flowers. Makes 10 servings.

Single-Crust Pastry: In a medium bowl stir together 1¼ cups all-purpose flour and ¼ teaspoon salt. In a small bowl combine ¼ cup fat-free milk and 3 tablespoons cooking oil; add all at once to flour mixture. Stir with a fork until a dough forms. Form into a ball.

On a lightly floured surface, roll dough from center to edge into a 13-inch circle. Ease into an 11-inch tart pan with removable bottom. Trim

to edge of pan. Prick bottom and side well with tines of a fork. Bake in a 450° oven for 10 to 12 minutes or until golden brown. Cool in pan on a wire rack.

NUTRITION FACTS PER SERVING:

216 calories
6 g total fat
1 g saturated fat
44 mg cholesterol
96 mg sodium
37 g carbohydrate
2 g fiber
5 g protein

252

cranberry tart

Tissue-thin layers of phyllo pastry form the crispy crust of this tart. Packaged frozen phyllo dough, readily available in supermarkets, is easy to use.

INGREDIENTS

- 1 cup cranberries
- ¼ cup sugar
- 1 tablespoon orange juice
- 1 8-ounce package reduced-fat cream cheese (Neufchâtel)
- ¼ cup sugar
- 1 egg
- 1 egg white

- 1 teaspoon vanilla
  Butter-flavored nonstick spray coating
- 4 sheets frozen phyllo dough, thawed
- 1 ounce white chocolate, melted (optional)

Prep time: 20 minutes
Baking time: 25 minutes
Cooling time: 1 hour
Chilling time: 4 hours

DIRECTIONS

1. In a small saucepan combine the cranberries, ¼ cup sugar, and the orange juice. Cook, uncovered, over medium heat until the cranberries pop and the mixture thickens slightly, stirring frequently. Remove from heat. Set aside.

2. In a food processor bowl combine the cream cheese, ¼ cup sugar, the egg, egg white, and vanilla. Cover and process until smooth. Set the mixture aside.

3. Spray a 9-inch tart pan or pie plate with nonstick coating. Spray 1 phyllo sheet with nonstick coating. Fold the sheet in half crosswise to form a rectangle (about 13×9 inches). Gently press the folded sheet of phyllo into the prepared tart pan, allowing ends to extend over edge of pan. Spray with nonstick coating. Spray and fold another sheet of phyllo; place across first sheet in a crisscross fashion. Spray with nonstick coating. Repeat with remaining 2 sheets of phyllo. (If desired, turn under edges of phyllo to form a crust.) Bake, uncovered, in a 350° oven for 5 minutes.

4. Spoon the cream cheese mixture into the phyllo crust, spreading evenly. Spoon the cranberry mixture over the cream cheese mixture. Using a knife, marble the mixtures together slightly.

5. Bake tart for 20 to 25 minutes or until the phyllo is lightly browned and the filling is set. Cool on a wire rack for 1 hour. Cover and chill for 4 to 24 hours. If desired, drizzle edges of phyllo with white chocolate before serving. Makes 10 servings.

NUTRITION FACTS PER SERVING:

192 calories
7 g total fat
4 g saturated fat
40 mg cholesterol
142 mg sodium
18 g carbohydrate
1 g fiber
4 g protein

253

summer fruit tart

A pudding-like mixture fills this fruit-topped tart. Use any type of in-season fruit you like.

INGREDIENTS

1 recipe Tart Pastry
¼ cup sugar
2 tablespoons cornstarch
1 12-ounce can evaporated fat-free milk
¼ cup refrigerated or frozen egg product, thawed
½ teaspoon vanilla
2 medium fresh nectarines or peeled peaches, thinly sliced
2 fresh plums, thinly sliced
2 kiwi fruit, peeled and sliced
½ cup fresh blueberries, raspberries, and/or blackberries
2 tablespoons honey
1 tablespoon rum or orange juice

Prep time: 35 minutes
Chilling time: 2 hours

DIRECTIONS

1. Prepare Tart Pastry. For filling, in a medium heavy saucepan combine sugar and cornstarch. Stir in evaporated milk and egg product. Cook and stir over medium heat until thickened and bubbly. Cook and stir for 2 minutes more. Remove from heat. Stir in vanilla. Cover surface with plastic wrap; chill for 1 hour.

2. Spread the filling in the baked tart shell. Arrange the nectarines, plums, and kiwi fruit on top of filling. Sprinkle with the berries. Combine the honey and rum or orange juice; brush over fruit. Cover and chill for up to 1 hour. Makes 10 servings.

Tart Pastry: In a medium bowl stir together 1¼ cups all-purpose flour and ¼ teaspoon salt. Using a pastry blender, cut in ¼ cup shortening until the mixture resembles fine crumbs. Sprinkle 1 tablespoon cold water over part of mixture; gently toss with a fork. Add 3 to 4 tablespoons more cold water, 1 tablespoon at a time, until the mixture is moistened. Form into a ball. On a lightly floured surface, roll dough from center to edge into a 13-inch circle. Ease into an 11-inch tart pan with removable bottom. Trim to edge of pan. Prick bottom and side well with fork. Bake in a 450° oven for 10 to 12 minutes or until golden. Cool in pan on a wire rack.

NUTRITION FACTS PER SERVING:

187 calories
6 g total fat
1 g saturated fat
1 mg cholesterol
84 mg sodium
31 g carbohydrate
2 g fiber
4 g protein

254

INGREDIENTS

- 3 cups sliced strawberries
- 2 tablespoons sugar
- 1⅔ cups all-purpose flour
- 1 tablespoon sugar
- 2 teaspoons baking powder
- ¼ teaspoon baking soda
- 3 tablespoons margarine or butter
- 1 beaten egg
- ½ cup buttermilk or sour fat-free milk
- 2 cups frozen light whipped dessert topping, thawed, or one 1.3-ounce envelope whipped dessert topping mix
- Strawberry fans (optional)

strawberry shortcake

Another time, use a combination of summer berries, such as raspberries, blackberries, and blueberries.

Prep time: 25 minutes
Chilling time: 1 hour
Baking time: 7 minutes

DIRECTIONS

1. In a medium bowl combine sliced berries and the 2 tablespoons sugar. Cover; chill for at least 1 hour.

2. In a medium mixing bowl stir together the flour, the 1 tablespoon sugar, the baking powder, and baking soda. Using a pastry blender, cut in the margarine or butter until the mixture resembles coarse crumbs. Combine the egg and buttermilk or sour milk; add to flour mixture all at once, stirring just until moistened.

3. Drop the dough from a tablespoon into 8 mounds on an ungreased baking sheet. Bake in a 450° oven for 7 to 8 minutes or until golden brown. Transfer the shortcakes to a wire rack and cool about 10 minutes. Meanwhile, if using topping mix, prepare according to package directions using fat-free milk.

4. To serve, cut shortcakes in half horizontally. Spoon the strawberries and half of the whipped topping over bottom layers. Replace tops. Spoon the remaining topping onto shortcakes. If desired, garnish with strawberry fans. Makes 8 servings.

To make a strawberry fan,

place the strawberry on a cutting board with the pointed end facing you. Using a paring knife, make 4 or 5 lengthwise cuts from the pointed end not quite to stem end. Fan the slices apart slightly, being careful to keep all slices attached to the cap.

NUTRITION FACTS PER SERVING:

206 calories
6 g total fat
1 g saturated fat
27 mg cholesterol
215 mg sodium
34 g carbohydrate
2 g fiber
4 g protein

255

country apricot tart

The flavor of this cornmeal crust is outstanding and—better yet—it's great for those who haven't mastered the art of making beautifully crimped pie edges. You simply fold the crust over the filling.

INGREDIENTS

1 recipe Cornmeal Crust

⅓ cup sugar

3 tablespoons all-purpose flour

¼ teaspoon ground nutmeg or cinnamon

3 cups sliced, pitted fresh apricots or 3 cups frozen, unsweetened peach slices, thawed (do not drain)

1 tablespoon lemon juice

2 teaspoons fat-free milk

Prep time: 30 minutes
Baking time: 40 minutes

DIRECTIONS

1. Grease and lightly flour a large baking sheet. Prepare the Cornmeal Crust. Place on the baking sheet; flatten the dough. Roll into a 12-inch circle. Set aside.

2. For filling, in a large bowl stir together the sugar, flour, and nutmeg or cinnamon. Stir in the apricots or peaches and the lemon juice. Mound the filling in center of crust, leaving a 2-inch border. Fold the border up over filling. Brush edge of crust with the 2 teaspoons milk.

3. Bake in a 375° oven about 40 minutes or until the crust is golden and the filling is bubbly. Loosely cover the edge of crust with foil the last 10 to 15 minutes of baking to prevent overbrowning. Serve warm. Makes 8 servings.

Cornmeal Crust: In a medium bowl stir together ¾ cup all-purpose flour, ⅓ cup cornmeal, 2 tablespoons sugar, 1 teaspoon baking powder, and ⅛ teaspoon salt. Cut in 3 tablespoons butter or margarine until the size of small peas. Sprinkle 1 tablespoon cold fat-free milk over part of mixture; gently toss with a fork. Add 3 to 4 tablespoons more fat-free milk, 1 tablespoon at a time, until dough is moistened (dough will be crumbly). On a lightly floured surface, knead gently 7 to 8 strokes or just until the dough clings together. Form into a ball.

NUTRITION FACTS PER SERVING:

176 calories
5 g total fat
3 g saturated fat
12 mg cholesterol
128 mg sodium
32 g carbohydrate
2 g fiber
3 g protein

INGREDIENTS

- 6 cups thinly sliced, peeled cooking apples (about 2 pounds total)
- ¼ cup sugar
- 1 teaspoon ground cinnamon
- 1 tablespoon cornstarch
- ⅛ teaspoon salt
- ¾ cup all-purpose flour or ½ cup all-purpose flour plus ¼ cup whole wheat flour
  Dash ground nutmeg
- 3 tablespoons margarine or butter
- 2 to 3 tablespoons cold water
  Fat-free milk

deep-dish apple pie

Bite into this all-American dessert and you'll experience some of our country's best from the past. Each forkful boasts a luscious cinnamon-apple filling and flaky pastry.

Prep time: 30 minutes
Baking time: 40 minutes

DIRECTIONS

1. Place apples in a 2-quart square baking dish.

2. In a small bowl combine the sugar and cinnamon; set aside 1 teaspoon of the mixture. Stir the cornstarch and salt into the remaining sugar mixture; sprinkle evenly over the apples in the baking dish.

3. In a medium bowl stir together the flour and nutmeg. Using a pastry blender, cut in the margarine or butter until mixture resembles coarse crumbs. Sprinkle 1 tablespoon of the water over part of mixture; gently toss with a fork. Add the remaining water, 1 tablespoon at a time, until the dough is moistened. Form into a ball.

4. On a lightly floured surface, roll the dough into a 10-inch square. Cut decorative vents in pastry. Carefully place pastry over apples. Using the tines of a fork, press edges to sides of dish. Brush pastry with milk and sprinkle with the reserved sugar mixture.

5. Bake in a 375° oven about 40 minutes or until the apples are tender and the crust is golden brown. Serve warm. Makes 8 servings.

NUTRITION FACTS PER SERVING:

171 calories
5 g total fat
1 g saturated fat
0 mg cholesterol
85 mg sodium
33 g carbohydrate
2 g fiber
1 g protein

strawberry bavarian pie

Naturally low-fat ladyfinger sponge cakes form the crust for this light, strawberry-flavored pie. Shop for soft ladyfingers at bakeries or grocery stores; the crispy ones will not work as well.

INGREDIENTS

- 3 **cups fresh strawberries**
- ¼ **cup sugar**
- 1 **envelope unflavored gelatin**
- 3 **slightly beaten egg whites**
- 1 **3-ounce package ladyfingers, split**
- 2 **tablespoons orange juice**
- ½ **of an 8-ounce container frozen light whipped dessert topping, thawed (about 1⅔ cups)**

Frozen light whipped dessert topping, thawed (optional)
Strawberry fans (see tip, page 255) (optional)

Prep time: 20 minutes
Chilling time: 2½ hours

DIRECTIONS

1. Place the 3 cups strawberries in a blender container or food processor bowl. Cover; blend or process until smooth. Measure the strawberries (you should have about 1¾ cups).

2. In a medium saucepan combine the sugar and gelatin. Stir in the blended strawberries. Cook and stir over medium heat until the mixture bubbles and the gelatin is dissolved.

3. Gradually stir about half of the gelatin mixture into the slightly beaten egg whites.

Return all of the mixture to the saucepan. Cook, stirring constantly, over low heat for 2 to 3 minutes or until slightly thickened. Do not boil. Pour into a mixing bowl. Chill just until the mixture mounds when dropped from a spoon, stirring occasionally.

4. Meanwhile, cut about half of the split ladyfingers in half crosswise; stand these on end around the outside edge of a 9- or 9½-inch tart pan with removable bottom or a 9-inch springform pan. Arrange the remaining split ladyfingers in bottom of pan. Slowly drizzle the orange juice over the ladyfingers.

5. Fold whipped topping into strawberry mixture; spoon into the ladyfinger-

lined pan. Cover and chill for at least 2 hours or until set. If desired, garnish with additional whipped topping and strawberry fans. Makes 10 servings.

258

NUTRITION FACTS PER SERVING:

98 calories
2 g total fat
2 g saturated fat
31 mg cholesterol
39 mg sodium
16 g carbohydrate
1 g fiber
3 g protein

INGREDIENTS

⅓ cup sugar
3 beaten eggs
1 12-ounce can (1½ cups) evaporated milk

⅓ cup sugar
1 teaspoon vanilla
Fresh fruit (optional)
Edible flowers (optional)

flan

Flan was imported directly from Spain. The inverted caramel custard is so well loved it's found on restaurant dessert menus everywhere. Canned evaporated milk gives the custard a rich flavor.

Prep time: 30 minutes
Baking time: 30 minutes
Chilling time: 4 hours

DIRECTIONS

1. To caramelize sugar, in a heavy skillet cook ⅓ cup sugar over medium-high heat until the sugar begins to melt, shaking skillet occasionally. Do not stir. Once the sugar starts to melt, reduce heat to low and cook about 5 minutes more or until all of the sugar melts and is golden brown, stirring as needed with a wooden spoon.

2. Remove skillet from heat. Immediately pour the caramelized sugar into an 8-inch flan pan or an 8×1½-inch round baking pan (or divide caramelized sugar among six 6-ounce custard cups). Working quickly, rotate pan or cups so sugar coats the bottom as evenly as possible. Cool.

3. In a medium mixing bowl combine the eggs, evaporated milk, ⅓ cup sugar, and vanilla. Place the pan or custard cups in a 13×9×2-inch baking pan on an oven rack. Pour the egg mixture into pan or custard cups. Pour the hottest tap water available into the 13×9×2-inch pan around the flan or 8-inch baking pan or custard cups to a depth of about ½ inch.

4. Bake in a 325° oven for 30 to 35 minutes for flan or 8-inch baking pan (35 to 40 minutes for custard cups) or until a knife inserted near the center comes out clean. Immediately remove pan or custard cups from hot water. Cool on a wire rack. Cover and chill for 4 to 24 hours.

5. To unmold flan, loosen edges with a knife, slipping end of knife down sides of pan to let in air. Invert a serving platter over the pan or dessert plates over each custard cup; turn dishes over together to release custard. Spoon any caramelized sugar that remains in pan or cups over top(s). If desired, serve with fresh fruit and garnish with edible flowers. Makes 6 servings.

Before the sugar begins to melt, shake the pan occasionally, but do not stir until melting begins. The sugar is caramelized when it is syrupy and golden brown.

NUTRITION FACTS PER SERVING:

202 calories
7 g total fat
3 g saturated fat
123 mg cholesterol
92 mg sodium
28 g carbohydrate
0 g fiber
7 g protein

259

fresh fruit with minted yogurt

With summer produce at its peak, you'll have no trouble finding your favorite fruits to mix and match in this "plum good" dessert.

INGREDIENTS

1 16-ounce carton plain low-fat yogurt
3 tablespoons honey
2 tablespoons snipped fresh mint
4 medium plums, pitted and thinly sliced (about 3 cups)
3 cups assorted fresh berries, such as blueberries, raspberries, and strawberries
   Fresh mint (optional)

Thinly sliced nectarines or peaches make an excellent substitute for the plums. Make sure you have about 3 cups sliced fruit.

Prep time: 15 minutes

DIRECTIONS

1. In a small mixing bowl stir together the yogurt, honey, and snipped mint. Cover and chill until ready to serve.

2. To serve, in a medium bowl combine the plums and assorted berries. Divide fruit mixture among 6 individual dessert dishes. Spoon yogurt mixture on top of each serving. If desired, garnish with additional fresh mint. Makes 6 servings.

NUTRITION FACTS PER SERVING:

144 calories
1 g total fat
0 g saturated fat
1 mg cholesterol
56 mg sodium
31 g carbohydrate
3 g fiber
5 g protein

autumn fruits with cinnamon custard

Lady apples and small Seckel pears combine for a comforting twosome, served with a cinnamony stirred custard. If Lady apples and Seckel pears aren't available, don't worry—this recipe works well with other varieties of these fruits.

INGREDIENTS

- 6 Seckel or Forelle pears
- 6 Lady apples
- ⅔ cup white vermouth, apple cider, or apple juice
- 3 whole star anise
- 3 tablespoons sugar
- 1 recipe Cinnamon Custard

Start to finish: 25 minutes

DIRECTIONS

1. If desired, core fruit. Quarter the pears lengthwise; halve the apples crosswise. Set aside. In a large skillet bring the vermouth, apple cider, or juice just to boiling; reduce heat. Gently add the pears, apples, and star anise to hot liquid. Sprinkle the sugar over the fruit. Cook, covered, about 5 minutes or until the fruit is just tender.

2. Using a slotted spoon, transfer fruit to 6 dessert dishes. Discard poaching liquid. Drizzle fruit with Cinnamon Custard. Serves 6.

Cinnamon Custard: In a small heavy saucepan combine 1 beaten egg, ⅔ cup milk, and 4 teaspoons sugar. Cook and stir over medium heat just until the mixture coats the back of a spoon. Stir in ½ teaspoon vanilla and dash ground cinnamon. Remove from heat. If desired, place in a pan of ice water to stop the cooking process.

To test the custard, dip a clean metal spoon into the cooked custard. The custard should coat the spoon. Using your finger, draw a line down the center of the back of the spoon. The edges of the custard along the path drawn should hold their shape.

NUTRITION FACTS PER SERVING:

188 calories
2 g total fat
1 g saturated fat
38 mg cholesterol
25 mg sodium
36 g carbohydrate
4 g fiber
3 g protein

summer fruit cups

A dessert this simple depends on the finest ingredients for its success. Start with juicy summer fruits, then drizzle on a syrup steeped with verbena leaves. The verbena lends a sweet, clean, lemon flavor.

INGREDIENTS

1 cup water
½ cup sugar
¼ cup fresh lemon verbena leaves
      or 1 teaspoon finely shredded
      lemon peel
¼ cup loosely packed fresh
      mint leaves
2 cups sliced fresh apricots
2 cups sliced fresh nectarines

1 cup fresh boysenberries,
      blackberries, and/or
      raspberries
¼ cup loosely packed fresh
      mint leaves

To ripen apricots, nectarines, plums, peaches, pears, or tomatoes, place fruit in a paper bag and let it stand at room temperature for a few days or until desired ripeness. Once the fruit is ripe, store in the refrigerator.

Start to finish: 40 minutes

DIRECTIONS

1. In a 1-quart saucepan combine the water, sugar, lemon verbena or lemon peel, and ¼ cup mint leaves. Cook and stir over medium heat until bubbly; reduce heat. Simmer, covered, for 10 minutes. Strain, discarding the lemon verbena and mint. Cool. Use at once or cover and chill for up to 3 days.

2. In a large bowl combine the fruit and ¼ cup mint leaves. Drizzle the cooled syrup over the fruit mixture. Serve at once or cover and chill for up to 3 hours. Makes 8 servings.

NUTRITION FACTS PER SERVING:

95 calories
0 g total fat
0 g saturated fat
0 mg cholesterol
2 mg sodium
24 g carbohydrate
2 g fiber
1 g protein

INGREDIENTS

Butter or margarine
Granulated sugar
½ cup chunk-style applesauce
2 tablespoons apple brandy or apple juice
1 tablespoon lemon juice
2 tablespoons butter or margarine

3 tablespoons all-purpose flour
¾ cup milk
4 beaten egg yolks
4 egg whites
½ teaspoon vanilla
¼ cup granulated sugar

french apple soufflé

Follow the baking time carefully to avoid overbaking, or the soufflé could water out and easily collapse.

Prep time: 30 minutes
Baking time: 35 minutes

DIRECTIONS

1. Butter the sides of a 1½-quart soufflé dish. Sprinkle the sides of the dish with a little sugar. Set aside.

2. In a small mixing bowl stir together the applesauce, apple brandy or apple juice, and lemon juice. Set aside.

3. In a small saucepan melt the 2 tablespoons butter or margarine. Stir in flour. Add milk all at once. Cook and stir over medium heat until thickened and bubbly. Remove from heat.

4. Gradually stir the hot mixture into the beaten egg yolks. Stir in the applesauce mixture. Set aside.

5. In a large mixing bowl beat egg whites and vanilla with an electric mixer on medium speed until soft peaks form (tips curl). Gradually add the ¼ cup sugar, about 1 tablespoon at a time, beating on medium to high speed until stiff peaks form (tips stand straight).

6. Fold about 1 cup of the beaten whites into applesauce mixture. Fold applesauce mixture into remaining beaten whites. Carefully transfer to prepared dish.

7. Bake in a 350° oven about 35 minutes or until a knife inserted near the center comes out clean. Serve at once. Makes 6 servings.

To serve your soufflé, insert two forks back to back, and gently pull the soufflé apart. Cut into serving-size wedges in this manner. Use a large serving spoon to transfer the portions to individual plates.

NUTRITION FACTS PER SERVING:

190 calories
9 g total fat
5 g saturated fat
158 mg cholesterol
109 mg sodium
19 g carbohydrate
0 g fiber
6 g protein

pecan ice-cream roll

Make this elegant, splurge dessert up to 2 weeks in advance and store it, tightly wrapped, in your freezer.

INGREDIENTS

⅓ cup all-purpose flour

¼ cup unsweetened cocoa powder

1 teaspoon baking powder

¼ teaspoon salt

4 egg yolks

½ teaspoon vanilla

⅓ cup granulated sugar

4 egg whites

½ cup granulated sugar

Sifted powdered sugar

1 quart fat-free vanilla ice cream, softened

¼ cup broken pecans

1 recipe Raspberry Sauce (optional)

Fresh raspberries (optional)

Fresh mint (optional)

Prep time: 45 minutes
Baking time: 12 minutes
Cooling time: 30 minutes
Freezing time: 4 hours

DIRECTIONS

1. Grease and flour a 15×10×1-inch baking pan. Stir together the flour, cocoa powder, baking powder, and salt. Set aside.

2. In a small mixing bowl beat the egg yolks and vanilla with an electric mixer on high speed about 5 minutes or until thick and lemon-colored. Gradually add the ⅓ cup sugar, beating on medium speed about 5 minutes or until sugar is almost dissolved. Thoroughly wash the beaters.

3. In a large mixing bowl beat the egg whites on medium to high speed until soft peaks form (tips curl).

Gradually add the ½ cup granulated sugar, beating until stiff peaks form (tips stand straight). Fold the yolk mixture into the egg white mixture. Sprinkle the flour mixture over the egg mixture; fold in gently just until combined. Spread the batter evenly in the prepared pan.

4. Bake in a 375° oven for 12 to 15 minutes or until the top springs back when lightly touched. Immediately loosen edges of cake from pan; turn out onto a towel sprinkled with powdered sugar. Starting from a short side, roll up cake and towel together into a spiral. Cool on a wire rack.

5. Unroll the cake. Spread softened ice cream onto cake to within 1 inch of edges. Sprinkle with pecans. Reroll

cake without towel. Wrap and freeze for at least 4 hours. To serve, if desired, drizzle Raspberry Sauce over serving plates. Slice cake; place on plates. If desired, garnish with raspberries and mint. Makes 10 servings.

Raspberry Sauce: In a saucepan combine ⅔ cup seedless raspberry spreadable fruit, 1 tablespoon lemon juice, and ¼ teaspoon almond extract. Cook and stir just until melted. Cool slightly.

NUTRITION FACTS PER SERVING:

211 calories
5 g total fat
1 g saturated fat
85 mg cholesterol
171 mg sodium
38 g carbohydrate
0 g fiber
6 g protein

INGREDIENTS

- 1½ cups egg whites (10 to 12 large eggs)
- 1½ cups sifted powdered sugar
- 1 cup sifted cake flour or sifted all-purpose flour
- 3 tablespoons unsweetened cocoa powder
- ¼ teaspoon ground cinnamon
- 1½ teaspoons cream of tartar
- 1 teaspoon vanilla
- 1 cup granulated sugar
- Chocolate-flavored syrup (optional)
- Strawberries (optional)

chocolate-cinnamon angel cake

A mild chocolate flavor accented with cinnamon sets this angel cake apart from others. However, it's still low in calories and fat-free. Chocolate purists can omit the cinnamon.

Prep time: 50 minutes
Baking time: 40 minutes
Cooling time: 3 hours

DIRECTIONS

1. In a extra-large mixing bowl allow the egg whites to stand at room temperature for 30 minutes.

2. Meanwhile, sift the powdered sugar, flour, cocoa powder, and cinnamon together 3 times. Set aside.

3. Add the cream of tartar and vanilla to the egg whites. Beat with an electric mixer on medium speed until soft peaks form (tips curl).

4. Gradually add granulated sugar, about 2 tablespoons at a time, beating on high speed until stiff peaks form (tips stand straight).

5. Sift about one-fourth of the dry mixture over the beaten egg whites; fold in gently. Repeat, folding in the remaining dry mixture by fourths. Pour into an ungreased 10-inch tube pan. Using a narrow metal spatula or knife, gently cut through the batter to remove any large air pockets.

6. Bake in a 350° oven on the lowest rack for 40 to 45 minutes or until the top of cake springs back when lightly touched.

7. Immediately invert cake (leave in pan); cool completely. When cool, loosen sides of cake from pan. Remove cake from pan. To serve, slice into wedges. If desired, serve cake drizzled with chocolate-flavored syrup and garnish with strawberries. Makes 16 servings.

NUTRITION FACTS PER SERVING:

125 calories
0 g total fat
0 g saturated fat
0 mg cholesterol
35 mg sodium
28 g carbohydrate
0 g fiber
3 g protein

mango mousse

For this recipe, look for mangoes that have a healthy red blush and feel slightly soft to the touch like a ripe tomato.

INGREDIENTS

2 ripe mangoes, seeded, peeled, and chopped
1 envelope unflavored gelatin
2 tablespoons sugar
2 teaspoons lemon juice
1 8-ounce container frozen light whipped dessert topping, thawed
   Mango and/or kiwi fruit slices (optional)

Removing a mango seed takes a little cutting know-how. Place the fruit on its blossom end and align a sharp knife slightly off-center of the stemmed end. Slice down through the peel and flesh, next to the seed. Repeat on the other side. Cut off the remaining flesh around the seed. Cut off the peel, then cut the mango into pieces as directed.

Prep time: 20 minutes
Freezing time: 45 minutes
Chilling time: 4 hours

266

DIRECTIONS

1. In a food processor bowl or blender container place the chopped mangoes. Cover and process or blend until smooth. Add enough water to make 2 cups puree. Transfer the mango mixture to a medium saucepan and bring to boiling.

2. In a large mixing bowl stir together the gelatin and sugar. Pour mango mixture over gelatin mixture and stir until gelatin dissolves. Stir in the lemon juice. Cover and freeze for 45 to 60 minutes or until the mixture mounds when dropped from a spoon, stirring occasionally.

3. Beat the mango mixture with an electric mixer for 2 to 3 minutes or until mixture is thick and light. Fold in the whipped topping.

4. Pipe or spoon the mango mixture into 6 dessert dishes or parfait glasses. Cover and chill until set. If desired, garnish with mango and/or kiwi fruit slices. Makes 6 servings.

NUTRITION FACTS PER SERVING:

149 calories
5 g total fat
0 g saturated fat
1 mg cholesterol
31 mg sodium
25 g carbohydrate
2 g fiber
1 g protein

INGREDIENTS

Nonstick spray coating

⅓ cup crushed vanilla wafers
     (8 wafers)

1½ 8-ounce tubs fat-free cream
     cheese, softened
     (12 ounces total)

½ cup sugar

1 tablespoon all-purpose flour

1 teaspoon vanilla

¼ cup frozen egg product, thawed

¾ cup fresh raspberries;
     blueberries; sliced, peeled
     kiwi fruit; sliced strawberries;
     sliced, pitted plums; and/or
     orange sections

Prep time: 20 minutes
Baking time: 18 minutes
Chilling time: 4 hours

DIRECTIONS

1. Spray ten 2½-inch muffin cups with nonstick coating. Sprinkle bottom and side of each cup with about 1 teaspoon of the crushed vanilla wafers. Set aside.

2. In a medium mixing bowl beat the cream cheese with an electric mixer on medium speed until smooth. Add sugar, flour, and vanilla. Beat on medium speed until smooth. Add egg product and beat on low speed just until combined. Divide mixture evenly among muffin cups.

3. Bake in a 325° oven for 18 to 20 minutes or until set.

Cool in pan on a wire rack for 5 minutes. Cover pan and chill for 4 to 24 hours. Remove the cheesecakes from the muffin cups. Just before serving, top the cheesecakes with fresh fruit. Makes 10 cheesecakes.

mini cheesecakes

Top these tiny cheesecakes with whatever fruit strikes your fancy. The small size makes perfect light desserts or party treats.

NUTRITION FACTS PER SERVING:

124 calories
4 g total fat
1 g saturated fat
5 mg cholesterol
25 mg sodium
16 g carbohydrate
0 g fiber
6 g protein

267

strawberry-topped cheesecake

To test for a perfectly baked, creamy cheesecake, gently shake the pan after the minimum baking time. The center should appear nearly set. If it still jiggles, bake it 5 minutes longer and test again.

INGREDIENTS

- ½ cup graham cracker crumbs
- 4 teaspoons margarine or butter, melted
- 2 8-ounce packages fat-free cream cheese (block style)
- 1 cup fat-free cottage cheese
- ¼ cup fat-free milk
- ¾ cup sugar
- 2 tablespoons all-purpose flour
- 1¼ teaspoons vanilla
- ½ teaspoon finely shredded lemon peel
- 3 eggs or ¾ cup refrigerated or frozen egg product, thawed
- ¼ cup fat-free or light dairy sour cream
- 2 teaspoons fat-free milk
- 1 teaspoon sugar
- 1 cup sliced strawberries

Prep time: 20 minutes
Baking time: 35 minutes
Cooling time: 2 hours
Chilling time: 4 hours

DIRECTIONS

1. In a small bowl stir together the graham cracker crumbs and melted margarine or butter. Press onto the bottom of an 8-inch springform pan. Set aside.

2. Cut up the cream cheese. In a large food processor bowl place the undrained cottage cheese and the ¼ cup milk. Cover and process until smooth. Add cream cheese, the ¾ cup sugar, the flour, 1 teaspoon of the vanilla, and the lemon peel. Cover; process until smooth. Add the eggs or egg product and process just until combined. Do not overprocess. Pour mixture into pan. Place on a baking sheet.

3. Bake in a 375° oven for 35 to 40 minutes or until set. Cool for 15 minutes. Using a narrow metal spatula, loosen the side of the cheesecake from pan. Cool 30 minutes more, then remove the side of pan. Cool completely. Cover and chill for at least 4 hours.

4. In a small bowl combine the sour cream, the 2 teaspoons milk, the 1 teaspoon sugar, and remaining vanilla. To serve, arrange berries on top of cheesecake; drizzle with sour cream mixture. Serves 12.

NUTRITION FACTS PER SERVING:

163 calories
3 g total fat
1 g saturated fat
62 mg cholesterol
92 mg sodium
22 g carbohydrate
0 g fiber
11 g protein

INGREDIENTS

Nonstick spray coating
½ cup water
2 tablespoons margarine or butter
½ cup all-purpose flour
2 eggs
1 4-serving-size package fat-free instant chocolate pudding mix or reduced-calorie chocolate pudding mix

⅛ teaspoon peppermint extract
1 cup sliced strawberries
Sifted powdered sugar (optional)
Fresh mint (optional)

mint-chocolate cream puffs

Watching your diet doesn't mean giving up chocolate. These minty chocolate puffs have loads of flavor—and only 126 calories and 4 grams of fat per serving.

Prep time: 25 minutes
Baking time: 30 minutes
Cooling time: 1 hour

DIRECTIONS

1. Spray a baking sheet with nonstick coating. Set aside. In a small saucepan combine the water and margarine or butter. Bring to boiling. Add the flour all at once, stirring vigorously. Cook and stir until mixture forms a ball. Remove from heat. Cool for 5 minutes.

2. Add the eggs, one at a time, beating after each addition. Drop the mixture into 8 mounds, about 3 inches apart, onto the prepared baking sheet.

3. Bake in a 400° oven about 30 minutes or until golden brown. Remove from oven. Split puffs and remove any soft dough from inside. Cool well on a wire rack.

4. Meanwhile, for filling, prepare the pudding mix according to package directions. Stir in peppermint extract. Cover the surface of pudding with plastic wrap and chill thoroughly.

5. To serve, spoon about ¼ cup of the filling into the bottom half of each cream puff. Top with the sliced strawberries. Replace the tops. If desired, dust with powdered sugar and garnish with fresh mint. Makes 8 servings.

After adding the flour, stir the dough vigorously until the mixture forms a ball that doesn't separate. Cool as directed. Add the eggs, one at a time. After each addition, use a wooden spoon to beat the dough until it is smooth.

NUTRITION FACTS PER SERVING:

126 calories
4 g total fat
1 g saturated fat
53 mg cholesterol
225 mg sodium
20 g carbohydrate
1 g fiber
2 g protein

brownie-fruit pizza

To make the brownie crust easier to cut, spray a pizza cutter or knife with nonstick spray coating.

INGREDIENTS

Nonstick spray coating

½ cup sugar

3 tablespoons margarine or butter, softened

¼ cup refrigerated or frozen egg product, thawed

¾ cup chocolate-flavored syrup

⅔ cup all-purpose flour

3 cups fresh fruit, such as sliced, peeled, and quartered kiwi fruit; sliced, peeled peaches; sliced nectarines or strawberries; raspberries; or blueberries

½ cup chocolate-flavored syrup

Prep time: 15 minutes
Baking time: 20 minutes
Cooling time: 2 hours

DIRECTIONS

1. Spray a 12-inch pizza pan with nonstick coating. Set aside.

2. For crust, in a medium mixing bowl combine the sugar and margarine or butter. Beat with an electric mixer on medium speed until creamy. Add the egg product; beat well. Alternately add the ¾ cup chocolate syrup and the flour, beating after each addition on low speed until combined. Spread in the prepared pizza pan.

3. Bake in a 350° oven about 20 minutes or until the top springs back when lightly touched. Cool in the pan on a wire rack.

4. To serve, cut the brownie into 12 wedges. Top each wedge with fruit and drizzle with the ½ cup chocolate syrup. Makes 12 servings.

NUTRITION FACTS PER SERVING:

169 calories
4 g total fat
1 g saturated fat
0 mg cholesterol
60 mg sodium
35 g carbohydrate
1 g fiber
2 g protein

INGREDIENTS

¼ of an 18-ounce roll refrigerated
    sugar cookie dough, sliced
    ¼ inch thick (8 slices)

½ cup frozen light whipped dessert
    topping, thawed

½ cup fat-free dairy sour cream

1 teaspoon finely shredded
    orange peel

3 cups fresh or frozen berries
    (such as raspberries,
    blackberries, or sliced
    strawberries), thawed
    and drained

Sifted unsweetened cocoa
    powder (optional)
Orange peel twists (optional)
Edible flowers (optional)

cookies and cream

This Italian dessert usually is laden with whipped cream and yogurt. To lighten the calorie load, we skipped the cream and yogurt and added fat-free sour cream to light dessert topping instead. We also used slice-and-bake cookies instead of a homemade dough to save you time.

Prep time: 20 minutes
Baking time: 8 minutes

NUTRITION FACTS PER SERVING:

222 calories
7 g total fat
3 g saturated fat
5 mg cholesterol
154 mg sodium
36 g carbohydrate
4 g fiber
3 g protein

DIRECTIONS

1. Bake sugar cookies according to package directions. Set aside to cool.

2. Meanwhile, combine the whipped topping and sour cream. Stir in the shredded orange peel. Cover and chill until serving time.

3. To assemble, place a cookie on each of 4 dessert plates. Top each cookie with about one-fourth of the berries, one-fourth of the sour cream mixture, another cookie, the remaining sour cream mixture, and the remaining berries. If desired, dust with cocoa powder and garnish with orange peel and edible flowers. Makes 4 servings.

271

apricot-cardamom bars

Applesauce and apricot nectar replace some of the fat in these moist snack bars.

INGREDIENTS

- 1 cup all-purpose flour
- ½ cup packed brown sugar
- ½ teaspoon baking powder
- ¼ teaspoon baking soda
- ¼ teaspoon ground cardamom or
  - ⅛ teaspoon ground cloves
- 1 slightly beaten egg
- ½ cup apricot nectar or
  - orange juice
- ¼ cup unsweetened applesauce
- 2 tablespoons cooking oil
- ½ cup finely snipped dried apricots
- 1 recipe Apricot Icing

Experiment with cardamom for a new

change of spice. Cardamom has a pungent and aromatic flowery sweetness that's a little like ginger but is much more subtle. Try it in place of some of your favorite spices, such as cinnamon, nutmeg, or ginger.

Prep time: 20 minutes
Baking time: 25 minutes
Cooling time: 2 hours

272

DIRECTIONS

1. In a medium mixing bowl stir together the flour, brown sugar, baking powder, baking soda, and cardamom or cloves; set aside. In a small mixing bowl stir together the egg, apricot nectar or orange juice, applesauce, and oil until combined. Add to dry ingredients, stirring just until moistened. Stir in apricots.

2. Spread batter in an ungreased 11×7×1½-inch baking pan. Bake in a 350° oven about 25 minutes or until a toothpick inserted near the center comes out clean. Cool in pan on a rack. Drizzle with Apricot Icing. Cut into bars. Makes 24 bars.

Apricot Icing: In a small bowl stir together ½ cup sifted powdered sugar and 1 to 2 teaspoons apricot nectar or orange juice. Stir in enough additional apricot nectar or orange juice, 1 teaspoon at a time, to make of drizzling consistency.

NUTRITION FACTS PER BAR:

63 calories
1 g total fat
0 g saturated fat
9 mg cholesterol
25 mg sodium
12 g carbohydrate
1 g fiber
1 g protein

cashew meringues

A drizzling of caramel and a sprinkling of cashews create a melt-in-your-mouth cookie that is simply irresistible.

INGREDIENTS

- 4 egg whites
- 1 teaspoon vanilla
- ¼ teaspoon cream of tartar
- 4 cups sifted powdered sugar
- 2 cups chopped cashews or mixed nuts
- 12 vanilla caramels, unwrapped
- 2 teaspoons milk

Prep time: 25 minutes
Baking time: 15 minutes per batch

DIRECTIONS

1. In a large mixing bowl allow egg whites to stand at room temperature for 30 minutes. Meanwhile, grease a cookie sheet; set aside.

2. Add vanilla and cream of tartar to egg whites. Beat with an electric mixer on medium speed until soft peaks form (tips curl). Gradually add the powdered sugar, about ¼ cup at a time, beating on medium speed just until combined. Beat for 1 to 2 minutes more or until soft peaks form. (Do not continue beating to stiff peaks.) Using a spoon, gently fold in the cashews or mixed nuts.

3. Drop egg white mixture by a rounded teaspoon about 2 inches apart onto prepared cookie sheet. Bake cookies in a 325° oven about 15 minutes or until edges are very lightly browned. Transfer cookies to a wire rack; cool.

4. In a small saucepan combine the caramels and milk. Heat and stir over low heat until the caramels are melted. Place cookies on a wire rack over waxed paper. Drizzle caramel mixture over cookies. If desired, sprinkle with additional chopped cashews or mixed nuts. Let stand until caramel mixture is set. Makes 60 cookies.

NUTRITION FACTS PER COOKIE:

61 calories
2 g total fat
1 g saturated fat
0 mg cholesterol
9 mg sodium
10 g carbohydrate
0 g fiber
1 g protein

citrus-hazelnut bars

Definitely a bar cookie with lots of appeal—these double citrus and nutty delights are not overly sweet. They make a great accompaniment to an afternoon tea break.

INGREDIENTS

- ⅓ cup butter
- ¼ cup granulated sugar
- 1 cup all-purpose flour
- ⅓ cup chopped toasted hazelnuts (filberts) or chopped almonds
- 2 eggs
- ¾ cup granulated sugar
- 2 tablespoons all-purpose flour
- 1 teaspoon finely shredded orange peel
- 1 teaspoon finely shredded lemon peel
- 2 tablespoons orange juice
- 1 tablespoon lemon juice
- ½ teaspoon baking powder
  Powdered sugar (optional)

Prep time: 20 minutes
Baking time: 30 minutes

DIRECTIONS

1. For the crust, beat the butter in a medium mixing bowl with an electric mixer on medium to high speed for 30 seconds. Add the ¼ cup granulated sugar. Beat until thoroughly combined. Beat in the 1 cup flour and about half of the nuts until mixture is crumbly.

2. Press mixture into the bottom of an ungreased 8×8×2-inch baking pan. Bake in a 350° oven for 10 minutes or until lightly browned.

3. Meanwhile, in a mixing bowl stir together the eggs, the ¾ cup granulated sugar, the 2 tablespoons flour, orange peel, lemon peel, orange juice, lemon juice, and baking powder. Beat for 2 minutes at medium speed or until combined. Pour over hot baked layer. Sprinkle with remaining nuts.

4. Bake about 20 minutes more or until light brown around the edges and the center is set. Cool on a rack. If desired, sifted powdered sugar over top. Cut into bars. Store bars, covered, in the refrigerator. Makes 20 bars.

NUTRITION FACTS PER BAR:

111 calories
5 g total fat
1 g saturated fat
25 mg cholesterol
43 mg sodium
16 g carbohydrate
0 g fiber
2 g protein

lemon bars with raspberries

Impressive and easy to make, this refreshingly tart dessert is a great ending for any meal.

INGREDIENTS

Nonstick spray coating
¾ cup all-purpose flour
3 tablespoons sugar
¼ cup margarine or butter
1 egg
1 egg white
⅔ cup sugar
2 tablespoons all-purpose flour
1 teaspoon finely shredded lemon peel (set aside)
2 tablespoons lemon juice
1 tablespoon water
¼ teaspoon baking powder
1½ cups fresh raspberries
2 tablespoons red currant jelly, melted

Prep time: 25 minutes
Baking time: 35 minutes
Cooling time: 1 hour

DIRECTIONS

1. Spray an 8×8×2-inch baking pan with nonstick coating. Set aside. In a small mixing bowl combine the ¾ cup flour and the 3 tablespoons sugar. Cut in the margarine or butter until crumbly. Pat the mixture onto the bottom of the prepared pan. Bake in a 350° oven for 15 minutes.

2. Meanwhile, for filling, in a small mixing bowl combine the egg and egg white. Beat with an electric mixer on medium speed until frothy. Add the ⅔ cup sugar, the 2 tablespoons flour, the lemon juice, water, and baking powder. Beat on medium speed about 3 minutes or until slightly thickened. Stir in lemon peel.

3. Pour over hot baked layer in pan. Bake for 20 to 25 minutes more or until edges are light brown and center is set. Cool completely in pan on a wire rack. Cut into 9 squares; cut each square diagonally to make a triangle. Top triangles with raspberries. Drizzle with the jelly. Makes 18 servings.

NUTRITION FACTS PER SERVING:

96 calories
3 g total fat
1 g saturated fat
12 mg cholesterol
42 mg sodium
17 g carbohydrate
1 g fiber
1 g protein

chocolate ricotta-filled pears

Discover all the wonderful flavors of the classic Sicilian ricotta-chocolate-fruit-filled cake called cassata—without turning on your oven or chopping a thing. Be sure the pears are ripe. Serve them with an Italian dessert wine, such as Vin Santo.

INGREDIENTS

- 1 cup ricotta cheese
- 1/3 cup sifted powdered sugar
- 1 tablespoon unsweetened cocoa powder
- 1/4 teaspoon vanilla
- 2 tablespoons miniature semisweet chocolate pieces
- 1 teaspoon finely shredded orange peel
- 3 large ripe Bosc, Anjou, or Bartlett pears
- 2 tablespoons orange juice
- 2 tablespoons slivered or sliced almonds, toasted (see tip, page 108)
- Fresh mint (optional)
- Orange peel curls (optional)

Ricotta cheese is a fresh, moist, white cheese that is very mild and semisweet. It has a soft and slightly grainy texture. Ricotta is available in whole milk, part-skim, light, or fat-free varieties, with the whole milk cheese having a creamier consistency and fuller flavor.

Prep time: 20 minutes

DIRECTIONS

1. In a medium mixing bowl beat together the ricotta cheese, sugar, cocoa powder, and vanilla with an electric mixer on medium speed until combined. Stir in chocolate pieces and the 1 teaspoon orange peel. Set aside.

2. Peel the pears; cut in half lengthwise and remove the cores. Remove a thin slice from the rounded sides so the pear halves will sit flat. Brush the pears all over with orange juice. Place the pears on dessert plates.

3. Spoon the ricotta mixture on top of the pears and sprinkle with the almonds. If desired, garnish with fresh mint and orange curls. Makes 6 servings

NUTRITION FACTS PER SERVING:

166 calories
6 g total fat
2 g saturated fat
13 mg cholesterol
52 mg sodium
24 g carbohydrate
3 g fiber
6 g protein

INGREDIENTS

- 4   small pears
- 2   tablespoons lemon juice
- 2   teaspoons vanilla
- ½   teaspoon ground cinnamon
- 2   tablespoons chocolate-flavored
     syrup

chocolate-sauced pears

Go ahead—splurge. These luscious pears contain less than 120 calories and only 1 gram of fat per serving.

Prep time: 15 minutes
Baking time: 30 minutes

DIRECTIONS

1. Core the pears from the bottom end, leaving the stems intact. Peel the pears. If necessary, cut a thin slice from the bottoms of pears to help stand upright.

2. Place the pears in a 2-quart square baking dish. In a small bowl stir together the lemon juice, vanilla, and cinnamon. Brush onto the pears. Pour any extra lemon juice mixture over pears.

3. Bake pears, covered, in a 375° oven for 30 to 35 minutes or until tender. Cool slightly.

4. To serve, place the warm pears, stem ends up, on dessert plates. Strain the baking liquid; pour the liquid into a small bowl. Stir in the chocolate-flavored syrup. Drizzle the chocolate sauce over the pears. Serve warm. Makes 4 servings.

Carefully insert an apple corer into the bottom end of each pear, leaving the stem intact. Twist and pull to remove the core.

NUTRITION FACTS PER SERVING:

116 calories
1 g total fat
0 g saturated fat
0 mg cholesterol
5 mg sodium
29 g carbohydrate
2 g fiber
1 g protein

pineapple-topped ice cream

Present this versatile dessert as flashy or as humbly as you like. Ignite the rum and serve as a sensational flambé. Or skip the rum, and crown it with light whipped dessert topping and a maraschino cherry.

INGREDIENTS

- ½ teaspoon finely shredded orange peel
- ¼ cup orange juice
- 2 teaspoons cornstarch
- ½ teaspoon ground ginger
- 1 20-ounce can crushed pineapple (juice pack), undrained
- 2 tablespoons light rum (optional)
- 1½ cups vanilla low-fat or light ice cream or frozen yogurt
  Orange peel strips (optional)

The freezer section is brimming with a variety of ice-cream-like treats in a multitude of tempting flavors. Which one is best for a healthy diet? Check out the fat contents listed on the packages of ice cream, ice milk, frozen yogurt, and sherbet to help you decide.

Start to finish: 12 minutes

DIRECTIONS

1. In a large skillet stir together the shredded orange peel, the orange juice, cornstarch, and ground ginger. Stir in undrained pineapple. Cook and stir until slightly thickened and bubbly. Cook and stir for 2 minutes more. Remove from heat.

2. If desired, in a small saucepan heat the rum over low heat just until warm. Using a long match, carefully ignite the rum. While it's still flaming, carefully pour the rum over the pineapple mixture. When the flame dwindles, serve immediately over the ice cream or frozen yogurt. If desired, garnish with orange peel strips. Makes 6 servings.

NUTRITION FACTS PER SERVING:

111 calories
2 g total fat
1 g saturated fat
5 mg cholesterol
30 mg sodium
24 g carbohydrate
1 g fiber
2 g protein

frozen berry yogurt

Kick off the ice-cream-making season with this frosty treat.

INGREDIENTS

- 1¼ cups sugar
- 1 cup water
- 3 cups fresh raspberries, blackberries, and/or strawberries
- 3 8-ounce cartons vanilla yogurt
- 1 teaspoon vanilla
- Fresh melon or other fruit, cut into thin slices (optional)

Prep time: 25 minutes
Chilling time: 8 hours
Freezing time: 45 minutes
Ripening time: 4 hours

DIRECTIONS

1. In a medium saucepan combine the sugar and water. Cook and stir over high heat until the mixture comes to a boil and the sugar dissolves. Remove from heat; cool.

2. In a blender container combine half of the sugar mixture and half of the berries. Cover and blend until almost smooth. Pour into a fine mesh sieve set over a bowl. Press the berry mixture through sieve; discard seeds.

Transfer the berry mixture to a large mixing bowl. Repeat with the remaining sugar mixture and the remaining berries. Stir in the yogurt and vanilla; mix until well combined. Cover and chill for at least 8 hours or overnight.

3. Freeze the mixture in a 2-quart ice-cream freezer according to manufacturer's directions. Ripen for 4 hours. If desired, cut melon or other fruit into long, thin ribbons with a vegetable peeler. Serve with scoops of frozen yogurt. Makes 6 to 8 servings.

Homemade frozen yogurt and
ice cream taste better and melt more slowly if they are ripened before serving. To ripen, follow the manufacturer's directions for your ice-cream freezer.

NUTRITION FACTS PER SERVING:

298 calories
2 g total fat
1 g saturated fat
6 mg cholesterol
67 mg sodium
67 g carbohydrate
3 g fiber
5 g protein

279

macaroons

Made from whipped egg whites, macaroons have long been a friend to dieters. A simple chocolate drizzle updates these feather-light morsels.

INGREDIENTS

Nonstick spray coating
3   egg whites
1   cup sugar
2   cups flaked coconut (about 5 ounces)
1   ounce semisweet chocolate
½   teaspoon shortening

To pipe chocolate easily,

transfer the slightly cooled melted chocolate mixture to a self-sealing plastic bag; seal bag. Cut a small hole in a corner of the bag. Pipe the chocolate through the hole over the cookies.

Prep time: 20 minutes
Baking time: 20 minutes
Cooling/Standing time: 1 hour

DIRECTIONS

1. Spray an extra-large cookie sheet with nonstick coating. Set aside.

2. In a large mixing bowl beat the egg whites with an electric mixer on high speed until soft peaks form (tips curl). Gradually add the sugar, 1 tablespoon at a time, beating until stiff peaks form (tips stand straight). Fold in the coconut.

3. Drop by rounded teaspoons, about 2 inches apart, onto prepared cookie sheet. Bake in a 325° oven about 20 minutes or until the edges are light brown. Transfer to a wire rack; let cool about 30 minutes.

4. To serve, in a small saucepan combine the chocolate and shortening. Cook and stir over low heat until melted. Cool slightly. Pipe chocolate mixture over cookies. Let stand about 30 minutes or until chocolate is set. Store cookies in an airtight container. Makes about 45 cookies.

NUTRITION FACTS PER COOKIE:

37 calories
1 g total fat
1 g saturated fat
0 mg cholesterol
4 mg sodium
6 g carbohydrate
0 g fiber
0 g protein

cinnamon meringues with fruit

INGREDIENTS

- 2 egg whites
- ½ teaspoon vanilla
- ½ teaspoon ground cinnamon
- ¼ teaspoon cream of tartar
- ½ cup sugar
- 2 cups sliced, peeled peaches or nectarines
- 2 tablespoons sugar
- 1 tablespoon cornstarch
- 2 cups fresh fruit, such as sliced peeled peaches, nectarines, or kiwi fruit; and/or sliced strawberries

You may either pipe the meringues from a pastry bag or simply spoon them onto the baking sheet. For crispy meringue shells, serve them right away. However, if you like softer, marshmallow-like shells, chill them for up to 2 hours before serving.

Prep time: 25 minutes
Baking time: 30 minutes
Standing time: 1 hour

DIRECTIONS

1. For meringue shells, cover a baking sheet with plain brown paper. Draw six 3-inch squares or six 3½-inch circles on the paper. In a small mixing bowl beat the egg whites, vanilla, cinnamon, and cream of tartar with an electric mixer on medium speed until soft peaks form.

Gradually add the ½ cup sugar, beating on high speed until stiff peaks form and sugar is almost dissolved.

2. Spoon meringue mixture into a decorating bag fitted with a star tip (about ¼-inch opening) or a medium plain-round tip. Pipe shells onto prepared baking sheet. (Or, using a spoon or a spatula, spread meringue mixture over the squares or circles on prepared baking sheet, building sides up to form shells.)

3. Bake in a 300° oven for 30 minutes. Turn off the heat and let the shells dry in the oven with the door closed for at least 1 hour. (Do not open oven.) Peel off paper.

4. For the sauce, place the 2 cups peaches or nectarines in a blender container or food processor bowl. Cover and blend or process until nearly smooth. Pour into a small saucepan. Combine the 2 tablespoons sugar and the cornstarch; add to saucepan. Cook and stir sauce over medium heat until thickened and bubbly. Cook and stir for 2 minutes more.

5. To serve, spoon the sauce into the meringue shells. Top with fresh fruit. Serve immediately or cover and chill for up to 2 hours. Makes 6 servings.

Use only brown paper that is specially made for baking purposes. Brown paper bags may contain materials that can catch fire in the oven and also may not be sanitary.

NUTRITION FACTS PER SERVING:

138 calories
0 g total fat
0 g saturated fat
0 mg cholesterol
19 mg sodium
34 g carbohydrate
3 g fiber
2 g protein

281

K-O

TIPS

Metric Cooking Hints

By making a few conversions, cooks in Australia, Canada, and the United Kingdom can use the recipes in this book with confidence. The charts on this page provide a guide for converting measurements from the U.S. customary system, which is used throughout this book, to the imperial and metric systems. There also is a conversion table for oven temperatures to accommodate the differences in oven calibrations.

Product Differences: Most of the ingredients called for in the recipes in this book are available in English-speaking countries. However, some are known by different names. Here are some common U.S. American ingredients and their possible counterparts:

• Sugar is granulated or castor sugar.
• Powdered sugar is icing sugar.
• All-purpose flour is plain household flour or white four. When self-rising flour is used in place of all-purpose flour in a recipe that calls for leavening, omit the leavening agent (baking soda or baking powder) and salt.
• Light-colored corn syrup is golden syrup.
• Cornstarch is cornflour.
• Baking soda is bicarbonate of soda.
• Vanilla is vanilla essence.
• Green, red, or yellow sweet peppers are capsicums.
• Golden raisins are sultanas.

Volume and Weight: U.S. Americans traditionally use cup measures for liquid and solid ingredients. The chart, below, shows the approximate imperial and metric equivalents. If you are accustomed to weighing solid ingredients, the following approximate equivalents will help.

• 1 cup butter, castor sugar, or rice = 8 ounces = about 230 grams
• 1 cup flour = 4 ounces = about 115 grams
• 1 cup icing sugar = 5 ounces = about 140 grams

Spoon measures are used for smaller amounts of ingredients. Although the size of the tablespoon varies slightly in different countries, for practical purposes and for recipes in this book, a straight substitution is all that's necessary. Measurements made using cups or spoons always should be level unless stated otherwise.

EQUIVALENTS: U.S. = AUSTRALIA/U.K.

⅛ teaspoon = 0.6 ml
¼ teaspoon = 1.25 ml
½ teaspoon = 2.5 ml
1 teaspoon = 5 ml
1 tablespoon = 1 tablespoon = 15 ml
¼ cup = 4 tablespoons = 2 fluid ounces = 60 ml
⅓ cup = ¼ cup = 5 tablespoons + 1 teaspoon = 3 fluid ounces = 80 ml
½ cup = ⅓ cup = 4 fluid ounces = 120 ml
⅔ cup = ½ cup = 10 tablespoons + 2 teaspoons = 6 fluid ounces = 160 ml
¾ cup = ⅔ cup = 6 fluid ounces = 180 ml
1 cup = ¾ cup = 8 fluid ounces = 240 ml
1¼ cup = 1 cup
2 cups = 1 pint = 16 fluid ounces
1 quart = 1 liter
½ inch = 1.27 cm
1 inch = 2.54 cm

BAKING PAN SIZES

American	Metric
8×1½-inch round baking pan	20×4-cm cake tin
9×1½-inch round baking pan	23×4-cm cake tin
11×7×1½-inch baking pan	28×18×4-cm baking tin
13×9×2-inch baking pan	32×23×5-cm baking tin
2-quart rectangular baking dish	28×18×4-cm baking tin
15×10×1-inch baking pan	38×25.5×2.5-cm baking tin (Swiss roll tin)
9-inch pie plate	22×4- or 23×4-cm pie plate
7- or 8-inch springform pan	18- or 20-cm springform or loose-bottom cake tin
9×5×3-inch loaf pan	23×13×8-cm or 2-pound narrow loaf tin or pâté tin
1½-quart casserole	1.5-liter casserole
2-quart casserole	2-liter casserole

OVEN TEMPERATURE EQUIVALENTS

Fahrenheit Setting	Celsius Setting*	Gas Setting
300°F	150°C	Gas Mark 2 (slow)
325°F	160°C	Gas Mark 3 (moderately slow)
350°F	180°C	Gas Mark 4 (moderate)
375°F	190°C	Gas Mark 5 (moderately hot)
400°F	200°C	Gas Mark 6 (hot)
425°F	220°C	Gas Mark 73.859
450°F	230°C	Gas Mark 8 (very hot)
Broil		Grill

*Electric and gas ovens may be calibrated using Celsius. However, for an electric oven, increase the Celsius setting 10 to 20 degrees when cooking above 160°C. For convection or forced-air ovens (gas or electric), lower the temperature setting 10°C when cooking at all heat levels.